IEUAN AP HYWEL SWRDWAL (fl.1430-1480). The MS tradition attributes this praise-poem, in early Modern English spelt in Welsh, to him. Primarily a Welsh-language writer, he is associated with the Cydewain district of Powys, and with Newtown. Some MSS have a prologue describing the poet as a Welshman at Oxford, all lack four lines.

THE PENIARTH POET (after 1484). His poem, 167 lines long, is one of five items in English in MS Peniarth 53.

ANONYMOUS (c.1521). Possibly a Welshman at the court of Henry VIII. The epitaph's subject is the son of Rhys ap Thomas, who is said to have slain Richard III at Bosworth.

MORRIS KYFFIN (c.1555-1598). Primarily a Welsh-language writer, probably born near Oswestry. His praise-poem to Elizabeth I dissociates him from the Babington plot, in which Welshmen were implicated.

JOHN DAVIES OF HEREFORD (c.1565-1618). Called the Welsh Poet, he was a Welsh-speaking Welshman born in Hereford, a well-known teacher of penmanship in London, and a copious poet in English. His praise-poem is for Henry Stuart, Prince of Wales.

HUGH HOLLAND (1569-1633). Born at Denbigh, he travelled widely, was a member of the Mermaid Club, and a poet in English and Latin.

LUDOVIC LLOYD (fl.1573-1610). A Welsh-speaking courtier probably born in Shropshire. His praise-poem is for Queen Elizabeth I.

EDWARD HERBERT (1583-1648), First Baron Herbert of Cherbury. Traveller, diplomatist, philosopher, born in Eyton-on-Severn of the powerful mid Wales family, who sent him to a tutor to learn Welsh.

RICHARD WILIAM (fl.1590-1630), *Syr Risiart y Fwyalchen*. Priest of a parish in east Glamorgan. He wrote in both Welsh and English.

GEORGE HERBERT (1593-1633). Younger brother of Edward, he became Rector of Bemerton, near Salisbury, also holding the sinecure of Llandinam. His poems are contained in *The Temple* (1633).

JAMES HOWELL (1594-1666). Born at Abernant, Carmarthen, he was Welsh-speaking, a traveller, linguist, diplomatist and letter-writer. His verse-letter was addressed to Ben Jonson.

DAVID LLOYD (1597-1663). Dean of St Asaph, he was born at Llanidloes, Mont. His picaresque poem *The Legend of Captain Jones* (1631) was extended and reprinted several times. Here he meets Prester John.

MORGAN LLWYD (1619-1659). Born Cynfal, near Llanffest-iniog, Merioneth, he was primarily a Welsh-language writer, but 31 of his 52 poems with their radical, apocalyptic and European vision, are in English.

THOMAS VAUGHAN (1621-1666). Alchemist, hermetic philosopher, Anglican parson, and occasional poet in English and Latin. Born a Welsh-speaker at Trenewydd, Brecon.

HENRY VAUGHAN (1621-1695), Silurist. Twin brother of Thomas, distantly related to George Herbert, and more closely by poetry. A physician in the Brecon area. The first two poems are from *Olor Iscanus* (1651), the others from the 1655 edition of *Silex Scintillans*.

ANONYMOUS (c.1632). The poem exists in various forms.

ANONYMOUS (c.1642). From Brogyntyn MS 27.

ROWLAND WATKYNS (fl.1634-1664). Born in Longtown, Herefordshire, became Rector of Llanfrynach, Breconshire, and published one volume of poetry, *Flamme sine Fumo* (1662).

ANONYMOUS (c.1664). From Brogyntyn MS 27. A thinner version occurs in MS Richard Morris, 1718.

THE BROGYNTYN POET (c.1690). From Brogyntyn MS 28.

JOHN DYER (1699-1757). Born at Llanfynydd in the Towy valley, he became a painter — in which capacity he visited Italy — and then an Anglican clergyman.

LEWIS MORRIS (1701-1765), *Llewelyn Ddu o Fôn*. Born in Llanfihangel Tre'r Beirdd, Anglesey, he was primarily a Welsh scholar and poet, and by occupation a surveyor.

WILLIAM WILLIAMS (1717-1791), Pantycelyn. Wales's greatest hymn writer, born in Llanfair-ar-y-bryn, Carmarthenshire. He produced two volumes of hymns in English: *Hosannah to the Son of David* (1759) and *Gloria in Excelsis* (1772), from which the following are taken.

EDWARD DAVIES (1718-1789). Born at Llandâf, of whose cathedral he became a prebendary. He has been described as 'an easy-going Protestant pluralist with a sense of humour.'

EVAN EVANS (1731-1788), *Ieuan Brydydd Hir*. Scholar and poet primarily in Welsh. Born at Lledrod, Cardiganshire, he became an Anglican cleric, whose curacies included Manafon.

EVAN LLOYD (1734-1776). Born at Bala, he became an Anglican parson and author of a number of verse satires which provoked some trouble.

EDWARD WILLIAMS (1747-1826), *Iolo Morganwg*. A stone-mason born in Llancarfan, he spent his life celebrating his native Glamorgan as a poet, antiquary and literary forger. Primarily a Welsh-language writer, he published *Poems Lyrical and Pastoral* in English in 1794.

DAVID SAMWELL (1751-1798). Born at Nantglyn, Denbighshire, he wrote verse in Welsh and English, became surgeon on the Discovery, and was an eyewitness of Cook's death.

RICHARD LLWYD (1752-1835). Called the Bard of Snowdon, he was born at Beaumaris, Anglesey. Bilingual, he became a student of Welsh MSS and genealogy.

JULIA ANN HATTON (1764-1838). Called Ann of Swansea, she was born a Kemble, the youngest sister of Sarah Siddons. She ran the Swansea Bathing House, and was a copious writer in English.

TALIESIN WILLIAMS (1787-1847), *Taliesin ab Iolo*. Son of Edward (above), and said to have been born in Cardiff Gaol. He became a schoolmaster, editor of his father's MSS, and a writer in both languages.

JOHN JONES (1788-1858). Called Poet Jones, he was born in Llanasa, Flintshire, and was a factory worker for most of his life. He published *Poems by John Jones* (1856).

JOHN L. THOMAS (1795-1871), *Ieuan Ddu*. Born at Pibwr Lwyd, Carmarthen, one of several towns where he kept a school. He wrote in both languages and published *Cambria upon Two Sticks* (1867), (i.e. the two languages of Wales).

JOHN LLOYD (1797-1875). Born at Brecon, a well known figure at contemporary eisteddfodau. He published a volume of poems in Latin and English in 1847.

JOHN JONES (1810-1869), *Talhaiarn*. A building supervisor in Wales, England and France, he was born at Llanfairtal-haearn, Denbighshire. He published extensively in Welsh, and *Gwaith Talhaiarn* (1869) includes the following songs in English.

FRANCIS HOMFRAY (fl. 1817). Presumably of the family of iron-masters of Penydarren, Merthyr Tydfil, he was an Anglican parson in Gwent.

RICHARD HALL (1817-1866). Born in Brecon, where he was a pharmacist. He published *A Tale of the Past and Other Poems* (1850).

ROWLAND WILLIAMS (1817-1870). *Goronva Camlan*. Anglican cleric, born at Halkyn, Flints, he became Vice Principal of St David's College, Lampeter, and was author of *Lays from the Cimbric Lyre* (1846).

THOMAS HUGHES (fl.1818-1865). Rector of Clocaenog, Ruthin. In 1865 he published *Poems by Hughes*, consisting of poems in Welsh, Latin and English by his father and himself.

THOMAS JEFFREY LLEWELYN PRICHARD (fl.1824-1861). Travelling actor born at Builth, and author of the early Anglo-Welsh novel *The Adventures of Twm Shon Catti*. The following is taken from *Welsh Minstrelsy* (1824).

JOHN MORGAN (1827-1903). Born at Newport, Pembs., an Anglican cleric, preaching and writing in both languages.

SIR LEWIS MORRIS (1833-1907). Born at Carmarthen, grandson of Lewis Morris (above), he is perhaps the first of many Anglo-Welsh poets associated with the University of Wales, for whose establishment he worked. His verse enjoyed considerable popularity during his lifetime.

ERNEST RHYS (1859-1946). Born in London but brought up in Carmarthen and on Tyneside. Qualified in mining, but moved to London and edited the Everyman Books, translated widely from the Welsh and became the first Anglo-Welsh 'man of letters'.

W. H. DAVIES (1871-1940). Born at Newport, Monmouth-shire. Went to America and became a hobo (*The Autobiography of a Super-Tramp*), losing a leg while jumping a train. Returned to Britain and wrote his first poems in a London doss-house. Later befriended by Edward Thomas.

E. HOWARD HARRIES (1876-1961). Born at Swansea, he taught almost all his life in Lancashire, retiring to Swansea, about which most of his poems are written.

OLIVER DAVIES (1881-1960). Born at Greenwich of a father from Cardiganshire. His career in the prison service involved the stewardship of three gaols, including Winchester. Author of five books of verse.

HUW MENAI (1887-1961). A Caernarfonshire man who moved south to work in the Rhondda collieries, later qualifying as a checkweighman for the Cambrian Coal Combine at Gilfach Goch. Bilingual, his first volume of poems was *Through the Upcast Shaft* (1921).

A.G. PRYS-JONES (1888-1987). Denbigh born, for many years H.M. Inspector of Schools in West Wales and Glamorgan. Bilingual, he edited the first exclusively Anglo-Welsh anthology of poems, *Poems of Wales* (1917).

WYN GRIFFITH (1890-1977). Born at Dolgellau, he became an officer of the Inland Revenue in London. During the First World War he was an officer in C Company, the 15th Batt. R.W.F. (David Jones was a private in B Company). His experiences are related in *Up to Mametz* (1931). Bilingual.

DUDLEY G. DAVIES (1891-1981). Born at Swansea, he entered the Indian Civil Service but resigned due to ill health in 1928. Entered the Church and became rector of Bletchingdon,

Oxon., 1935-1955. The poem 'Carmarthenshire' was written in India in 1920.

DAVID JONES (1895-1974). Born in Kent of a father from north Wales. A distinguished painter and poet, best known for *In Parenthesis* (1937), based in part on his experiences in the First World War.

EILUNED LEWIS (1900-1979). Born at Newtown, Montgomeryshire, she became a journalist and was assistant editor of *The Sunday Times* 1931-1936. Her novel *Dew on the Grass* (1934) won the Gold Medal of the Book Guild.

THEODORE NICHOLL (1902-1973). Born at Llanelli, son of a Welsh rugby international, and distantly descended from Welsh poet Lewis Morris (above). He became a journalist and writer, and was one of six winners of the Festival of Britain Poetry Competition in 1951.

EVAN J. THOMAS (1903-1930). Born at Penarth, but moved at an early age to Yorkshire. He worked in London as a journalist on denominational newspapers. A Socialist.

GWYN WILLIAMS (1904-1990). Born at Port Talbot. For many years Professor of English at universities in Cyrenaica and Istanbul. Bilingual. A gifted translator from the Welsh.

IDRIS DAVIES (1905-1953). Born at Rhymney, and a colliery worker from the age of fourteen. Later a teacher in London and elsewhere. Died early of cancer. Bilingual.

GLYN JONES (1905-1995). Born in Merthyr, he taught all his life in Bridgend and in Cardiff. Poet, novelist, story-writer, translator from the Welsh. Bilingual.

VERNON WATKINS (1906-1967). Born at Maesteg but lived from childhood on the Gower coast. A bank employee for all his working life until his renown as a poet led to visiting professorships at universities.

LYNETTE ROBERTS (b.1909). Brought up in Buenos Aires. Married Keidrych Rhys (below), she continues to live in Carmarthenshire. Her books include *Poems* (1944) and *Gods with Stainless Ears* (1951).

JEAN EARLE (b. 1909). Came to the Rhondda as a child and lived for many years in Pembrokeshire. Wrote no poetry until the late 1970s.

KEN ETHERIDGE (1911-1981). Taught art for most of his life in Ammanford, Carmarthenshire, where he was born. A painter and dramatist as well as a poet.

TOM EARLEY (b.1911). Born in Aberpennar, but taught for many years in London, where he now lives.

ELWYN DAVIES (1912-1994). A native of Cardiff who taught in Pembroke Dock and in the Netherlands.

BRENDA CHAMBERLAIN (1912-1971). Born at Bangor. A student at the Royal Academy and primarily a painter, but also distinguished in prose.

R.S. THOMAS (b.1913). Born in Cardiff but moved to Anglesey in early life. Rector of Manafon, Eglwysfach and Aberdaron in turn, he has now retired. In 1964 he won the Queen's Gold Medal for Poetry. Bilingual.

DYLAN THOMAS (1914-1953). Born in Swansea. His sole intention was to be a poet, and his *Eighteen Poems* made him famous at twenty. After some time in London he lived largely in Laugharne, Carmarthenshire, but died in New York during a reading tour.

CLIFFORD DYMENT (1914-1970). Born in Derbyshire because his mother visited her sister there for the birth. His childhood home was Caerleon. Wrote for the BBC on books and the countryside. An occasional film director.

ALUN LEWIS (1915-1944). Born at Cwmaman, Aberdare; a student at UCW Aberystwyth and Manchester University. He taught for a short time in south Wales, then enlisted in 1940. His service took him to England, India and Burma, where he died tragically young without seeing action.

CYRIL HODGES (1915-1974). Born in Cardiff. Became a freelance journalist, and later a successful businessman who was a generous patron of literature and the arts.

KEIDRYCH RHYS (1915-1987). A native of Llangadog, he emerged in 1937 as editor of the influential magazine *Wales*. At first a polemicist, he was a significant influence upon English language writing in Wales. Bilingual.

ROLAND MATHIAS (b.1915). Born at Talybont-on-Usk, Breconshire, he taught for much of his life in England and Wales. He was a founder of *The Anglo-Welsh Review*, which he edited between 1961 and 1976.

EMYR HUMPHREYS (b.1919). Former teacher and BBC Drama Producer born at Trelawnyd, Flintshire. He is a distinguished novelist, whose works have won the Somerset Maugham and Hawthornden Prizes. Bilingual.

JOHN STUART WILLIAMS (b.1920). A native of Mountain Ash, for many years Head of English and Drama at the South Glamorgan Institute of Higher Education. A composer and a poet, his last collection of poems was *Banna Strand* (1975).

HARRI WEBB (1920-1994). Born at Swansea, he spent most of his professional life as a librarian, latterly in Mountain Ash. His poetry was particularly influential in the late sixties and early seventies. Bilingual.

ROBERT MORGAN (1920-1994). Born in the Cynon Valley, he spent twelve years as a collier before becoming a teacher. Long resident in Hampshire, he was also a painter.

LESLIE NORRIS (b.1921). Born in Merthyr Tydfil. A teacher, headmaster and lecturer, he has on many occasions been a visiting professor in America. Author of an acclaimed book of stories, *Sliding*.

T. HARRI JONES (1921-1965). Born near Llanafan, Breconshire, he became a lecturer at an Australian university, a move which strengthened his ambivalent feelings towards Wales. He drowned in 1965.

RUTH BIDGOOD (b.1922). Born at Seven Sisters, Glamorgan, she worked as a WRNS coder and on Chambers' Encyclopaedia in London. A local historian, she now lives at Abergwesyn, Powys.

DANNIE ABSE (b.1923). Born into a Jewish family in Cardiff, he worked in London as a doctor specialising in chest complaints, but devoted much time to writing and the support of literature. Also an acclaimed playwright and novelist, he maintains a home in Ogmore-by-Sea, Glamorgan.

JOHN ORMOND (1921-1990). Born at Swansea, he was for many years a BBC producer and film maker. His subjects included the poets Dylan Thomas, Vernon Watkins, Alun Lewis and R.S. Thomas.

ALISON BIELSKI (b.1925). A largely experimental poet, born in Newport, Monmouthshire, whose work combines words with graphic images and explores Welsh folk-lore and mythology.

RAYMOND GARLICK (b.1926). Born in London of English parents, but brought up and educated in Wales. He was the first editor of *Dock Leaves*, later the *Anglo-Welsh Review* (1949-1960). He was for many years Principal Lecturer in English Studies at Trinity College, Carmarthen.

JOHN TRIPP (1927-1986). Born in Bargoed, but brought up in Cardiff, he worked in London as a journalist and public relations officer, returning to Wales in the late sixties as a freelance writer.

JOSEPH P. CLANCY (b.1928). An American of Irish descent, and a Professor of English in Manhattan for over thirty years. His translations from the Welsh are widely acclaimed; his most recent volume of poems is *Here and There: Poems 1984-93*.

DOUGLAS PHILLIPS (b.1929). Born in Carmarthen, as his poem shows, he has taught for many years in Derbyshire.

BRIAN MORRIS (b.1930). Lord Morris of Castle Morris. Born in Cardiff, he was Professor of English at Sheffield University, and until recently Principal of St. David's University College, Lampeter.

ANTHONY CONRAN (b.1931). Born in India, but moved to north Wales in 1939, where he was later a Tutor in English at UCNW Bangor. His collected translations in *The Penguin Book of Welsh Verse* (1967) established his reputation and stressed the importance of praise-poetry in the Welsh tradition. His own poetry brought this canon into modern Anglo-Welsh writing.

GLORIA EVANS DAVIES (b.1932). A native of west Wales who has lived mostly in Brecon. Her books include *Her Name Like the Hours* (1974).

HERBERT WILLIAMS (b 1932). Born in Aberystwyth, he trained as a journalist and worked on *The South Wales Echo* before becoming a radio producer and film maker.

BRYAN ASPDEN (b.1933). Born in Blackburn but resident near Conwy for many years. A retired local government officer who speaks Welsh fluently, he is the author of two volumes of poetry, most recently *Blind Man's Meal* (1988).

JON DRESSEL (b.1934). Born in Saint Louis, Missouri of Welsh descent. Since 1976 he has been Director of Studies for American students at Trinity College, Carmarthen. His *Cerddi Ianws* (with T. James Jones) was judged the best entry for the Crown at the 1979 National Eisteddfod, but was disqualified for its dual authorship.

SAM ADAMS (b.1934). Born at Gilfach Goch, Glamorgan, he was a teacher and lecturer before becoming H.M. Inspector of Schools. A past editor of *Poetry Wales*.

PETER GRUFFYDD (b.1935). Born in north Wales, he has taught English, Drama and Liberal Studies in several schools in Wales and England. His volume *The Shivering Seed* was published in 1972.

SALLY ROBERTS JONES (b.1935). Born in London, but one of many exiles who returned to Wales in the late sixties. A librarian by profession, she now manages her own publishing house, Alun Books.

PETER PREECE (b.1936). Born at Stackpole, Pembrokeshire, he became a teacher in England and Holland. Some years after returning to Wales failing eyesight has diminished his output of poetry.

GILLIAN CLARKE (b.1937). Brought up in Cardiff, where she read English at the University College. She published no poetry before 1970 but has since become a writer of repute within Wales and without. Her *Selected Poems* was published in 1985.

ALUN REES (b.1937). Born in Merthyr Tydfil, he left university without a degree to become a journalist. Formerly a sports columnist with *The Sunday Telegraph*, he is now a freelance football writer.

J. P. WARD (b.1937). Born in Suffolk, he was for many years a lecturer in Education at UCW Swansea, living on the Gower for much of this time. From 1975 to 1980 he was editor of *Poetry Wales*.

EVAN GWYN WILLIAMS (b.1938). Born at Penderyn, Breconshire, and educated by the WEA and Coleg Harlech, he is now a teacher, having worked in a quarry, a steelworks, a psychiatric hospital and in the Civil Service.

JOHN IDRIS JONES (b.1938). A native of Llanrhaeadr-ym-Mochnant, Denbighshire, he has been both teacher and publisher.

MEIC STEPHENS (b.1938). Born in Pontypridd and educated at Aberystwyth he was, briefly, a teacher and a journalist before becoming Literature Director for the Welsh Arts Council, from 1968 to 1990. He founded *Poetry Wales* in 1965 and was its first editor.

GRAHAM ALLEN (b.1938). A teacher and lecturer from Swansea who has been for some years Senior Tutor in English and Vice-Warden at Coleg Harlech.

PETER THOMAS (b.1939). Born in Manchester but moved to south Wales during his childhood. He has been a lecturer at the University of New Brunswick, Canada, for many years now.

BRAMWELL JONES (b.1939). A college lecturer born in Llanelli. He was taught at the Birmingham School of Music, and later studied English at Coleg Harlech.

CHRIS TORRANCE (b.1941). Born in Edinburgh and brought up in Surrey, he arrived in west Wales in 1970. At first a full-time writer, he now teaches creative writing for a University Extra-Mural Department.

JEREMY HOOKER (b.1941). Born near Southampton, he taught English at UCW Aberystwyth for many years. He has written extensively about Anglo-Welsh poetry and published several volumes of poetry himself. He now lectures in Bath.

JOHN POOK (b.1942). A native of the Swansea area, he is a teacher and lecturer, now based in Clwyd.

CHRISTINE EVANS (b.1943). Born in Yorkshire but a teacher for many years in her father's native Llyn, where she lives near Aberdaron. She has published four collections of poetry, the most recent being *Island of Dark Horses* (1995).

CLIFF JAMES (b.1943). Born in Pembroke Dock, he now teaches in Gwent.

GRAHAM THOMAS (b.1944). Born at Abertillery, where he still lives. A teacher of physics and chemistry at a local school, his first collection of poems, *The One Place*, appeared in 1983.

JOHN DAVIES (b.1944). Born in Port Talbot, Glamorgan, he now teaches in Prestatyn, in north Wales. His own books apart, he has recently published an anthology of prose and poetry for schools.

NIGEL WELLS (b.1944). Brought up in Essex and Hampshire, he moved to Wales in 1972, working on farms, in forestry and as a builder.

RICHARD POOLE (b.1945). Born in Bradford, he has been Tutor in English at Coleg Harlech since 1970 and has written extensively on Richard Hughes. He is currently the editor of *Poetry Wales*. Bilingual.

TONY CURTIS (b.1946). Proferssor of Poetry at the University of Glamorgan, he was born in Carmarthen. He won an Arts Council Young Poets Prize in 1974; his most recent collection is *War Voices* (1995).

DUNCAN BUSH (b.1946). Born in Cardiff, he was educated at universities in Wales, England and America and has worked at a number of occupations. Also a novelist, *Masks*, his most recent poetry collection was ACW Book of the Year, 1995.

PETER FINCH (b.1947). Born in Cardiff, he was editor of *Second Aeon* for a number of years, and organiser of the No Walls poetry readings. He is now manager of the specialist poetry bookshop HMSO Oriel. Chiefly an experimental and concrete poet. Bilingual.

PAUL GROVES (b.1947). Born in Monmouth but lives now in the Forest of Dean. A witty poet, widely published, his most recent book of poems is *Ménage à Trois* (1995).

PHILIP OWENS (b.1947). Born in Wrexham, and ordained into the Ministry of the Church in Wales in 1971. He served at Colwyn Bay and Wrexham and is at present a vicar in Suffolk. His last book of poems was *Look, Christ* (1979).

STEVE GRIFFITHS (b.1949). Now a researcher in social conditions, living in London, he was born in Anglesey, the inspiration for his first book, *Anglesey Material* (1980).

NIGEL JENKINS (b.1949). Brought up on the Gower, he became a journalist in the Midlands before travelling extensively, and studying film and literature at Essex University. A winner of the Arts Council's Young Poets Prize in 1974, he has returned to live on the Gower. Bilingual.

SHEENAGH PUGH (b.1950). Born in Birmingham of Welsh and Irish parents, she previously worked in the Welsh Office at Cardiff. Her *Selected Poems* appeared in 1990.

HILARY LLEWELLYN-WILLIAMS (b.1951). Has lived in west Wales since 1982, the countryside and its associated legends being a fertile source for her work. The author of two collections: *The Tree Calendar* (1987) and *Book of Shadows* (1990).

PETER THABIT JONES (b.1951). Born and educated in Swansea, where he still lives.

ROBERT MINHINNICK (b.1952). Born in Neath but brought up in the village of Pen-y-fai, Bridgend. A prize-winning poet he is also a longstanding campaigner on environmental issues. His most recent collection was *Hey Fatman* (1994).

MIKE JENKINS (b.1953). Born in Aberystwyth, where he read English at the University College. He has returned to Wales to teach in Merthyr Tydfil after posts in Northern Ireland and West Germany. Bilingual.

CHRISTOPHER MEREDITH (b.1954). Born in Tredegar and educated at Aberystwyth and Swansea. Now lecturing in the University of Glamorgan after periods in the steel industry and teaching. Author of a collection of poems, *Snaring Heaven* (1990), and two prize-winning novels, *Shifts* and *Griffri*.

CATHERINE FISHER (b.1957). A native of Newport, Gwent, where she teaches in a primary school. In addition to two books of poems, she has published a number of prize-winning novels for children.

Introduction

THIS is an anthology of the poetry of Wales composed in the English language, not of poems translated from the Welsh. By long usage the term Welsh poetry is properly understood to denote poetry in the Welsh language. To apply it to the poetry of Wales composed in English is confusing and, to some Welsh-language writers and readers, offensive. The English-medium literature of Wales is conveniently described by the term Anglo-Welsh, the first element of the compound being understood to specify the language and the second the provenance of the writing. Though for some it has become almost *de rigeur* to deprecate the use of the term, while nonetheless employing it, it is in fact a linguistic precision witnessing to the bilingual nature of literary activity in Wales. The term was first employed in this context in 1922, by Sir Idris Bell, and its widespread usage since that time testifies to the need for so convenient a locution.

The two compilers of this anthology were among the founders, in 1949, of the literary periodical now known as *The Anglo-Welsh Review*, and edited it successively until 1976: the magazine continues, of course, to the present day. It was in the pages of that periodical more than thirty years ago that this anthology had its point of origin. In the editorial of the spring 1952 number the hope was expressed that ''someone will persuade a publishing house to put forth a badly-needed anthology of Anglo-Welsh poetry from the seventeenth century to the twentieth'' such as might be used in school and college courses. When they were invited to put together the present book the compilers made it a condition that it must be available in a paperback edition in the hope that it would lie within the means of students.

Over the past thirty years various attempts have been made to meet this need, notably the second part of Professor Gwyn Williams's *Presenting Welsh Poetry* (1959), Gerald Morgan's useful teaching anthology *This World of Wales* (1968), and the booklet *Some Early Anglo-Welsh Texts* (1972) published by Trinity College, Carmarthen, for use in its own courses. The definitive anthology of twentieth century Anglo-Welsh poetry up to the time of its publication was certainly *The Lilting House* (1969), edited by John Stuart Williams and Meic Stephens.

In 1952 it seemed that the range of a comprehensive anthology of Anglo-Welsh poetry must run "from the seventeenth century to the twentieth". However, in the following year the Introduction to a delightful and scholarly pocket-volume, *A Book of Wales* edited by D. M. and E. M. Lloyd, contained a startling piece of information:

> The earliest effort at literary composition in English by a Welshman, of which we have any record, is very much a *tour-de-force*. It is an eulogistic poem to the Virgin by an Oxford student, composed in the fifteenth century.

The *Transactions* of the Honourable Society of Cymmrodorion for the next session, published in 1955, carried a conflated text of the poem in question, 'The Hymn to the Virgin', together with an exhaustive linguistic study of it by Dr E. J. Dobson of Jesus College, Oxford. This took the presumed origins of Anglo-Welsh poetry back by more than a century. In conjunction with a major work of reference, *Y Bywgraffiadur Cymreig hyd 1940*, which had appeared in 1953, it stimulated investigation of the Anglo-Welsh writing of previous centuries by the compilers of the present anthology in such essays as *An Introduction to Anglo-Welsh Literature* (1970, 1972) and 'Thin Spring and Tributary' in *Anatomy of Wales* (1972). The forthcoming *Oxford Companion to the Literatures of Wales*, edited by Meic Stephens, will be the obvious and authoritative source of the latest information about writers represented in the present anthology.

In the context of the slight knowledge available thirty years ago of the Anglo-Welsh poetry of past centuries, as reflected in its thin and arbitrary representation (then as now) in the standard anthologies of British poetry, it was natural to take the seventeenth century as the point of departure. After all, the Herberts and the Vaughans were indubitably Welsh and had written poetry in English. Whichever side of the border they were born (and one of the earliest sources, Izaak Walton, who had friends in common with George Herbert, states that he was born in Montgomery Castle), the Herbert brothers were certainly born into a family for which Welshness had significance. In his *Autobiography* Edward Herbert records:

> After I had attained the age of nine . . . my parents thought fit to send me to some place where I might learn the Welsh tongue, as believing it necessary to enable me to treat with those of my friends and tenants who understood no other language.

As for George Herbert, we are grateful to Sam Adams for the information that, among the memorial verses prefaced to the 1674 edition of *The Temple*, two celebrate him as a Welshman. In one he is referred to as 'Phoenix of Wales', while the other contains these lines:

> What Province hath produced a greater soul
> Between the Arctic and Antarctic Pole
> Than Wales hath done? where Herbert's Church shall be
> A lasting pyramid for him and thee.

It is in George Herbert's own celebration of his spiritual home that his Welshness is most evident. No English poet of the time, writing about the Church of England, would call it 'The British Church'. As in Kyffin's "British poets" and Holland's "Britons brave", it is the preferred epithet for Welsh. Davies of Hereford's reference to "Scots and Britons" shows that they are not at all the same thing, and indeed nearly thirty years after the first publication of *The Temple*, in the terminology of the State itself, British and English are mutually exclusive. The Act of Uniformity of 1662 contains a provision

> That the Book [of Common Prayer] hereunto annexed be truly and exactly translated into the British or Welsh tongue.

In a recent collection of 'Essays on the English poets of Wales' in the twentieth century, entitled *The Cost of Strangeness* (1982), Anthony Conran puts forward the idea that what he calls a "seepage" has taken place "on all cultural levels between the two language-groups of Wales". Elsewhere in the book, writing about the praise-poetry of Dylan Thomas as one of a number of instances of such seepage (and writing too as a distinguished translator of medieval Welsh poetry), he draws attention to the implications of the word *bardd*:

> In Welsh, of course, *bardd* simply means poet; but since a poet in Wales was a man who specialised in a certain kind of

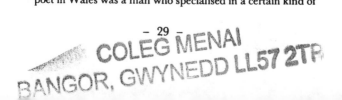

praise, the word has overtones which are different from those of the English word "poet". The bard is a poet dedicated to praise, to giving honour.

He goes on to refer to "the inborn Welsh feeling, which is still all around us, that praise is what poetry should be about".

Of the first nine poems in the present anthology, eight might be considered in some sense praise-poems: of the Virgin, of a Welsh aristocrat, of Elizabeth Tudor, of Henry Stuart, of Owen Tudor, and so forth. And though in the nature of things the content of George Herbert's poetry, the universals of Christianity in their Anglican particulars, can have no obviously Welsh characteristics, Herbert might be thought of as exemplifying what Dylan Thomas later claimed, namely that his poems were written "for the love of Man and in praise of God". Indeed, in his long poem 'Providence' Herbert creates an image which defines the Welsh view of a poet's function: he is "secretary of thy praise". Moreover, since Herbert was a Welshman, and was thought of as such, and came of a family which attached significance to the Welsh language, it might be argued that his work illustrates a seepage of characteristic devices of bardic craft. Examples of this are his creation of compound words ("Christ-side-piercing"), and *dyfalu* (which also characterizes Henry Vaughan's poem 'Sondayes') – the heaping up of some twenty-seven comparisons in the sonnet 'Prayer'.

In his brief but illuminating book *Dylan Thomas* (1972) in the Writers of Wales series, Walford Davies too faces the phenomenon of the "survival of a radically Welsh mode of thought or sensibility beyond the anglicization of a second generation", and comes to the conclusion that his poet's Welsh-speaking parents "relayed unconsciously another and older culture into his life". He goes on to make a general point of some interest:

> A Welshman, it seems fair to argue, whether he speaks Welsh or not, has ingrained in him a certain view of his art – a kind of collective sense of his responsibility towards form.

George Herbert might be thought to attempt to discharge this responsibility by apparently believing that almost every poetic statement has a unique form in which its precision must be articulated: it is said that of the 164 poems in *The Temple* 116 are in forms which are not repeated. The most obvious of these are the shaped poems, 'Easter Wings' and 'The Altar', which presumably lie behind Henry Vaughan's 'The Waterfall' (where the shape conveys the movement of the Usk), and Dylan Thomas's geometrical shapes in 'Now' and 'Vision and Prayer'. Another sort of shaping is seen in Herbert's 'Paradise', where the rhyming word of each triplet is successively pared of its first two consonants in the second and third lines of each stanza. Walford Davies uses the concept of "welcome obstacles" to describe similar self-imposed formal constraints in the poetry of Dylan Thomas, and observes

> A nation to whom *englynion* seem as much art as craft is in the end right in recognizing in Thomas one of her own.

The first seven stanzas of 'The Hymn to the Virgin' are, of course, *englynion*, before the poem moves into six stanzas in *awdl* metres, and in the old MS collections of Welsh poetry the occasional *englyn* in English is to be found. Perhaps the best comment on them is embodied in such an *englyn* by one of the finest Welsh-language poets of the twentieth century, Waldo Williams, whose first language was in fact English:

> Yes, Idwal, it is oddish; – it is strange;
> It is true outlandish –
> Not a fowl nor yet a fish,
> An englyn writ in English.

In contemporary Anglo-Welsh poetry the *englyn* is written memorably, as one might expect, by Anthony Conran – in such a poem as his 'Elegy for Sir Ifor Williams', for example. There is an appropriate symmetry in the circumstance that the sense of responsibility towards form should articulate itself in this particular way at both ends of the present anthology. And indeed one of its compilers, in the Introduction to an earlier anthology – *Green Horse* (1978), an anthology of work by Anglo-Welsh poets then aged forty or under, edited by Meic Stephens and Peter Finch – made a comment which might sum up this brief discussion of the topic here:

> One of the great differences to be noted between an Anglo-Welsh anthology and its English counterpart is the affection it continues to demonstrate for comparatively severe structural forms.

In a remarkable editorial prefaced to the first number of his magazine *Wales*, published in 1894, Sir O. M. Edwards wrote:

> There is a strong desire for a literature that will be English
> in language but Welsh in spirit . . . Why should the land of
> Henry Vaughan and George Herbert be less fond of
> literature than the land of Islwyn and Ceiriog? . . . Why
> should not the English literature of Wales have charac-
> teristics of its own – like Scotch (*sic*) literature and
> American literature?

It has been suggested so far that such characteristics might
be the concept of poetry as praise, celebration, and a
strong awareness of form, technique, wrought language.
Are there any other marks which appear to characterize
Anglo-Welsh poetry? Perhaps it is worth noting that the
duty to praise also implies its opposite, what R. S.
Thomas has called "the winnowing of the people". This
is sometimes embodied in a genre well represented in
Anglo-Welsh poetry, the portrait poem (e.g. Evan
Lloyd's 'Portrait of a Bishop'), perhaps witnessing to a
characteristically Welsh openness to and curiosity about
other people. Moreover, the assumption of the right to
praise or blame implies something about the poet's role.
Alun Richards, in the Introduction to his Penguin collec-
tion of Welsh and Anglo-Welsh short stories, makes the
following comment:

> English writers, it has been said, are often refugees from
> society, but almost all the stories in this book written by
> Welsh men and women show a concern for a particular
> landscape or community. It is as if Welsh writers cannot
> escape this involvement.

Certainly many Anglo-Welsh poets seem to assume that
their function is not primarily to explore the private world
of their own thoughts and feelings but to address their
community and, in R. S. Thomas's words, "to beautify,
to purify and to enlarge" its way of life – as Welsh-
language poets have always assumed.

The celebration of particular landscapes, the sense of
place, the naming of locations, mark many of their
poems. In his history of Wales, *Land of My Fathers* (1974),
Dr Gwynfor Evans makes the point that from very early
times

> the eastern border, which is the only land border Wales has,
> was close to the line later taken by Offa's Dyke and the edge
> of modern Wales. Of very few nations can it be said, as it
> can be said of the Welsh, that their territory has remained
> the same for most of the last three millenia. The probable

result of this unusual Welsh situation is that it can be claimed that the majority of the Welsh of this generation are descended from the people who inhabited the country when Ostorius and his legions came here in 47 A.D.

In the context of such territorial stability and continuity attachment to, affection for, celebration of, place is hardly surprizing. Moreover, this sense of place is often associated with a sense of time – sometimes a personal past (as in 'Fern Hill'), but more often a national past, the immensely venerable continuity of the history of Wales. Gwynfor Evans notes that

> Recorded Welsh history begins about fifteen years after the crucifixion of Christ with the attack of Ostorius upon the Silurians and the Ordovicians,

the inhabitants of south and mid Wales, as recorded by Tacitus; and of course Welsh myth and legend recede into Celtic prehistory beyond this. So long and unbroken a sweep of history not unnaturally gives rise to a tendency to look back (intensified in some, no doubt, by an unsatisfactory national present, and an uncertain future). Its continuity allows a telescoping effect whereby such figures as Magnus Maximus, Arthur, Glyndwr, such events as Camlan, Catraeth, Cilmeri, can be referred to quite naturally in contemporary contexts ranging from political discourse to pop songs. Certainly the presentness of the past broods over Anglo-Welsh poetry, often offering an obstacle to the outside reader – for whom the language is lucid and accessible but, unless he has done his homework and can pick up the allusions, the poem remains opaque or yields only part of its meaning. The reader for whom the name Cynddylan has no resonances will not know that he has failed to gain complete entry into R. S. Thomas's poem 'Cynddylan on a Tractor'.

As Poet Jones observes, "Industry's children are the sons of Wales", and the Anglo-Welsh industrial poem begins appropriately enough in the mid eighteenth century with Lewis Morris's 'Miner's Ballad' (probably a lead miner) and Edward Davies's evocation of the iron foundry in Tintern Abbey nine years before Wordsworth's first visit. Its most compelling twentieth century articulation is in the poetry of Idris Davies, raising its great cry

O what is man that coal should be so careless of him,
And what is coal that so much blood should be upon it?

Yet it is surprizing that in a Wales the majority of whose population lives in the industrial townships of the south, poems which are in many ways versions of the pastoral should still predominate. No doubt this is in part because, above the urban communities of the great industrial valleys, the open mountains are immediately accessible and still largely unspoilt; but it may also be an abiding witness to the fact that Celtic culture is not an urban one and does not feel the contempt for the countryman reflected in such words as "yokel", "clown", "bumpkin", "hick", and their equivalents in other modern European languages. R. S. Thomas's "peasant" is certainly not a term of diminishment or patronage.

Here and there are found adverse reflections upon London, which Morgan Llwyd invites to come down to the dust and Iolo Morganwg describes as "Folly's hateful sphere", and it would be idle to pretend that from time to time there are not anti-England sentiments. 'The Hymn to the Virgin' appears to have originated as an anti-English demonstration at Oxford, and Davies of Hereford's *croeso* extravaganza – whereby the Roman ruins of Wales are to be refurbished "That Scots and Britons may mixed live therein" – makes it quite clear who is not to be invited. With Henry Stuart as Prince, Davies delicately observes, Wales will "be eased/ Of what in former times hath her displeased". Evan Evans reminds his readers that

> The false historians of a polished age
> Show that the Saxon has not lost his rage

and exhorts them to "Beware of Saxons still" (having Lord Lyttleton particularly in mind); and in his satirical account of the deracinating tendencies of a bourgeois Welsh education Ieuan Ddu ironically concedes that perhaps "the English tongue/ Alone can save our skins from English wrong". If in our own time Harri Webb's observances at the putative grave of Dafydd ap Gwilym:

> I kept my vow, prayed for my country,
> Cursed England, came away

may seem to have a certain perfunctory quality, possibly tongue in cheek, it must be said that there are plenty of contemporary Anglo-Welsh poems not in this anthology whose glances across the border are not inspired by uncritical adulation.

If political comment in any real sense can be attributed to Anglo-Welsh poetry up to the Civil War, it is praise of the established order – reinforced in Morris Kyffin, perhaps, by an urgent awareness that any hesitations could hang, draw and quarter him. For Morgan Llwyd, however, Charles was "the last king of Britain", and with him begins a line of occasional radical criticism lasting to the present day. He sharply attacks the callousness of the establishment of his time:

> Our king, queen, prince and prelates high their merry
> Christmas spent
> with brawny hearts, when yet their dogs could Lazarus
> lament.

Though English was his second language, his choice of the epithet "brawny" shows that he was a true poet in it. This forthrightness is echoed in our own time by Harri Webb's portrait poem embodying the characteristics that went to make "all our dead princes":

> He is a gambler, a drinker, a doggy-boy,
> Better at drawing the dole than earning a wage.

Idris Davies and Herbert Williams (in 'Like Father?') are among other contemporary poets who engage in radical social comment.

Of the first forty-two poets represented in this anthology, that is to say those up to roughly 1900 and including Sir Lewis Morris, more than half were Welsh-speaking and at least a third wrote in Welsh – some of course being much better known as Welsh writers. Writing in 1867, Ieuan Ddu seems to articulate their view that the life of Wales is supported on the two languages, that the total Welsh statement involves both; that English, in short, is a language of Wales:

> Reader! here thou dost behold
> On her sticks thy Cambria old;
> One of Oak time-proof and tough,
> Th'other Ash and lithe enough:
> And to such as dare abuse
> Her customs, she can either use –
> Or on occasion both.

In some of the earlier poets we see English, their second language, heavily under the influence of Welsh: the Welsh metric and orthography of 'The Hymn to the Virgin', and to a lesser extent the Peniarth Poet and Sir

Richard the Blackbird. In others, from Morgan Llwyd to our own time, there is the occasional line, phrase or word in Welsh. As for their English, its spelling, punctuation and the forms of place-names having on the whole been modernized, we are left with an essentially standard form of the language: the English of the Welsh professional class, from whom more often than not the Anglo-Welsh poets have been drawn. Few of the distinctive words and phrases recorded by the Survey of Anglo-Welsh Dialects (which has been conducted for some years by the Department of English at University College, Swansea) will be found in Anglo-Welsh poetry, such is the strength of its linguistic tradition: on the other hand, quite a number are evident in the Anglo-Welsh novel, short story and drama, essentially twentieth century forms.

It is not their use of language but their fascination with it as a subject that, as in Wales at large, most distinctively characterizes Anglo-Welsh poets when compared with American or English ones. It seems likely that the presence of two languages, whether or not one has access to them both, is responsible for a heightened sense of language as a marvellous human phenomenon, especially for those whose work lies with the word. There is a sense in which 'The Hymn to the Virgin' is a poem in praise of language, and in a number of poems from James Howell's bustling verse-letter to our own time we see one language being used to celebrate the other, English praising Welsh. In others English is used to draw the attention of a wider public to the dangers threatening Welsh. Particularly interesting in this context is the poem 'Education in Wales' by the pseudonymous and unidentified Goronva Camlan, who appears to have been a Welsh don at Cambridge. The slim volume in which it appears was published in 1846, the year in which the commissioners were working their way through Wales preparing for the Treachery of the Blue Books of 1847, and the poem shows the enlightened – and surprizingly modern – attitude to language learning of an English-writing Welsh academic. In our own day Sam Adams's poem 'Hill Fort, Caerleon' is perhaps the most powerful of a number of articulations of the sense of linguistic alienation and its relationship to identity which is, at least at a subconscious level, probably widespread in contemporary Wales.

While often showing a concern for Welsh, it seems that at least from the second half of the sixteenth century – when the distinguished scholar and antiquary Humphrey Llwyd, himself a Welsh-speaker, referred to "our English tongue" – Anglo-Welsh writers have seen English as a language of Wales, one of the two ways of communicating Welshness. "I like our language," writes George Herbert, and goes on to celebrate it lyrically:

> Lovely enchanting language, sugar-cane,
> Honey of roses.

In our own day Glyn Jones, with characteristic commonsense and urbanity, has reiterated the lack of any contradiction between writing English and being Welsh:

> While using cheerfully enough the English language, I have never written in it a word about any country other than Wales, or any people other than Welsh people.

This is, as it were, the classical Anglo-Welsh position; but it might be argued that wherever, whatever, whoever an Anglo-Welsh writer writes about, what he writes is informed by a Welsh sensibility, by approaches, assumptions, standpoints, perceptions, which differ from those of an American, an Anglo-Irish or an English writer. It must be said, however, that in Welsh life in general and in education in particular there is a curious failure to examine the positive and creative role, historical and contemporary, of English as a language of Wales. In the schools, by and large, it continues to be presented as the language and literature of anywhere else but Wales.

The attitude of one contemporary poet of Wales in English to the language in which he writes perhaps best demonstrates the contradictions which can arise. "Despite our speech we are not English" writes R. S. Thomas in a poem called 'Border Blues', and indeed statistically those whose mother-tongue is English are most likely to be Americans. Obviously, too, English as a native language can define a variety of other identities – Scots, Australian, Canadian and so forth. Though in answer to a questionnaire in the magazine *Wales* in 1946 R. S. Thomas had written

> The question of a writer's language is a mere matter of historical accident, and will be seen to have little ultimate significance,

six years later a poem entitled 'The Old Language' opens with the cry

> England, what have you done to make the speech
> My fathers used a stranger at my lips?

This train of thought finds a quite astounding conclusion in the last poem of a small collection published in 1974, whose title asks the question *What is a Welshman?* Here English is seen as the destroyer of Wales and Welsh, the language of commerce and the industrialists who came

> burrowing
> in the corpse of a nation
> for its congealed blood. I was
> born into the squalor of
> their feeding and sucked their speech
> in with my mother's
> infected milk, so that whatever
> I throw up now is still theirs.

These lines from the poem 'It hurts him to think' convey a unique and paradoxical expression of anguish. Here we see one of the most distinguished living poets in the English language, whose work has extended its grace and precision of statement, in a mood of intense revulsion towards that language and his achievement in it. It too is a quintessentially Anglo-Welsh utterance, though unparallelled in any other writer of Wales in English. In this poet the bruising of Wales by the misuse of English as an instrument of political, economic and cultural oppression has reached to the very bone.

However, it is a part of the reality, and when in 1946 R. S. Thomas was asked for whom he wrote he answered with the words of Yeats: "for my own race/ And the reality". Though, centuries before, Davies of Hereford had proposed an interpretative role for the Anglo-Welsh poet, addressing not Wales but the outside world as a voice of Wales –

> I speak for those whose tongues are strange to thee
> In thine own tongue,

the main tradition of Anglo-Welsh poetry has avoided the dangers of exaggeration and pandering to stereotyped expectations that this position can give rise to, and has addressed Wales as naturally and directly as Welsh-language poetry has done.

What opera is to Italy, ballet to Russia, theatre to England, symphonic music to Germany, painting to the Netherlands, poetry is to Wales: the supreme and defining art form. However, no one who has any acquaintance with the ultimately untranslatable splendours of Welsh-language poetry, and its millenium and a half of magnificence, will entertain for one moment any notion of Anglo-Welsh poetry as a possible rival. Though it seems to have originated a century and more before the language was taken to the New World, there eventually to give rise to a new and major literature, the articulation of yet another life quite distinct from that of England, Anglo-Welsh literature in its fullest flowering is essentially a modern phenomenon. It is not a rival to Welsh but a younger partner, a complement. On the other hand, it is not our intention to sell it short. No one, whichever his mother tongue, has a full entry into Wales and its national heritage who is ignorant of Anglo-Welsh poetry.

It is necessary, however, to understand why the full flowering of Anglo-Welsh literature was so long delayed. Until the later nineteenth century, of course, no more than a small proportion of the inhabitants of Wales had English as their first language. That in the seventeenth century important poets like George Herbert and Henry Vaughan emerged from the ranks of the English-educated gentry must be attributed both to the unpredictability of the appearance of natural talent and to the spiritual and political crisis which engulfed their times. A crisis usually precipitates strong convictions and strong convictions produce their own confidence. Both the convictions and the confidence, after the days of Herbert and Vaughan, were largely missing from Anglo-Welsh poetry. Before their time, the political inheritors of Geoffrey of Monmouth and his compulsive Plantagenet myth had been sustained by Bosworth, the suzerainty of the Tudor monarchy, and the "seniority" of Wales in the union with England. As late as James Howell's day the legacy of ancient Wales was a matter for pride rather than apology. But as the seventeenth century wore on and the tribulations of the Civil War were succeeded by an insensitive Restoration, that pride faded into defensiveness and apology, just as the confidence of the Welsh as a people faded. In the nadir of the eighteenth century the widespread literacy achieved by the Circulating Schools and the new enthusiasm of the Methodists brought back confidence to many of the social aspects of the life of the *gwerin* and to the Welsh language, but they left writing in English in even greater need to apologize for itself. During the early nineteenth century, as in the late eighteenth, the strongest voices heard were those of English Romantics and Celtophiles. For the Welsh, except in rare instances, English was a language in which the achievements of Welsh literature must be publicized, but which was not seen as a natural vehicle for the creativity of Welshmen. Individuals fought against this, but for the gentry class as a whole, absentee or resident amongst relative poverty and decay, there was no longer sufficient nerve to proclaim a Welsh identity in English. This situation did not change until the vast English immigrations after 1850 provided a substantial population in Wales whose identity had inevitably to be rendered in the only language they were ever likely to learn.

The surprizing thing is that even when secondary education in English began to be available (after the County Schools were established in 1895 and the years following), and when a probable forty per cent of the population had no language other than English, creative writing in that language was slow to reappear. One or two reasons for this may be advanced. An immigrant section of any community takes time to accustom itself to its new location and lacks the ancient ties out of which love and confidence grow. The secondary education on offer was very selective (in terms of numbers), narrowly academic and nervous of inferiority most of all in its reverence for English norms and its anxiety to go by the book. What brought about the twentieth century flowering of Anglo-Welsh writing was a factor directly related to English immigration and an education in English for all Welsh children, but nevertheless distinct: it was the blow that immigration and its consequences in Welsh industry and society had administered to the confidence of Welsh-speaking parents in South Wales: their children, often brought up to believe that English was the only language of opportunity, were still impregnated with the radical values inherent in a Welsh-speaking society and were sad enough, resentful enough, conscious of difference enough, to use the English language in an un-English way and proclaim their difference confidently to English

readers. It was, first with Glyn Jones about 1934, and
then with Dylan Thomas, Vernon Watkins, Keidrych
Rhys and Idris Davies, that the new Anglo-Welsh, freed
from the echoing classicism of their predecessors, made
their mark.

This explanation is necessary because the order of the
poems in this anthology, based upon the birth-dates of the
poets, substantially obscures the points just made. The
compilers do not apologize for their poem-order. Any
other scheme proliferates difficulties of other kinds. But it
has to be understood that a pronounced feature of Anglo-
Welsh writing is its avoidance of precocity, an avoidance
which in itself underlines the slow growth from
unconfidence and a determination to experience life in
some fullness before seeking to comment on it. Dylan
Thomas, in writing some 350 poems in his little red
notebook before he was nineteen, was an outrageous ex-
ception. Much more characteristic are David Jones and
Gwyn Williams, who wrote scarcely at all in their twenties
and early thirties. David Jones's first literary work, *In
Parenthesis*, was published in 1937. Gwyn Williams's first
translations from the Welsh appeared in 1950 and his own
poetry not till 1970. Jean Earle, whose poetic style may
strike the reader as "very modern" for her place in the
date-order, did not publish a volume of poetry until 1980.
Harri Webb and Leslie Norris (despite some early bur-
geonings from the latter) did not write seriously until 1965
or later. In some instances the lateness of the development
has reference to the lateness of any substantial improve-
ment in Welsh publishing, but for this and other related
factors this Introduction is not the place. Readers of this
anthology, in effect, would be well advised, upon the
issues of date-order and the historical development of
Anglo-Welsh poetry (in the twentieth century, in par-
ticular), to acquaint themselves with Roland Mathias's
'Thin Spring and Tributary' in *Anatomy of Wales* (1972) or
his 'Literature in English' in *The Arts in Wales 1950-75*
(1979).

One other factor should perhaps be mentioned in a
twentieth century context. Of the poets from Ernest Rhys
onwards six out of eighty-four can confidently be de-
scribed as Welsh-speaking from birth and fully literate in
the Welsh language. Another eight have learned that
language, amongst them R. S. Thomas, and are fully

competent to write in it, if not, they feel, to write creatively. As many as ten more have acquired an ability to read and write Welsh rather less than perfectly. As may be expected, the original fully bilingual six belong to the earliest generation represented in this century, the next ten largely to that generation of reaction against the first direction taken by Anglo-Welsh writing (chiefly in prose), which saw Wales as an antediluvian society whose eccentricities would fascinate English readers. Those who have a partial knowledge of Welsh are scattered, without any generally ascertainable cause, throughout the period from 1900 to 1980. Amongst poets under forty, however, only three can be noted with any significant mastery of Welsh and it may be, in the context of the renewed enthusiasm of students for the Welsh language which has characterised the last twenty years, that potential Anglo-Welsh poets have been drawn into linguistic studies and away from creativity in their first language. However this may be, there is considerable ground for thinking that younger Anglo-Welsh poets are drawn from a background increasingly separated from and ignorant of the Welsh heritage. That they are also few in number may be related more closely to the tardiness of poetic development already referred to, but it is a fact that no poet under thirty finds a place in this anthology.

It would be possible, but less than honest, to explain this by reference to the relative crowdedness of the more established Anglo-Welsh scene and the difficulty the compilers have faced in including as many poets as they have. The exigencies of space have indeed curtailed the more generous circle of original choice: another fourteen poets, at the very least, might have been included. But the compilers felt, and feel, that it is of more service to the reader to acquaint him with the variety and breadth of the writing of poets of some stature than to increase the number of single-poem entries. In this respect personal regret has to give way to literary judgment. In the interest of breadth too, and cohesion, poems have not infrequently been chosen which, over the whole range of the anthology, take for subject matter material already treated in other poems, sometimes of widely separated times. Thus there are, for example, several poems about waterfalls, and St. Ursula makes two appearances. Rightly or wrongly, the compilers believe that such correspondences will help the serious reader to draw together both the history and the natural features of the poetry.

One last point, not unconnected with the first part of the paragraph preceding, needs explanation. Some comment has already been made on the development of the term Anglo-Welsh in this century. But it has to be understood that within the definition given at the outset of this Introduction several closer definitions are possible. One may, for example, apply with rigour the criterion of *birth in Wales*, and to a large extent that application is reasonable and necessary. But a total strictness about this may well make eligible a T. E. Lawrence who has no interest in Wales and ineligible a David Jones whose life is moved by it. From the very beginning the compilers of this anthology have had to face the fact that one of them, though English by birth and blood, has generally been recognised as Anglo-Welsh by virtue of long involvement with Wales and with the English writing of Wales. It is accordingly impossible to be rigid about the matter of birth. The only workable criterion seems to be "a commitment to the identity of Wales and to Anglo-Welsh writing" or to some form of words not dissimilar. Because the complications belong to the twentieth century, the term Anglo-Welsh must find a place in any such definition, and within that definition poets like Jeremy Hooker and J. P. Ward can no more be excluded than the Welsh-Americans Jon Dressel and Joseph Clancy. Admittedly, there are poets in this anthology whose commitment is more marginal and for whom long residence in Wales has to complement the qualification, just as there is one – Evan J. Thomas – whose birth qualification is undisputed but whose real right to inclusion is much more the powerful feeling his work evokes of an essentially Welsh family settled in the Pennines. The ultimate line has to be drawn by instinct as much as anything else and even instinct may, on occasion, be mistaken. But the compilers believe that the anthology they have put together is one in which the poets, though in no sense confined to writing *about* Wales, nevertheless either had indissoluble connections with the Wales of the past or see themselves as part of the Welsh literary scene in the present. If this is too generous an interpretation of the term Anglo-Welsh, so be it: but in the view of the compilers any other would prove, in the work-out, to be far more arbitrary and meaningless.

Of the direction taken by the most recent writing, if one can be discerned, the reader must form his own judgment, most of all in the context of the survival of those characteristics earlier Anglo-Welsh writing inherited from its ancestor in Welsh. He must bear in mind that the compilers may have influenced his conclusions as much by their choice of poems as he influences them by his prejudices. The road to objectivity is strewn with such rocks.

Raymond Garlick & Roland Mathias

IEUAN AP HYWEL SWRDWAL

(*fl.* 1430 – 1480)

The Hymn to the Virgin

I

O michti ladi, owr leding/tw haf
at hefn owr abeiding:
yntw ddy ffest efrlesting
i set a braents ws tw bring.

II

I wann ddys wyth blys, ddy blesing/off God
ffor iwr gwd abering,
hwier i bynn ffor iwr wyning
syns kwin, and iwr swnn ys king.

III

Owr ffadyrs ffadyr, owr ffiding,/owr pop,
on iwr paps had swking;
yn hefn-blys i haf thys thing,
atendans wythowt ending.

IV

Wi sin ddy bricht kwin wyth kwning/and blys,
ddy bloswm ffruwt bering;
ei wowld, as owld as ei sing,
wynn iwr lwf on iwr lofing.

V

Kwin od off owr God, owr geiding/mwdyr,
maedyn notwythstanding,
hwo wed syts wyth a ryts ring
as God wod ddys gwd weding.

VI

Help ws, prae ffor ws, preffering/owr sowls;
Asoel ws at owr ending.
Mak ddat awl wi ffawl tw ffing
iwr swns lwf, owr syns lefing.

VII

As wi mae ddy dae off deiing/resef
owr safiowr yn howsling;
as hi mae tak ws waking
tw wwn yn hys michti wing.

VIII

Michti, i twk, mi ocht tw tel
owt, sowls off hel tw soels off hicht.
Wi aes wyth bwk, wi wys wyth bel,
tw hefn ffwl wel tw haf on fflicht
    awl dids wel dwn,
    tabeit te bwn—
    a god-mat trwn,
       a gwd, mit wricht;
    and si so swn
    and north and nwn
    an swnn an mwn
       an swnn on micht.

XII

   *   *   *   *   *
   *   *   *   *   *

O trysti Kreist tat werst a krown,
er wi dei down, aredi dicht
    tw thank tw thi
    at te rwt-tri.
    Dden went awl wi,
       ddein own, tw licht.
    Tw grawnt agri,
    amen, wy mi,
    ddat ei mae si
       ddi tw mei sicht!

XIII

Owr lwk, owr king, owr lok, owr kae—
mei God, ei prae, mei geid wpricht!
Ei sik, ei sing, ei siak, ei sae,
ei wer awae, a wiri wicht.
    Agast ei go,
    mei ffrynds mi ffro.
    Ei ffond a ffo,
       wy ffynd ei fficht;
    eil sing awlso
    yn welth an wo
    (ei kann no mo)
       tw kwin o micht.

IEUAN AP HYWEL SWRDWAL

The Hymn to the Virgin

(A literal version)

I

O mighty lady, our leading / to have
at heaven our abiding:
to bring us unto the everlasting feast
ye planted a branch (= of Jesse's tree).

II

Ye won this with bliss, the blessing / of God
for your good child-bearing,
where ye are for your reward
since queen, and your Son is king.

III

Our father's father, our feeding, / our pope,
was nourished at your breast;
in heaven's bliss ye have this thing (namely)
service without ending.

IV

We see the bright queen with wisdom / and bliss,
the blossom bearing fruit;
I would for as long as I sing
win your love in praising you.

V

Sole queen of our God, our guiding / mother,
maiden notwithstanding,
who wed such with a rich ring
since God desired this good wedding.

VI

Help us, pray for us, favouring /our souls;
Absolve us at our ending.
Grant that we all consent to accept
your Son's love, our sins leaving.

VII

So that we may the day of dying / receive
our saviour in communion;
that he may take us wakeful
to dwell in his mighty wing.

VIII

Mighty, he took (I must tell it
out) souls from hell to regions on high.
We ask with book, we wish with bell,
to heaven full well to have in flight
  all well-done deeds,
  to abide the reward —
  a throne made by God,
    a good, true craftsman;
   and see thus soon
 both north and noon
 and sun and moon
   and the Son in might.

XII

 *   *   *   *   *
 *   *   *   *   *

O trusty Christ that wearest a crown,
ere we die down, already dressed
  to give thee thanks
  at the rood-tree.
  Then wend all we,
   thine own, to light.
  To grant agree,
  amen, with me,
  that I may see
   thee to my sight!

XIII

Our luck, our king, our lock, our key —
my God, I pray, my upright guide!
I seek, I sing, I shake, I speak,
I wear away, a weary wight.
  Aghast I go,
  far from my friends.
  I find a foe,
   with fiend I fight;
  I'll sing also
  in wealth and woe
  (I can do no more)
   to the queen of might.

THE PENIARTH POET

(after 1484)

from *A Drinking Song*

Loke that none of you departe
Tyll he be sur of a quarte
All the whyle the mowth ys dry
The tong may schew no melody
But hong styll as a clapyr
Anoynt hym wele with good ale
And then of many a dyvers tale
He wyll begyn to clater
Of all oyntmentys hyt ys the beste
When a man goth to hys reste
When that hyt ys nyght
Hyt makyth hym mery at hys herte
And kepyth his body yn good quarte
And makyth hym to slepe aryght
There may no harper myrth make
Withowte that he thys oyntment take
To anoynte hym withall
Nothyr no mynstrell scew game
But he be anoyntyd with the same
Hys song wyl sone a fall

ANONYMOUS

(c. 1521)

The Epitaph of Sir Griffith ap Rhys

When I revolve in my remembrance
This life fugitive and the world transitory,
It moveth my heart, it pricketh my conscience
Little to regard this world's vanity,
Seeing nothing remaineth in stability,
But every creature here natural
Suddenly slippeth hence by chance mortal.

Sole as I stood late towards a night
The sun beholding, how it went to rest,
A griffith came flying fair in my sight   (*griffin*
From the mountains of Wales by south west,
And direct over me as he came exprest
Before me he let fall suddenly
This heavy and lamentable epitaphy:

Farewell, England! Farewell, Wales!
I take my leave now at this tide.
Farewell Calais and English Pales!
Farewell, King Henry! I may not abide,
Death hath me lanced into the side.
Farewell knighthood, farewell chivalry!
Of the courteous court farewell good company!

Farewell my lady! your heart is sore:
At our departing we thought not of this,
A hard chance for here we meet no more.
Be of good comfort though ye do me miss:
God shall provide for your solace and bliss
Better chance for you though ye be left alone,
Far from your country and friends everyone.

The late loss of your child was a great grievance,
But nothing to this comparable.
Be you of good comfort, thus turneth the balance
From life to death which is inevitable.
O sorrowful chance so lamentable!
Now shall I no more my lady see,
Sole mourning left in a strange country.

I would ye should not for me weep and wail,
My own true lady, but me recommend
To God by prayer which may me avail
My pain to slake and comfort you send.
Though death of me thus have made an end,
In my lusty time no longer I may dwell,
Be you of good comfort and thus fare ye well.

To my old master now will I be gone,
Prince Arthur with him still to abide.
It slacketh my sorrows to think upon
My chance is to lie so nigh to his side.
What should I more wish in this world wide
But in rest perpetual to make merry
With that noble prince in eternal glory?

Yet all my fellows that was with Prince Arthur
In service with me full diligent,
For old love I pray you to procure
To good King Henry the Eighth by one assent
That it will please him of his grace most excellent

To my wife and children good lord to be;
For all service past I ask none other fee.

And remember how sudden this life doth slide,
Ye may all take ensample by me.
Beware death cometh sudden and not espied,
When ye think least he will do his villainy.
O that I had not forecast his slighty subtlety!   (*sly*
Now ye be warned, ye may take better heed,
Of his sudden dart ye shall have less dread.

MORRIS KYFFIN
(c. 1555 – 1598)

from *The Blessednes of Brytaine*

Adore November's sacred seventeenth day,
Wherein our second sun began her shine:
Ring out, loud sounding bells; on organs play;
To music's mirth let all estates incline:
    Sound drums and trumpets, rending air and ground;
    Stringed instruments, strike with melodious sound.

Ye mighty men of Mars, ennobled knights,
Advance yourselves on fiery foaming steeds:
Revive this time's remembrance, with all rights,
In armour bright and gorgeous warlike weeds:
    At tilt and tourney, trying martial might,
    And battering strokes, at barriers forceful fight.

Ye country folk, forth stalking in your fields,
Loud carols sing to celebrate this time;
Show signs of joy (as country manner yields)
In sporting games, with dance and rural rhyme:
    Each swain and shepherd sound his piping reed
    For joy, enjoying fields and flocks to feed.

Ye British poets, repeat in royal song
(With weighty words, used in King Arthur's days)
Th'imperial stock from whence your Queen hath sprung;
Install in verse your Princess' lasting praise:
    Pencerddiaid, play on ancient harp and crowde;   (crwth, *fiddle*
    Atceiniaid, sing her praises piercing loud.

Let hills and rocks rebounding echoes yield
Of Queen Elizabeth's long lasting fame;
Let woody groves and watery streams be filled,
And creeks and caves, with sounding of the same:
  O Cambria, stretch and strain thy utmost breath,
  To praise and pray for Queen Elizabeth.

Her third time ten years reign we now possess;
Thrice three times ten God grant her grace may reign
To this her realm's long wished for wealfulness,
Whereby each long erst loss it may regain:
  And so redound, the happiest realm for aye,
  Unturned from truth ev'n till the latter day.

JOHN DAVIES OF HEREFORD
(*c.* 1565 – 1618)

called The Welsh Poet

from *Cambria*

Great Grandame Wales, from whom those ancestors
Descended from whom I (poor I) descend,
I owe so much to my progenitors
And to thee, for them, that until mine end
Thy name and fame I'll honour and defend:
Sith joy doth passage to thy speech deny
(For that thy Prince thine honour doth commend),
Lest that thy silence might be ta'en awry
Mine artless pen shall thy tongue's want supply.

From Owen Tudor, who from Camber came
(From Camber son of Brute who came from Troy),
Art thou descended; and thy bellsire's name
Was Tudor: let us Britons then enjoy
Our own in thee, in thee our only joy.
We have been long afflicted and oppressed
By those that sought our whole race to destroy;
Then sith we are in thee so highly blessed,
Let's have our own, thyself, to give us rest.

But should I instance in particular
What truth doth warrant for the Britons' glory,
I could perhaps run up their race as far

As Jove, and find them famoused in story:
But — for in me it may be thought vainglory,
Since being one, myself I seem to praise —
I will desist, although my soul be sorry
I should desist from that which many ways
Might Camber crown with everlasting bays.

If thou wilt come to us thou well shalt see
We'll spare no pain that may effect thy pleasure,
For each one will be busy as a bee
To yield thee honied joy by weight and measure,
And shun as hell the cause of thy displeasure.
We'll plant our mountains with the rarest trees
That may be culled from Pomona's treasure,
And all our hedgerows shall be ranked with these,
To please thine eye with what with taste agrees.

We'll root up all our roughs, our heaths, our furze,
And in their place make grass and cowslips grow:
We will remove what thy dislike incurs
And with the mountains fill the vales below,
If by man's power and pain they may be so.
Nought shall offend thee, be it what it will
(Be it but mortal), if we it may know;
For we'll bring down the proudest he or hill
That thou shalt doom to be scarce good, or ill.

Then live with us, dear Prince, and we will make
Our wildest wastes jet-coloured garden plots,
So Flora will her flowered meads forsake
To set flowers there, in many curious knots,
To please thee and our other selves the Scots:
We'll turn our villages to cities fair
And share them twixt the Scots and us by lots,
Whereto both one and other may repair
To interchange commodities or air.

We'll cleave the mountains Neptune to let in,
That ships may float where now our sheep do feed:
And whatsoe'er industrious hands may win
Shall not be lost, that may thy pleasure breed
Or richer make our intermixed seed:
And whereas now two towns do scarce appear
Within the largest prospect, then with speed
They shall be built, as if one town they were,
That we may be to each as near as dear.

Those pleasant plots where erst the Romans built
Fair cities for their legions to live in,
Whose gorgeous architecture was oregilt,
That by the civil sword have ruined been
("Which ruins are the monuments of sin"),
These will we now repair, fair as before,
That Scots and Britons may mixed live therein:
Caerleon where King Arthur lived of yore
Shall be rebuilt, and double gilt once more.

O could I tune my tongue unto thine ear,
That so my words might music seem to it,
That so thou might'st alone the burden bear
Which it requires, as it is requisite,
Then should my note be noted to be fit.
I speak for those whose tongues are strange to thee
In thine own tongue: if my words be unfit,
That blame be mine; but if Wales better be
By my disgrace, I hold that grace to me.

Then come, sweet Prince, Wales wooeth thee by me
(By me her sorry tonguesman) to be pleased
To live with her, that so she may by thee
Be ruled in love, and ruled so, be eased
Of what in former times hath her displeased.
The sheep their owner's keeping most approve
For he will cure them, when they are diseased,
With love's right hand; but hirelings, truth doth prove,
Do keep the flock for lucre more than love.

HUGH HOLLAND
(1569 – 1633)

Owen Tudor

The gentle Owen was a man well set;
Broad were his shoulders, though his waist but small;
Straight was his back, and even was his breast,
Which no less seemly made him shew than tall,
Such as Achilles seemed among the rest
Of all his army clad in mighty brass;
Among them such (though all they of the best)
The man of Mone, magnifique Owen, was.

He seemed another oak among the briers;
And as in stature, so did he surpass
In wit and active feats his other peers.
He nimbly could discourse, and nimbly dance,
And aged he was about some thirty years.

Epitaph on Henry Prince of Wales

Lo, where he shineth yonder,
   A fixed star in heaven,
Whose motion here came under
   None of the planets seven.
If that the Moon should tender
   The Sun her love, and marry,
They both could not engender
   So sweet a star as Harry.

On William Shakespeare

Those hands which you so clapped, go now and wring
You Britons brave, for done are Shakespeare's days;
His days are done that made the dainty plays
Which made the Globe of heaven and earth to ring:
Dried is that vein, dried is the Thespian spring,
Turned all to tears, and Phoebus clouds his rays.
That corpse, that coffin, now bestick those bays
Which crowned him poet first, then poet's king.
If tragedies might any prologue have,
All those he made would scarce make one to this,
Where Fame, now that he gone is to the grave
(Death's public tiring-house), the Nuntius is:
   For though his line of life went soon about,
   The life yet of his lines shall never out.

LUDOVIC LLOYD
(*fl.* 1573 – 1610)

from *Sidanen*

Flee, stately Juno, Samos fro,
From Delos straight, Diana go.
Minerva Athens must forsake,
Sidanen Queen your seat must take.   (*the silken one*

Sidanen conquers kings with quill,
Sidanen governs states at will.
Sidanen fears her foes with pen,
With peace Sidanen conquers men.

In Colchos had Sidanen been
The golden fleece then should she win.
To Ida had Sidanen gone
The golden apple she had won.

With palm in hand, with laurel crowned,
With olive decked she first was found.
In Parnasse mount with Muses nine
The tenth Sidanen there did shine.

From Brutus brood, from Dardane line,
Sidanen is that Phoenix fine.
From Camber's soil, from Hector's seed
Sidanen princely doth proceed.

The eagle's youth I wish this queen,
Acanthus-like to flourish green.
As serpents old do cast their skin,
Then she being old may youth begin.

With joyful days and Nestor's years
I wish to her and to her peers
That when Sidanen dyeth I crave
Mausolus tomb Sidanen have.

EDWARD HERBERT
(1583 – 1648)

called Lord Herbert of Cherbury

The Thought

If you do love as well as I,
Then every minute from your heart
    A thought doth part;
And wingëd with desire doth fly
Till it hath met, in a straight line,
    A thought of mine
So like to yours, we cannot know
Whether of both doth come, or go,
    Till we define
Which of us two, that thought doth owe.

I say then, that your thoughts which pass,
Are not so much the thoughts you meant,
    As those I sent:
For as my image in a glass
Belongs not to the glass you see,
    But unto me;
So when your fancy is so clear
That you would think you saw me there,
    It needs must be
That it was I did first appear.

Likewise, when I send forth a thought,
My reason tells me, 'tis the same
    Which from you came,
And which your beauteous image wrought.
Thus while our thoughts by turns do lead,
    None can precede;
And thus, while in each other's mind
Such interchangëd forms we find,
    Our loves may plead
To be of more than vulgar kind.

May you then often think on me,
And by that thinking know 'tis true
    I thought on you;
I in the same belief will be:
While, by this mutual address,
    We will possess
A love must live, when we do die,
Which rare and secret property
    You will confess
If you do love as well as I.

RICHARD WILIAM
(fl. 1590 – 1630)

called Sir Richard the Blackbird

Sir Richard's Confession

1 j haf latly, bing tw bysy
   jn law maters, lost my fethers
2 and haf bing dwl, jn my yowthffwl   (*having been*
   daes and livyd, disgontentyd
3 my tym j spent, off profferment
   most ungodly, and karlesly

4 that j dar not, hard hys my lot
  tak my ffry wyl, withowt peryl
5 j ffynd in ags, bwt smal kwrags
  ffor tw venter, any mater
6 and vaen siffting, is no living
  lawffwl and ffyt, ffor my kredyt
7 beter yt ys, in god sarvis
  tw lern to dy, and lyf godly
8 then tw pwrchas, by malin kas
  lands and livins, with gred kwrsins   (great cushions?
9 and my gray hers, mak my travers
  my fformen dawns, by repentawns
10 god gif my gras, my mesias
  tw lif kontent, with my talent
11 by law off lat, j got swmat
  thoch no living, ffor my kawling
12 yt hows and land, ffor a hwsband
  that in tyling, has swm kwning
13 yff yt wyl ples, god my nywnes
  off liff upon, my swbmysion
14 j wld ever, lif hier affter
  in godly sort, tw my kwmffort
15 and kraf daely, tw haf marsy
  wyth god giwstys, ffor offensys   (justice
16 or els j ffer, that my maker
  my sowl wyl rent, with giwst gidment   (judgment
17 and hys thretnings, in many things
  ffor deservyd, ffawts j dowtyd
18 yt swit jesu, j pray thy vyw
  how j awlter, liff and maner
19 j apeal lord, tw thy konkord
  thy wyl by dwn, ffor my pardwn
20 j wyl never, by a wandrer
  in my offys, ffrom thy sarfys
21 bwt in demywr, godly plesywr
  tw lern tw dwel, with thy gosbel
22 and set my lyms, with pwr pilgryms
  tw seck affter my Redymer
23 thus thy servant, jldeth konstant
  tw lif and dy, in thy marsy

GEORGE HERBERT
(1593 – 1633)

The British Church

I joy, dear Mother, when I view
Thy perfect lineaments and hue
      Both sweet and bright.

Beauty in thee takes up her place
And dates her letters from thy face
      When she doth write.

A fine aspect in fit array,
Neither too mean nor yet too gay,
      Shows who is best.

Outlandish looks may not compare,
For all they either painted are,
      Or else undressed.

She on the hills, which wantonly
Allureth all in hope to be
      By her preferred,

Hath kissed so long her painted shrines
That even her face by kissing shines,
      For her reward.

She in the valley is so shy
Of dressing that her hair doth lie
      About her ears;

While she avoids her neighbour's pride,
She wholly goes on th'other side,
      And nothing wears.

But, dearest Mother, (what those miss)
The mean thy praise and glory is,
      And long may be.

Blessed be God whose love it was
To double-meat thee with his grace,
      And none but thee.

Easter Wings

Lord, who createdst man in wealth and store,
　Though foolishly he lost the same,
　　Decaying more and more,
　　　Till he became
　　　Most poor:

　　　With thee
　　　O let me rise,
　　As larks, harmoniously,
　And sing this day thy victories:
Then shall the fall further the flight in me.

My tender age in sorrow did begin;
　And still with sicknesses and shame
　　Thou didst so punish sin
　　　That I became
　　　Most thin:

　　　With thee
　　　Let me combine,
　　And feel this day thy victory;
　For if I imp my wing on thine,　　　　　　　(*mend*
Affliction shall advance the flight in me.

The Altar

A broken altar, Lord, thy servant rears,
Made of a heart, and cemented with tears:
　Whose parts are as thy hand did frame;
　No workman's tool hath touched the same.
　　　　　A　　heart　　alone
　　　　　Is　　such　　a　　stone
　　　　　As　　nothing　　but
　　　　　Thy power doth cut.
　　　　　Wherefore each part
　　　　　Of　my　hard　heart
　　　　　Meets　in　this　frame
　　　　　To praise thy name.
That, if I chance to hold my peace,
These stones to praise thee may not cease.
O, let thy blessed sacrifice be mine,
And　sanctify　this　altar　to　be　thine!

Prayer

Prayer: the Church's banquet, angels' age,
   God's breath in man returning to his birth,
The soul in paraphrase, heart in pilgrimage,
   The Christian plummet sounding heaven and earth;

Engine against th'Almighty, sinner's tower,
   Reversed thunder, Christ-side-piercing spear,
The six-days world transposing in an hour,
   A kind of tune which all things hear and fear;

Softness, and peace, and joy, and love, and bliss,
   Exalted manna, gladness of the best,
   Heaven in ordinary, man well dressed,
The Milky Way, the bird of paradise,
   Church-bells beyond the stars heard, the soul's blood,
   The land of spices; something understood.

Paradise

I bless thee, Lord, because I grow
Among thy trees, which in a row
To thee both fruit and order owe.

What open force or hidden charm
Can blast my fruit or bring me harm
While the enclosure is thine arm?

Enclose me still, for fear I start;
Be to me rather sharp and tart
Than let me want thy hand and art.

When thou dost greater judgements spare
And with thy knife but prune and pare,
Even fruitful trees more fruitful are.

Such sharpness shows the sweetest friend,
Such cuttings rather heal than rend,
And such beginnings touch their end.

from *Providence*

O sacred Providence, who from end to end
Strongly and sweetly movest! shall I write,
And not of thee, through whom my fingers bend
To hold my quill? shall they not do thee right?

Of all the creatures both in sea and land,
Only to man thou hast made known thy ways,
And put the pen alone into his hand,
And made him secretary of thy praise.

Beasts fain would sing; birds ditty to their notes;
Trees would be tuning on their native lute
To thy renown: but all their hands and throats
Are brought to man, while they are lame and mute.

Man is the world's high priest: he doth present
The sacrifice for all while they below
Unto the service mutter an assent,
Such as springs use that fall, and winds that blow.

He that to praise and laud thee doth refrain
Doth not refrain unto himself alone,
But robs a thousand who would praise thee fain,
And doth commit a world of sin in one.

The beasts say, Eat me; but if beasts must teach,
The tongue is yours to eat but mine to praise:
The trees say, Pull me; but the hand you stretch
Is mine to write as it is yours to raise.

Wherefore, most sacred Spirit, I here present
For me and all my fellows praise to thee;
And just it is that I should pay the rent,
Because the benefit accrues to me.

The Forerunners

The harbingers are come. See, see their mark:
White is their colour, and behold my head.
But must they have my brain? must they dispark
Those sparkling notions which therein were bred?
　　　　Must dullness turn me to a clod?
Yet have they left me *Thou art still my God.*

Good men ye be to leave me my best room,
Even all my heart, and what is lodged there;
I pass not, I, what of the rest become,   *(care not*
So *Thou art still my God* be out of fear.
        He will be pleased with that ditty,
And if I please him I write fine and witty.

Farewell sweet phrases, lovely metaphors.
But will ye leave me thus? When ye before
Of stews and brothels only knew the doors,
Then did I wash you with my tears, and more –
        Brought you to church well-dressed and clad:
My God must have my best, even all I had.

Lovely enchanting language, sugar-cane,
Honey of roses, whither wilt thou fly?
Hath some fond lover 'ticed thee to thy bane?
And wilt thou leave the church and love a sty?
        Fie, thou wilt soil thy broidered coat,
And hurt thyself and him that sings the note.

Let foolish lovers, if they will love dung,
With canvas, not with arras, clothe their shame:
Let folly speak in her own native tongue.
True beauty dwells on high: ours is a flame
        But borrowed thence to light us thither.
Beauty and beauteous words should go together.

Yet if you go I pass not; take your way:
For *Thou art still my God* is all that ye
Perhaps with more embellishment can say.
Go, birds of spring: let winter have his fee,
        Let a bleak paleness chalk the door,
So all within be livelier than before.

The Sonne

    Let foreign nations of their language boast
    What fine variety each tongue affords;
    I like our language, as our men and coast;
    Who cannot dress it well want wit not words.
    How neatly do we give one only name
    To parents' issue and the sun's bright star!
    A son is light and fruit; a fruitful flame

Chasing the father's dimness, carried far
From the first man in the east to fresh and new
Western discoveries of posterity.
So in one word our Lord's humility
We turn upon him in a sense most true:
  For what Christ once in humbleness began,
  We him in glory call the Son of Man.

The Flower

      How fresh, O Lord, how sweet and clean
Are thy returns! even as the flowers in spring
      To which, besides their own demean,
The late-past frosts tributes of pleasure bring.
          Grief melts away
          Like snow in May,
  As if there were no such cold thing.

      Who would have thought my shrivelled heart
Could have recovered greenness? It was gone
      Quite undergound – as flowers depart
To see their mother-root when they have blown,
          Where they together
          All the hard weather,
  Dead to the world, keep house unknown.

      These are thy wonders, Lord of power –
Killing and quickening, bringing down to hell
      And up to heaven in an hour;
Making a chiming of a passing-bell.
          We say amiss
          This or that is:
  Thy word is all, if we could spell.

O that I once past changing were,
Fast in thy paradise where no flower can wither!
Many a spring I shoot up fair,
Offering at heaven, growing and groaning thither;
    Nor doth my flower
    Want a spring shower,
My sins and I joining together.

But while I grow in a straight line,
Still upwards bent, as if heaven were mine own,
Thy anger comes and I decline:
What frost to that? what pole is not the zone
    Where all things burn,
    When thou dost turn
And the least frown of thine is shown?

And now in age I bud again,
After so many deaths I live and write;
I once more smell the dew and rain
And relish versing. O my only light,
    It cannot be
    That I am he
On whom thy tempests fell all night.

These are thy wonders, Lord of love,
To make us see we are but flowers that glide;
    Which when we once can find and prove,
Thou hast a garden for us where to bide.
    Who would be more,
    Swelling through store,
Forfeit their paradise by their pride.

JAMES HOWELL
(1594 – 1666)

Upon Dr Davies's British Grammar

'Twas a tough task, believe it, thus to tame
A wild and wealthy language, and to frame
Grammatic toils to curb her, so that she
Now speaks by rules, and sings by prosody;
Such is the strength of art rough things to shape,
And of rude commons rich enclosures make.
Doubtless much oil and labour went to couch
Into methodic rules the rugged Dutch;

The Rabbis pass my reach, but judge I can
Something of Clenard and Quintilian;
And for those modern dames, I find they three
Are only lops cut from the Latian tree,
And easy 'twas to square them into parts,
The tree itself so blossoming with arts.
I have been shown for Irish and Bascuence
Imperfect rules couched in an accidence:
But I find none of these can take the start
Of Davies, or that prove more men of art,
Who in exacter method and short way
The idioms of a language do display.
   This is the tongue the bards sung in of old,
And Druids their dark knowledge did unfold;
Merlin in this his prophecies did vent,
Which through the world of fame bear such extent.
This spoke that son of Mars and Britain bold
Who first amongst Christian worthies is enrolled.
This Brennus who, to his desire and glut,
The mistress of the world did prostitute.
This Arviragus and brave Catarac,
Sole free, when all the world was on Rome's rack;
This Lucius, who on angel's wings did soar
To Rome, and would wear diadem no more;
And thousand heroes more which should I tell,
This new year scarce would serve me, so farewell.

DAVID LLOYD
(1597 – 1663)

from *The Legend of Captain Jones*

> *'Twas well the wars were done before,*
> *Lost in Lluellin and Glendore.*
> *Had Jones lived then, in vain th'assails*
> *Of Saxons: Wales had still been Wales.*

Roses and tulips Flora gathers here
When we have none, to crown her golden hair,
And here Medea picked (if Jones speaks truth)
Those herbs which turned antiquity to youth:
The only phoenix deigns to weather here,
The only place like her without a peer.

Lest all these sweets should want sweet harmony
A numerous quire of nightingales comply
To warble forth the sweet Amara's praise,
Who turns their mourning notes to merry lays...

Such is Amara, such is Tempe field,
Elysium on earth unparalleled:
'Twas here this royal priest now kept his court,
A place well suiting with his fame and port.
And here comes Jones, where having made's address,
Letters of credence given at his access
In Latin writ: in the same tongue he gives
Jones gracious words, which language Jones conceives
To be Arabic, for the Latin tongue
He ne'er endured to learn nor old nor young.
But that's all one: there's no reply expected;
Unto a rich pavilion he's directed
By men of state, where he is well attended
With all that's rich, and to his rest commended.
Some few days spent, and time for audience got,
When Prester John in royal state was set:
Jones, studying how t'express his eloquence
In some strange language which might pose the Prince,
Now trouls him forth a full mouthed Welsh oration
Boldly delivered as became his nation.
The plot proved right, for not one word of sense
Could be picked from't; which vexed the learned Prince.
His learned linguists are called in to hear,
Who might as well have stopped each other's ear
For aught they understood, and all protest
It was the very language of the Beast.
Jones hath his end, and then to make it known
He had more tongues t'express himself than one,
In a new tone he speaks, not half so rich
But better known: 'twas English; unto which
An English Factor is interpreter
Between our Captain and John Presbyter.
His business takes effect (what e'er it was)
And great expresses of respect do pass
To Jones from him, as one he thought most rich
In unknown tongues expressed in his first speech,
And so admires him for he knows not what:
But Jones may thank his mother-tongue for that.

MORGAN LLWYD
(1619 – 1659)

1648

1. The Excuse

Though truth be gold in any mould, and talents all for use,
and much of scripture given in verse, and some delight in muse;

I shall not sing but others say that I misspend my time.
They spy a mote and pick my coat and scorn my hopping rhyme.

But I must sing of Christ my king, and sessions of that man;
for such a summer was not seen, not since the world began.

All English swans that are alive, and Scottish cuckoos, sing;
and some Welsh swallows chirp and chime to welcome pleasant
    spring.

The chickens now are lifted up upon that eagle's wing.
The very stones will echo forth if men be dull this spring.

Hosanna cry, King Jesus comes, he'll summer with him bring:
a meek, just, strong, fair, lasting Prince. Again Hosanna sing.

Your hearts spread freely in his way, make heaven and earth to
    ring
with acclamations, and clap hands to welcome Christ the King.

In this our Anno of four parts, the winter and the spring,
the summer and the harvest last, news true and great I bring.

2. *from* The Winter

A thousand days great Beelzebub and Pope his son and fool
made Christendom their slaughterhouse, the church their
    dancing school.

Brave Huguenots, stiff Mordecais, stout Lollards, you stood
    fast;
*a glana iw'r gelynen wyrdd** that scorned the Romish blast.

and holiest is the holly green

These nations drunk the health of Rome long till their wits were
  drowned,
and then a cup of their own blood must pass the table round.

Our British climate was so cold, souls frozen were to death:
we were for want of light and zeal a barren tedious heath.

Our north-east cut to Indies' mines, I mean to heavenly gold,
we missed it – summer was so short and winter was so cold.

Our king, queen, prince and prelates high their merry
  Christmas spent
with brawny hearts, when yet their dogs could Lazarus lament.

Our Reformation mangled was, our blossomed truths were
  ripped
as errors and as heresies, our Christian freedom clipped.

The Just Judge sent us blessed news by Peter, Paul and John
that winter shall not always last: now pleasant spring come on.

3. *from* The Spring

God's twins (the testaments) speak loud
that Michael long shall reign,
nor bard nor devil can it deny.
It is so sure and plain.

Both Jews and Greeks expect a star,
and Rome (that witch) doth quake:
the nations are on potters' wheels,
the ancient thrones do shake.

The Judge was long since at the door
and do you understand?
The town prepares, they sweep the hall:
that session is at hand.

O glorious Lamb, thou King of saints,
we praise and worship thee
that gave us leave to live in spring.
Lord, let us summer see.

4. *from* The Summer

Sing on a brittle sea of glass!
Sing in a furne of fire!   *(furnace*
In flames we leap for joy, and find
a cave a singing choir.

Sight, sense and reason, hold your peace;
our guides no longer be.
Word, faith and spirit stand instead –
things now unseen we see.

It's true we differ in small points,
as clocks in cities do;
some travellers do lag behind
who yet to Salem go.

Men's faces, voices, differ much –
saints are not all one size;
flowers in one garden vary too:
let none monopolize.

Out of these all will Christ compound
an army for himself:
so Satan gets of all these sects
the parings and the pelf.

Come down, O London, to the dust:
let Christ sit on the throne.
And be not drunk with wit and wealth,
else sit with Tyre alone.

O Wales, poor Rachel, thou shalt bear;
sad Hannah, now rejoice.
The last is first, the summer comes
to hear the turtle's voice.

Christ is in arms. The day is hot:
now Beelzebub retreat.
When that great summer is once past
next comes that harvest great.

5. *from* The Harvest

The field is large, the barn at hand,
the reapers quick and wise.
The stubble flames, and sinful souls
lie down and never rise.

In Gog and Magog hell shall spew
that last and filthy foam,
and before winter comes again
we shall be all at home.

I tire thee, friend; I make an end.
But see thou bend thy line
and heart to sing in this thy spring
of Christ thy King and mine.

from *Charles The Last King of Britain*

The law was ever above kings
    and Christ above the law:
unhappy Charles provoked the lamb –
    to dust he must withdraw.

Not his fair words, but all his swords
    enraged by his command,
that sheathe themselves in Christians' hearts,
    should make you understand.

Look not too much on few late things:
    view all from first to last
since James his days, and wonder not
    that such a sentence passed.

Though this pen loathes to touch dead Charles,
    it warns the living all,
lest any stumble at his corpse
    and break their necks withal.

Make not, O kings, your curbs too sharp,
    but truth and justice seek!
O land, avoid king's evil now;
    O Parliament, be meek!

from *Awake, O Lord, Awake Thy Saincts*

Awake, O Lord, awake thy saints,
   unite them all in one,
and use them now against thy foes:
   Lord, take thy sling and stone!

Let Wales and England roused be!
   O churches, sleep no more,
and be not drunk with wealth or wrath –
   hark how the nations roar.

Holland begins to pledge you all
   and sip the wrathful cup,
and peace with them you shall not make
   lest you with Ahab sup.

Now wanton France is in a trance,
   the English dance they find;
they seek themselves, they mind not Christ:
   but Christ himself doth mind.

Woe is to Europe! Now the day
   approacheth very nigh
of plague, flame, sword and hailstones great.
   Woe Europe, blind and high!

Come Wisdome Sweet

Come wisdome sweet, my spirit meet, for at thy feet I fall:
Oh chiefest thing, my wealth, my wing, my rest, my ring, my all.

My love, my light, my song, my sight, my bread, my bright
   eternal one:
He doth not cease to give increase, with peace and ease in one.

Sin, Death and Satan, crabbed foes, are kings of woes and wrath –
As wind, fire, brimstone join in one. Our Christ all conquered hath.

O drymmed cri, a wnaethem ni, pe basit ti o Dduw
Heb ladd y tri, ath laddodd di, in llwyddo ni i fyw.*

    *O heavy cry we would have made, hadst not thou, O God,
    Killed the three who killed thee, to enable us to live.

THOMAS VAUGHAN
(1621 – 1666)

from On The Death of an Oxford Proctor

When he did read how did we flock to hear:
Sure some professors became pupils there.
He would refine abstractions: it was he
That gave the text all its authority,
As if the Stagyrite resigned his pen
And took his censure not his comment then.
And though with some the science goes for pelf,
His lectures made it to transcend itself.
He used the creatures as a scale to storm
The spiritual world, and though 'twas torn
And broken with uncertainties, yet he –
By reason, as by faith – a Deity
Could apprehend and reach. Thus having traced
These secondary things, his soul made haste
To view the Cause and then began to plod,
Nothing being left to puzzle him but God,
Whose mysteries he reached, as far as he
Of his great self had made discovery.
He plundered not the heavens, nor brought he down
Secrets from thence which were before unknown;
Yet some there are believe their wits so ripe
That they can draw a map of the Archetype,
And with strange optics tutored they can view
The emanations of the mystic Jew.
In this his pious ignorance was best
And did excel his knowledge of the rest.
But he is gone and Providence took him
To add to heaven another cherubim.
This to our tears may minister relief:
'Tis this preferment that does cause our grief.

HENRY VAUGHAN
(1621 – 1695)

called Silurist

from An Invitation to Brecknock

Since last we met, thou and thy horse, my dear,
Have not so much as drunk or littered here.
I wonder, though thyself be thus deceased,

Thou hast the spite to coffin up thy beast;
Or is the palfrey sick, and his rough hide
With the penance of one spur mortified?
Or taught by thee (like Pythagoras's ox)
Is then his master grown more orthodox?
Whatever 'tis, a sober cause't must be
That thus long bars us of thy company.
The town believes thee lost, and didst thou see
But half her sufferings, now distressed for thee,
Thou'ldst swear (like Rome) her foul, polluted walls
Were sacked by Brennus and the savage Gauls.
Abominable face of things! here's noise
Of banged mortars, blue aprons, and boys,
Pigs, dogs, and drums, with the hoarse hellish notes
Of politically deaf usurers' throats,
With new fine Worships, and the old cast team
Of Justices vexed with the cough and phlegm...
    Come! leave this sullen state, and let not wine
And precious wit lie dead for want of thine:
Shall the dull market landlord with his rout
Of sneaking tenants dirtily swill out
This harmless liquor, shall they knock and beat
For sack, only to talk of rye and wheat?
O let not such preposterous tippling be
In our metropolis! May I ne'er see
Such tavern sacrilege, nor lend a line
To weep the rapes and tragedy of wine!
Here lives that chimick, quick fire which betrays   (transmuting
Fresh spirits to the blood and warms our lays.
I have reserved against thy approach a cup
That, were thy muse stark dead, shall raise her up
And teach her yet more charming words and skill
Than ever Celia, Chloris, Astrophil
Or any of the threadbare names inspired
Poor rhyming lovers with a mistress fired.
Come then! and while the slow icicle hangs
At the stiff thatch, and winter's frosty pangs
Benumb the year, blithe (as of old) let us
'Midst noise and war, of peace and mirth discuss.
This portion thou wert born for: why should we
Vex at the times' ridiculous misery –
An age that thus hath fooled itself, and will
(Spite of thy teeth and mine) persist so still?
Let's sit then at this fire, and while we steal

– 74 –

A revel in the town let others seal,
Purchase or cheat, and who can, let them pay,
Till those black deeds bring on the darksome day.
Innocent spenders we! a better use
Shall wear out our short lease and leave th'obtuse
Rout to their husks. They and their bags at best
Have cares in earnest: we care for a jest.

from *Upon A Cloke Lent Him*

Here, take again thy sackcloth! and thank heaven
Thy courtship hath not killed me. Is't not even
Whether we die by piecemeal or at once,
Since both but ruin; why then for the nonce
Didst husband my afflictions, and cast o'er
Me this forced hurdle to inflame the score?
Had I near London in this rug been seen,
Without doubt I had executed been
For some bold Irish spy, and cross a sledge
Had lain messed up for their four gates and bridge.
When first I bore it, my oppressed feet
Would needs persuade me 'twas some leaden sheet;
Such deep impressions and such dangerous holes
Were made that I began to doubt my soles,
And every step (so near necessity)
Devoutly wished some honest cobbler by.
Besides, it was so short the Jewish rag
Seemed circumcised, but had a Gentile shag.
Hadst thou been with me on that day when we
Left craggy Beeston and the fatal Dee,
When beaten with fresh storms and late mishap
It shared the office of a cloak and cap,
To see how 'bout my clouded head it stood
Like a thick turban or some lawyer's hood,
While the stiff hollow pleats on every side
Like conduit-pipes rained from the bearded hide,
I know thou wouldst in spite of that day's fate
Let loose thy mirth at my new shape and state,
And with a shallow smile or two profess
Some Saracen had lost the clouted dress.   (*patched*
Didst ever see the good wife (as they say)
March in her short cloak on the Christening day,
With what soft motions she salutes the Church
And leaves the bedrid mother in the lurch?

Just so jogged I, while my dull horse did trudge
Like a circuit-beast plagued with a gouty judge.

But I have done. And think not, friend, that I
This freedom took to jeer thy courtesy.
I thank thee for't, and I believe my Muse
So known to thee, thou'lt not suspect abuse:
She did this 'cause (perhaps) thy love paid thus
Might with my thanks outlive thy cloak and us.

The Morning-Watch

O joys! Infinite sweetness! with what flowers
And shoots of glory my soul breaks and buds!
            All the long hours
            Of night and rest,
            Through the still shrouds
            Of sleep and clouds,
            This dew fell on my breast;
            O how it bloods
And spirits all my earth! Hark! In what rings
And hymning circulations the quick world
            Awakes and sings;
            The rising winds
            And falling springs,
            Birds, beasts, all things
            Adore him in their kinds.
            Thus all is hurled
In sacred hymns and order, the great chime
And symphony of nature. Prayer is
            The world in tune,
            A spirit voice
            And vocal joys
            Whose echo is heaven's bliss.
            O let me climb
When I lie down! The pious soul by night
Is like a clouded star whose beams, though said
            To shed their light
            Under some cloud,
            Yet are above
            And shine and move
            Beyond that misty shroud.
            So in my bed,
That curtained grave, though sleep like ashes hide
My lamp and life, both shall in thee abide.

HENRY VAUGHAN

The Pursuite

Lord! what a busy, restless thing
    Hast thou made man:
Each day and hour he is on wing,
    Rests not a span;
Then having lost the sun and light
    By clouds surprised,
He keeps a commerce in the night
    With air disguised.
Hadst thou given to this active dust
    A state untired,
The lost son had not left the husk
    Nor home desired:
That was thy secret, and it is
    Thy mercy too,
For when all fails to bring to bliss
    Then this must do.
Ah, Lord! and what a purchase will that be –
To take us sick, that sound would not take thee.

Sondayes

Bright shadows of true rest! some shoots of bliss,
                    Heaven once a week;
The next world's gladness prepossessed in this;
                    A day to seek

Eternity in time; the steps by which
We climb above all ages; lamps that light
Man through his heap of dark days; and the rich
And full redemption of the whole week's flight.

The pulleys unto headlong man; time's bower;
                    The narrow way;
Transplanted paradise; God's walking hour;
                  The cool o'th'day;

The creature's jubilee; God's parle with dust;
Heaven here; man on those hills of myrrh and flowers;
Angels descending; the returns of trust;
A gleam of glory after six-days-showers.

The Church's love-feasts; time's prerogative,
                    And interest
Deducted from the whole; the combs and hive
                    And home of rest.

The Milky Way chalked out with suns; a clue
That guides through erring hours; and in full story
A taste of heaven on earth; the pledge and cue
Of a full feast; and the out-courts of glory.

The Waterfall

With what deep murmurs through time's silent stealth
Doth thy transparent, cool and watery wealth
                    Here flowing fall
                    And chide, and call,
As if his liquid, loose retinue stayed
Lingering, and were of this steep place afraid:
                    The common pass
                    Where, clear as glass,
                    All must descend
                    Not to an end
But, quickened by this deep and rocky grave,
Rise to a longer course more bright and brave.

            Dear stream! dear bank, where often I
            Have sate and pleased my pensive eye,
            Why, since each drop of thy quick store
            Runs thither whence it flowed before,
            Should poor souls fear a shade or night
            Who came (sure) from a sea of light?
            Or since those drops are all sent back
            So sure to thee that none doth lack,
            Why should frail flesh doubt any more
            That what God takes he'll not restore?
            O useful element and clear!
            My sacred wash and cleanser here,
            My first consigner unto those
            Fountains of life where the Lamb goes:
            What sublime truths and wholesome themes
            Lodge in thy mystical, deep streams!
            Such as dull man can never find
            Unless that Spirit lead his mind

Which first upon thy face did move
And hatched all with his quickening love.
As this loud brook's incessant fall
In streaming rings restagnates all,
Which reach by course the bank and then
Are no more seen, just so pass men.
O my invisible estate,
My glorious liberty, still late!
Thou art the channel my soul seeks,
Not this with cataracts and creeks.

The Book

Eternal God! maker of all
That have lived here since man's fall:
The Rock of ages! in whose shade
They live unseen when here they fade.

Thou knew'st this paper when it was
Mere seed, and after that but grass;
Before 'twas dressed or spun, and when
Made linen, who did wear it then;
What were their lives, their thoughts and deeds,
Whether good corn or fruitless weeds.

Thou knewest this tree when a green shade
Covered it, since a cover made,
And where it flourished, grew and spread,
As if it never should be dead.

Thou knew'st this harmless beast when he
Did live and feed by thy decree
On each green thing; then slept (well fed)
Clothed with this skin which now lies spread
A covering o'er this aged book;
Which makes me wisely weep and look
On my own dust: mere dust it is,
But not so dry and clean as this.
Thou knew'st and saw'st them all, and though
Now scattered thus, dost know them so.

O knowing, glorious Spirit! when
Thou shalt restore trees, beasts and men,
When thou shalt make all new again,
Destroying only death and pain,
Give him amongst thy works a place
Who in them loved and sought thy face.

Death

Though since thy first sad entrance by
                    Just Abel's blood
'Tis now six thousand years well nigh,
And still thy sovereignty holds good,
Yet by none art thou understood.

We talk and name thee with much ease
                    As a tried thing,
And everyone can slight his lease
As if it ended in a spring
Which shades and bowers doth rent-free bring.

To thy dark land these heedless go:
                    But there was one
Who searched it quite through to and fro,
And then returning, like the sun,
Discovered all that there is done.

And since his death we throughly see
                    All thy dark way;
Thy shades but thin and narrow be,
Which his first looks will quickly fray:
Mists make but triumphs for the day.

As harmless violets, which give
                    Their virtues here
For salves and syrups while they live,
Do after calmly disappear,
And neither grieve, repine nor fear:

So die his servants; and as sure
                    Shall they revive.
Then let not dust your eyes obscure
But lift them up, where still alive
Though fled from you their spirits hive.

ANONYMOUS

(c. 1632)

There were Three Jovial Welshmen

There were three jovial Welshmen,
  As I have heard men say,
And they would go a-hunting
  Upon St David's Day.

All the day they hunted
  And nothing could they find
But a ship a-sailing,
  A-sailing with the wind.

One said it was a ship,
  The other he said Nay.
The third said it was a house
  With the chimney blown away.

And all the night they hunted
  And nothing could they find
But the moon a-gliding,
  A-gliding with the wind.

One said it was the moon,
  The other he said Nay.
The third said it was a cheese
  And half of it cut away.

And all the day they hunted
  And nothing could they find
But a hedgehog in a bramble bush,
  And that they left behind.

The first said it was a hedgehog,
  The second he said Nay.
The third said it was a pincushion
  And the pins stuck in wrong way.

And all the night they hunted
  And nothing could they find
But a hare in a turnip field,
  And that they left behind.

The first said it was a hare,
  The second he said Nay.
The third said it was a calf
  And the cow had run away.

And all the day they hunted
  And nothing could they find
But an owl in a holly tree,
  And that they left behind.

One said it was an owl,
  The other he said Nay.
The third said 'twas an old man
  And his beard growing grey.

ANONYMOUS
(c. 1642)

from *An Eccho*

Eccho, tell me: on what's religion grounded? .... Roundhead
Who are its professors most considerable? .... rabble
How do these prove themselves to be the godly? .... oddly
Who are their preachers, common men or women? .... women
Came they from any university? .... city
Do they not learning from their doctrine sever? .... ever
Yet they pretend that they do edify .... O fie
What do they always in their conventicle? .... tickle
What churches have they, and what pulpits? .... pits
As for the temples, they with zeal embrace them .... race them
Nor will they leave us any ceremonies .... or moneys
How stand they affected to the government civil? .... evil
But to the king they say they are most loyal .... lie all
Then God keep king and state from these same men .... Amen

ROWLAND WATKYNS
(*fl.* 1635 – 1664)

Golden Grove, Carmarthen

If I might where I pleased compose my nest,
The Golden Grove should be my constant rest.
This curious fabric might make us believe
That angels there, or men like angels, live.

I must commend the outside; but within
Not to admire, it were almost a sin.
Of fertile ground the large circumference
With admiration may confound the sense;
Which ground, if things were rightly understood,
From paradise came tumbling in the flood,
And there the water left it, therefore we
Find here of pleasures such variety.
Wise Nature here did strive, and witty Art,
To please the curious eye and longing heart.
The neighbouring river Towy doth o'erflow
Like pleasant Nilus the rich meads below.
Hence come great store, and various kind of fish
So good as may enrich the empty dish.
Fowls thither flock as if they thought it fit
They should present themselves unto the spit.
Here gardens are composed, so sweet, so fair,
With fragrant flowers as do perfume the air.
Hard by a grove doth stand, which doth defeat
Cold winter storms and the dry summer's heat.
There merry birds their pleasant carols sing,
Like sweet musicians to the wanton spring.
There are parks, orchards, warrens, fish-ponds, springs:
Each foot of ground some curious object brings.
There lives a noble earl, free, just and wise,
In whom the elixir of perfection lies.
His heart is good as balsam, pure as gold,
Wise as a serpent, as a lion bold.

The Common People

The many-headed Hydra, or the People,
Now build the church, then pull down bells and steeple:
Today for learned bishops and a king
They shout with one consent – tomorrow sing
A different note. One while the people cry
To Christ Hosanna; then him crucify.
And thus the wavering multitude will be
Constant in nothing but inconstancy:
When these together swarm, the kingdom fears;
They are as fierce as tigers, rude as bears.

ROWLAND WATKYNS

The Blackamoors

We many men from Mauritania see
To England come, as black as ravens be.
Into yourselves look with a curious eye
And you shall find you are more black than they.
Then wonder not at them so black in skin
But at yourselves so foul, so black by sin.

Peace and War

Peace is like salt which seasons all our meat,
Till envious war doth poison all we eat.
War, like the horseleech, calls for human blood
And ruins all things like the unruly flood
Or raging fire. I do prefer by far
An unjust peace before the justest war.
Welcome, sweet peace, which makes all things complete
And gives us grapes from our own vines to eat.
That land is blest and hath a golden day
Where drums and trumpets cease, and organs play.
Peace breedeth plenty, war consumes a nation;
Peace bringeth joy, war causeth lamentation.
Pray to the God of peace that we may have
The love and peace of God unto the grave.

The Shrew

Behold her lip, how thin it is; her nose
How sharp, her voice how shrill, which doth disclose
A froward shrew. Who hath her by mishap
Shall surely hear a constant thunder-clap:
Silence is her disease, for like a mill
Her clapper goes, and never standeth still.
By night hobgoblins houses haunt: this sprite
Doth vex and haunt the house both day and night.
The rack, the wheel, the Spanish Inquisition
Torments not like her tongue. A sad condition
Her husband lives in: like a coward he
Must leave the field and always vanquished be.
He must commend what she doth well approve,
And disallow of what she doth not love.
We tame wild fowls, bears, lions, but no art
To tame a shrew could any yet impart.

ANONYMOUS
(*c.* 1664)

Sence and Nonsence

I saw a peacock with a flaming tail,
I saw a blazing comet rain down hail;
I saw a cloud begirt with ivy round,
I saw a shady oak creep on the ground.
I saw a pismire swallow up a whale,   (*ant*
I saw the brackish sea brimful of ale;
I saw a Venice glass sixteen yards deep,
I saw a well full of men's tears that weep.
I saw men's eyes all on a flaming fire,
I saw an house big as the moon and higher;
I saw the sun all red, even at midnight:
I saw the man that saw this dreadful sight.

THE BROGYNTYN POET
(*c.* 1690)

On the Welch

The guile and softness of the Saxon race
In gallant Briton's soul had never place;
Strong as his rocks, and in his language pure,
In his own innocence and truth secure:
Such is the bold, the noble mountaineer,
As void of treason as he is of fear.
He scorns supplanting arts and crafts as base,
But like his hero ancestors he loves the manly chase.
His soil abounds with nature's choicest store,
His mountains' entrails stuffed with precious ore;
Yet sordid avarice could ne'er invade
The well-tuned soul, for love and music made.
Music and amorous poetry inspire
The natural bard as soon as genial fire.
With equal appetite his lively mate
(Blooming and fair as nature's unsoiled state)
Affords him joys as vigorous as their blood
When with delight they calm its raging flood.
Scarce fancied blessings could with his compare,
Did he not with us griping bondage share;
But till (as fatal prophecies have spoke)

By his roused valour all our chains are broke,
Silent he lies beneath the galling yoke.
So hidden mines their horrid fate conceal
Till well-timed fire the mighty force reveal:
At heaven and liberty the powder aims
And mounts in glorious and destroying flames.

JOHN DYER
(1699 – 1757)

Grongar Hill

Silent nymph! with curious eye
Who the purple evening lie
On the mountain's lonely van
Beyond the noise of busy man,
Painting fair the form of things,
While the yellow linnet sings
Or the tuneful nightingale
Charms the forest with her tale;
Come, with all thy various hues,
Come and aid thy sister Muse:
Now while Phoebus, riding high,
Gives lustre to the land and sky,
Grongar Hill invites my song.
Draw the landscape bright and strong –
Grongar in whose mossy cells
Sweetly musing Quiet dwells;
Grongar in whose silent shade
For the modest Muses made
So oft I have, the evening still,
At the fountain of a rill
Sat upon a flowery bed
With my hand beneath my head
While strayed my eyes o'er Towy's flood,
Over mead and over wood,
From house to house, from hill to hill,
Till Contemplation had her fill.
  About his chequered sides I wind
And leave his brooks and meads behind,
And groves and grottos where I lay,
And vistas shooting beams of day.
Wide and wider spreads the vale,
As circles on a smooth canal:

The mountains round, unhappy fate,
Sooner or later of all height
Withdraw their summits from the skies
And lessen as the others rise.
Still the prospect wider spreads,
Adds a thousand woods and meads;
Still it widens, widens still,
And sinks the newly risen hill.

Now I gain the mountain's brow,
What a landscape lies below!
No clouds, no vapours intervene,
But the gay, the open scene
Does the face of Nature show
In all the hues of heaven's bow
And, swelling to embrace the light,
Spreads around beneath the sight.

Old castles on the cliffs arise,
Proudly towering in the skies;
Rushing from the woods, the spires
Seem from hence ascending fires;
Half his beams Apollo sheds
On the yellow mountain-heads,
Gilds the fleeces of the flocks
And glitters on the broken rocks.

Below me trees unnumbered rise,
Beautiful in various dyes:
The gloomy pine, the poplar blue,
The yellow beech, the sable yew,
The slender fir that taper grows,
The sturdy oak with broad-spread boughs,
And beyond the purple grove –
Haunt of Phillis, queen of love –
Gaudy as the opening dawn
Lies a long and level lawn
On which a dark hill, steep and high,
Holds and charms the wandering eye.
Deep are his feet in Towy's flood,
His sides are clothed with waving wood
And ancient towers crown his brow,
That cast an awful look below;
Whose ragged walls the ivy creeps
And with her arms from falling keeps,
So both a safety from the wind
On mutual dependence find.

'Tis now the raven's bleak abode;
'Tis now th'apartment of the toad;
And there the fox securely feeds,
And there the poisonous adder breeds
Concealed in ruins, moss and weeds,
While ever and anon there falls
Huge heaps of hoary mouldered walls.
Yet Time has seen, that lifts the low
And level lays the lofty brow,
Has seen this broken pile complete,
Big with the vanity of state:
But transient is the smile of Fate!
A little rule, a little sway,
A sunbeam in a winter's day,
Is all the proud and mighty have
Between the cradle and the grave.

And see the rivers how they run
Through woods and meads in shade and sun!
Sometimes swift and sometimes slow,
Wave succeeding wave, they go
A various journey to the deep,
Like human life to endless sleep:
Thus is Nature's vesture wrought
To instruct our wandering thought;
Thus she dresses green and gay
To disperse our cares away.

Ever charming, ever new,
When will the landscape tire the view!
The fountain's fall, the river's flow,
The woody valleys warm and low;
The windy summit, wild and high,
Roughly rushing on the sky;
The pleasant seat, the ruined tower,
The naked rock, the shady bower;
The town and village, dome and farm,
Each give each a double charm,
As pearls upon an Ethiop's arm.

See on the mountain's southern side,
Where the prospect opens wide,
Where the evening gilds the tide,
How close and small the hedges lie,
What streaks of meadows cross the eye!
A step methinks may pass the stream,
So little distant dangers seem;

So we mistake the future's face
Eyed through Hope's deluding glass;
As yon summits soft and fair,
Clad in colours of the air
Which to those who journey near
Barren, brown and rough appear:
Still we tread the same coarse way;
The present's still a cloudy day.

O may I with myself agree
And never covet what I see;
Content me with an humble shade,
My passions tamed, my wishes laid;
For while our wishes wildly roll
We banish quiet from the soul:
'Tis thus the busy beat the air
And misers gather wealth and care.

Now, even now, my joys run high
As on the mountain turf I lie,
While the wanton Zephyr sings
And in the vale perfumes his wings;
While the waters murmur deep,
While the shepherd charms his sheep,
While the birds unbounded fly
And with music fill the sky –
Now, even now, my joys run high.

Be full, ye courts! be great who will;
Search for Peace with all your skill:
Open wide the lofty door,
Seek her on the marble floor:
In vain ye search, she is not there;
In vain ye search the domes of Care!
Grass and flowers Quiet treads
On the meads and fountainheads,
Along with Pleasure close allied,
Ever by each other's side,
And often by the murmuring rill
Hears the thrush, while all is still,
Within the groves of Grongar Hill.

from *The Ruins of Rome*

Enough of Grongar and the shady dales
Of winding Towy, Merlin's fabled haunt,
I sung inglorious. Now the love of arts
And what in metal or in stone remains
Of proud Antiquity, through various realms
And various languages and ages famed,
Bears me remote o'er Gallia's woody bounds,
O'er the cloud-piercing Alps remote, beyond
The vale of Arno purpled with the vine,
Beyond the Umbrian and Etruscan hills,
To Latium's wide champaign, forlorn and waste,
Where yellow Tiber his neglected wave
Mournfully rolls. Yet once again, my Muse!
Yet once again, and soar a loftier flight;
Lo! the resistless theme, imperial Rome.

Fallen, fallen, a silent heap! her heroes all
Sunk in their urns; behold the pride of pomp,
The throne of nations, fallen! obscured in dust;
Even yet majestical: the solemn scene
Elates the soul, while now the rising sun
Flames on the ruins in the purer air
Towering aloft upon the glittering plain,
Like broken rocks, a vast circumference!
Rent palaces, crushed columns, rifled moles,
Fanes rolled on fanes, and tombs on buried tombs!

LEWIS MORRIS
(1701 – 1765)

called Llewelyn Ddu o Fôn

The Fishing Lass of Hakin

Ye sailors bold both great and small
That navigate the ocean,
Who love a lass that's fair and tall,
Come hearken to my motion;
You must have heard of Milford Haven,
All harbours it surpasses,
I know no port this side of heaven
So famed for handsome lasses.

In Milford on your larboard hand
We found a town called Hakin,
The snuggest place in all the land
For lads inclined to raking;
There all the girls were cleanly dressed,
As witty as they are pretty,
But one exceeded all the rest,
And this was charming Betty.

A fisherman her father was,
Her mother a fishwoman,
And she herself a fishing lass
Perhaps possessed by no man;
She'd bait her hook with lug or crab,
No fisherman so nimble,
And at her oar she was a dab,
But never at her thimble.

Assist me, all the watery tribe,
I find my wit a-flagging
As I endeavour to describe
This precious pearl of Hakin;
Ye mermaids tune my merry song,
And Neptune bless my darling,
Your smoking altars shall ere long
Be spread with sole and sparling.

Her fishing dress was clean and neat,
It set me all a-quaking,
I loved her and could almost eat
This maiden ray of Hakin;
If ere you saw a cuttle fish,
Her breasts are more inviting,
Like shaking blubbers in a dish,
And tender as a whiting.

Her cheeks are as a mackerel plump,
No mouth of mullet moister,
Her lips of tench would make you jump,
They open like an oyster;
Her chin as smooth as river trout,
Her hair as rockfish yellow,
God's Sounds! I view her round about
But never saw her fellow.

When hungry people write for bread,
Whom they call poetasters,
They talk of fires in topmast head,
Of Pollax and of Castor's;
Her eyes afford a brighter mark
Than all those flashy meteors,
Like Milford Lights even in the dark
Revealing all her features.

Whene'er a smile sits on her lip
I'm brisk as bottled cider,
I quite renounce and leave my ship
And never can abide her;
Whene'er she speaks, so sweet her tone
I leap like spawning salmon,
And when she sings I'm all her own,
I serve no Jove nor Mammon.

But if she frowns I'm gone to pot,
As dead as pickled herring,
The muscles of my heart must rot
And split from clew to earring;
Then in my hammock sink me deep
Within the sight of Hakin,
Then sure she'll melancholy weep
As turtles at their taking.

Let doctors kill, let merchants cheat,
Let courtiers cog and flatter,   (deceive
Let gluttons feed on costly meat,
Let me have Betty's platter;
To mess with her I'd spend my days
On pilchard and on poor-John,
Let richer folks have if they please
Their turbot and their sturgeon.

The Miner's Ballad

I am a jovial miner,
I wander up and down,
I have no settled station
In country or in town,
    Then a-mining we will go.

I work in Pluto's regions
Where riches are in store,
And when I spend my gettings
I go and dig for more.

When soldiers run from cannon
To live another day,
We live in smoke of powder
And never run away.

When merchants lose their substance
By tempest or by floods,
We feel no change of weather
But safely land our goods.

When criminals at Tyburn
Of ropes do stand in fear,
We hang in ropes so often
We fear no Tyburn here.

Though nobles drive in chariots
They often run in debt;
We drive upon a level
And seldom overset.

When death in silent trenches
Imprisons lords and kings,
We in our graves live merry
And laugh at all his stings.

Some pick the nations' pockets
As others did before,
But we maintain their credit
By picking rocks and ore.

With odd conceits and whimsies
Some do their fortunes sink;
Our whimsies raise us money,
And money raises drink.

Your sailors when a-sinking
Have many a trembling heart;
We sink to live in plenty,
Then call ye t'other quart.

They talk of peace in palaces,
I'm sure there's no such thing;
Then who hath most contentment –
A miner or a king?
  Then a-mining we will go.

WILLIAM WILLIAMS
(1717 – 1791)

called Pantycelyn

from *Hymn XVII*

What is the world, and what is life,
  And what are honours vain,
When thou art absent from my soul
  But only grief and pain.

I ask not those seraphic flames
  That ravish thrones above,
Nor what the perfect spirits taste
  Of that immortal love.

But bliss that thou art wont to give,
  And promised in thy word;
Communion with thyself alone
  Is all I want, my Lord.

O! let me see those beams of light,
  Feel that celestial spark,
That veils the beauties of the world
  In an eternal dark.

Hymn XLI

Now the shadows flee and vanish,
  And the blessed morning came
When ten thousand silver trumpets
  Free salvation shall proclaim;
    All the islands
    Through the world shall hear the sound.

Now the living branch of Jesse
  Shall with glorious beauty shine,
And the negro and the Indian
  Look unto the Man divine;
    And with rapture
    Sing the glorious theme of love.

Now shall cease and wholly vanish
  Every meaner base delight;
Jesus, the desire and object
  Of the black and of the white,
    To the chiefest
    Sinners, grace shall more abound.

Come unto the living fountain,
  Sinners therefore haste away;
Hear the call and do not squander
  Precious moments thus away:
    Eat and welcome,
    Drink the pure delicious wine.

EDWARD DAVIES
(1718 – 1789)

from *Chepstow: A Poem*

Will no young British bard, on rhyme intent,
Step forth and sing the beauties of Cas Gwent?
Her various charms in polished lines rehearse,
And deck her with the ornaments of verse?
At their full length in colours bright lay down
The castle, bridge, the river and the town?
Prove her from Roman Venta's ashes sprung,
And like a new-burnt phoenix, paint her young?
Shew how she still her mother's charms retains,
How still the love of freedom warms her veins,
And her old hospitable laws maintains?
Who, like Ravenna, when with her we dine,
Instead of water fobs us off with wine.
Show how her walls a semi-circle form,
A guard designed 'gainst every adverse storm;
How with the aid of her good neighbour Wye,
Chepstow may all her enemies defy?

How the white rocks that skirt the river's side
Majestic rise, like ramparts o'er the tide;
And how her figure represents a bow,
Her walls the handle, Wye the string below?
Whoe'er on Tut's-Hill takes his airy stand
Will thence the platform of the town command;
So interspersed with fruit trees that in May
It looks like famed Damascus, blooming gay;
Seems one vast sheet of pure, unsullied white,
Sweet to the smell and pleasing to the sight.
Will not a scene like this inspire to sing,
Provoke some able bard to stretch his wing?

With admiration view yon castle there!
Hung by some necromancer in the air:
High o'er the rocks see how it lifts its head!
To guard the river Vaga in her bed,
Who far beneath in perfect saftey lies,
While her tall giant never shuts his eyes.
Above the castle gate, forever green,
A vast wide-spreading ivy bush is seen,
Where the grave owl in solemn silence sleeps
And safe from boys and birds her station keeps,
But quits at night her venerable house
To find for supper a fat Chepstow mouse;
When found, in haste she stoops upon her prey,
Then back on wobbling wings her murky way
Explores, to shun the dazzling glare of day.
Thus poachers, pest of sportsmen, nightly prowl,
Taught in the dark to murder by the owl.

No better cider does the world supply
Than grows along thy borders, gentle Wye;
Delicious, strong, and exquisitely fine,
With all the friendly properties of wine.
A vast extent of country owns the sway
Of sweet Pomona, blooming queen of May,
Who guards from blights thy apple-planted vales
From Chepstow upwards to the alps of Wales.

Where cider ends, there ale begins to reign
And warms on Brecknock hills the Cambrian swain;
High on the summit of King Arthur's Chair
He quaffs his ale and breathes untainted air;

Looks down on Hereford with scornful eyes,
Esteems himself a native of the skies:
Puffed with the thoughts of his exalted birth
He scorns the humble mushroom sons of earth;
His high descent from time's first dawn can trace,
From Gomer down to Owen Tudor's race;
Thinks none so great on this terraqueous ball –
Himself the ragged emperor of all.
This mountain prince outflies ballooning kings,
A cloud his car, the winds his whistling wings.

Above Lancaut in a sequestered dell
Where monks in former days were wont to dwell,
Enclosed with woods and hills on every side,
Stands Tintern Abbey, spoiled of all her pride,
Whose mournful ruins fill the soul with awe,
Where once was taught God's holy saving law;
Where mitred abbots fanned the heavenly fire
And shook with hymns divine the heavenly choir.
Though now the fallen roof admits the day
She claims our veneration in decay;
Looks like a goodly matron, drowned in tears,
By friends forsaken and broke down with years.
Her fine old windows, arches, walls, unite
To fill the mind with pity and delight,
For from her splendid ruins may be seen
How beautiful this desecrated place has been.
Round the old walls observe the ivy twine –
A plant attached to grandeur in decline.
The tottering pile she clasps in her embrace,
With a green mask conceals its furrowed face
And keeps it standing on its time-worn base.

Here now no bell calls monks to morning prayer,
Daws only chant their early matins here;
Black forges smoke and noisy hammers beat
Where sooty cyclops, puffing, drink and sweat;
Confront the curling flames nor back retire,
But live like salamanders in the fire.
For at each stroke that's by the hammer given,
From the red iron fiery sparks are driven:
In all directions round the forge they fly,
Like lightning flash and quick as lightning die.

Here smelting-furnaces like Etna roar
And force the latent iron from the ore;
The liquid metal from the furnace runs
And, caught in moulds of sand, forms pots or guns;
Oft shifts its shape, like Proteus, in the fire –
Huge iron bars here dwindle into wire;
Assume such forms as suit the calls of trade,
Plough-share or broad-sword, pruning-hook or spade:
To all impressions the kind metal yields,
Thimbles for ladies makes, for heroes shields.
These fruits of industry enrich the place,
Where plenty smiles in every busy face.

Here, in the hollow caverns of the rocks,
Skulks in security the wily fox:
Snug in his fronzy kennel Reynard lies
And all the snares of men and dogs defies.
In vain the hounds attempt to storm his cave –
Some enter but alas! there find a grave;
Some tumble down the rocks and perish in the wave.
Confusion reigns: enraged, the baying pack
Loud and more loud renews the vain attack.
In vain the huntsmen shout and wind the horn –
The fox triumphant laughs them all to scorn.

Next round the Chapel farm our course we shape
And double here the last projecting cape;
But who can paint our wonder and surprise
When bridge and castle both at once arise
And stand before our fascinated eyes!
Where rocks, woods, water, castle, bridge unite
To form a scene of exquisite delight.
The great Lorrain, unrivalled in his art,
Whose brilliant landscapes captivate the heart,
To copy these grand objects would decline
And own they were inimitably fine:
So grand and beautiful in every part,
They triumph o'er the impotence of art.

He who by land would enter Chepstow town
Must quit his horse and lead him gently down:
The long descent so rugged is and steep
That even post-boys here for safety creep;
The sloping road demands our utmost care –
Hawker when living never galloped here.

Cats with sharp claws and nanny-goats in dread
Descend the shelving street and cautious tread.
What must we men then do to walk secure?
Observe the good old proverb – slow and sure;
For if we careless walk the slippery street
Our prostrate nether-ends the pavement greet;
And paying oft such honour to the stones
Will fix domestic prophets in our bones:
For when old bruises ache, they full as well
As corns and whip-cord change of weather tell.
But though in fear the street the stranger treads,
Within he'll find sure footing and soft beds;
The inns will furnish every want and wish,
For there he'll find good flesh, good fowl, good fish;
And those who on crimp salmon wish to feast,
In great perfection there will find it dressed.
Here is good ale, good cider and good wine
So that like sons of kings we here may dine.
In this snug town good meat and drink abound
But, strange to tell, there cannot here be found
One single inch of horizontal ground:
To social joys folks therefore here incline,
By way of exercise sit down to dine,
Grow plump and rosy, like the god of wine.

If strait the gate and narrow be the way
That leads from earth to realms of endless day,
Then through this town must be the road to heaven,
Whose gate is strait, streets narrow and uneven.
Such is the town of Chepstow, rugged, steep,
But a choice place to revel in, and sleep.

EVAN EVANS
(1731 – 1788)

called Ieuan Brydydd Hir

from *The Love of Our Country*

Whatever clime we travel or explore,
To love our country still is nature's lore;
No less with Icelanders its force obtains
Than with Italians on their temperate plains.

The self-same language, manners, customs prove
That the wild Indian bears his country love.
So willed the wise Creator; and his will
Is nature's law, and men obey it still.
This in all ages has remained the same
And proves the origin from whence it came;
For what more just than to embrace that earth
That like a second mother gave us birth?
Hence all societies their source derive,
All are descended from one common hive:
Old Babel's jumble joined with cement strong
The infant union by one common tongue.
Each chose its spot, as Providence ordained,
And called it Country, which each tribe maintained –
Till drove by force superior from its right,
By lawless tyrants and the dint of might.
Hence first the hero and the patriot came,
Whose names are listed in the rolls of fame,
Who bravely struggled in their country's cause,
Who formed its manners and who planned its laws.

When Heaven offended sent the Saxon o'er,
And weak Gwrtheyrn Britain's sceptre bore,
The brave Ambrosius for his country stood
And made his sword drink deep of hostile blood.
Anon great Arthur, Britain's glory, rose,
For valour formed, the terror of his foes:
Immortal bards his virtue still rehearse
And each true patriot kindles at the verse.
Urien and Maelgwn, ancient heroes, shine
In thy famed odes, Taliesin the divine.
Old Llywarch and Aneirin still proclaim
How Britons fought for glory and for fame;
Whole troops of Saxons in the field they mowed,
And stained their lances red with hostile blood.

Let annals tell how Cambria's princes fought,
The Saxon victories how dearly bought,
And how for liberty they bravely strove
As if they had their sanction from above.
The bards extolled in lasting verse their praise,
In lofty numbers and in sweetest lays,
While to the lyre's sweet harmony they sung
Each warrior's hall with feats heroic rung.

Let England in her Alfred's high renown
Boast of a monarch worthy of her crown;
But let not Cambrian science be forgot –
How Asser taught, how Alfred learning got.
Monsters ingrate, how can you barbarous call
The men that taught the brightest of you all?
The false historians of a polished age
Show that the Saxon has not lost his rage,
Though tamed by arts his rancour still remains:
Beware of Saxons still, ye Cambrian swains.

EVAN LLOYD
(1734 – 1776)

Portrait of a Bishop

He in Christ's doctrine deals by way of trade,
Money by preaching poverty is made –
Whose labours were bestowed upon the head,
Whose heart, that found itself neglected, fled,
And now a mere, mere head he lives, with Greek
Carved on his skull and furrowed in his cheek;
Be-greeked, be-latined and be-hebrewed too,
Yet from no tongue has learnt what he should do:
Who lives as if life's business was to write
Learned materials for a schoolboy's kite;
Whose left hand cannot one good action quote,
And all the merit of his right – a Note.
A commentator sage, a critic nice,
A cobwebbed library his paradise –
Who though our gracious Master has foretold
The everlasting doors are shut 'gainst gold,
Yet still digs on for gold in Mammon's mines
And heaps up precious ruin, for it shines;
Thinking he may elude what Christ decreed
And though a camel fail, that he'll succeed,
And worn with avarice hopes like chaff to fly
And squeeze to heaven through a needle's eye.

from *The Powers of the Pen*

Drawn by old Homer's hand, the rose
Still on the cheek of Helen blows.
Her beauty suffers no decay
Nor moulders for the worm a prey;
Time's chisel cuts no wrinkles in
The velvet smoothness of her skin,
Nor can the thirst of old age sip
The dewy moisture of her lip;
And now her eyes as brilliant show
As Paris saw them long ago.
For though her beauteous body must
Have crumbled into native dust,
Yet still her features live in song,
Like Hebe, ever fair and young.

EDWARD WILLIAMS
(1747 – 1826)

called Iolo Morganwg

from *The Happy Farmer*

I live on my farm in a beautiful vale –
Ye lovers of Nature attend to my tale;
No pride or ambition find room in my breast,
Those venomous foes of contentment and rest;
From sound healthy sleep I rise up every morn
To toil in my fields with my cattle and corn,
And prefer, whilst of rural employments I sing,
The life of a farmer to that of a king.

On the fruits of my labour I look with delight –
My meadows are weedless and gladden the sight;
The flocks in my pastures are fair to behold,
Fine cows with large udders replenish my fold;
My fields yield abundance, in tillage complete,
Good barley, rich clover and excellent wheat:
The seasons attend through their changeable round
In toils that with plenty's rich blessings are crowned.

My house is convenient, and whitened all o'er,
An arbour of jessamine fronting the door;
My flourishing orchard abundantly bears
Fine plums, golden pippins and bergamot pears;
The rose, the sweet pink, in my garden are found,
Where dainties of health for my table abound;
My mind, when fatigued, here I often unbend,
Peruse a good book or converse with a friend.

With rural amusements in sober delight
I brighten my thoughts, their long labours requite;
And over my stubbles when harvest is done
I range in the morn with my dog and my gun;
Now course the fleet hare on the fern-covered hill,
Or angle for trout in a neighbouring rill;
And sometimes at eve, to enliven my soul,
I sing with my friend o'er a temperate bowl.

Where flocks and large herds in my pastures are seen,
The cowslips or daisy bespangle the green;
I view my gay lambs nimbly frolic and play
Whilst under their feet spring the beauties of May,
Whilst joyful, observing my flourishing corn,
The blackbird and linnet sing loud on the thorn:
Nor would I my peaceful employments lay down,
Or quit my green fields, for the pomp of a crown.

from *Stanzas Written in London in 1773*

Why, Cambria did I quit thy shore,
    The scenes I loved so dear?
With wounded feelings rankling sore
I languish, and thy loss deplore
    In Folly's hateful sphere.

Dear native land! though thoughtless pride
    Contemns thy peaceful plains,
By virtue's energy supplied
The joys of nature still abide
    Amongst thy cheerful swains.

Sad memory recalls the day
    When o'er thy lawns alone,
Exploring Fancy's mazy way,
My muse first tried her infant lay,
    Made first her efforts known.

Applauded by th'unlettered swain
    She felt her pinions grow;
She pleased the beauties of the plain,
Whilst Nature bade her simple strain
    In artless numbers flow.

Thus in Glamorgan's happy land
    I spent my blissful time;
My rural sonnet playful planned,
The novel charm of nature scanned,
    New subject of my rhyme.

Glamorgan, boast thy sky serene,
    Thy health-inspiring gales,
Thy sunny plains luxuriant green,
Thy graceful mountains' airy scene,
    Their wild romantic vales.

With nature's wealth supremely blessed,
    With peace, with plenty crowned;
In thy white cots, a cheerful guest,
Pure joy dilates the glowing breast
    And gladness smiles around.

Receive thy bard! he speeds again
    With truth-replenished mind
To range once more thy humble plain
And pass through life a rural swain,
    To heaven's high will resigned.

O London! let me turn away
    From thee my saddened eyes;
With drooping soul, to grief a prey,
Long have I spent the joyless day
    Beneath thy tainted skies.

DAVID SAMWELL
(1751 – 1798)

The Negro Boy

An African prince, having been asked what he had given for his watch, answered: "What I will never give again – I gave a fine boy for it".

When avarice enslaves the mind
    And selfish views alone bear sway,
Man turns a savage to his kind
    And blood and rapine mark his way.
        Alas! for this poor simple toy
        I sold a hapless negro boy.

His father's hope, his mother's pride,
    Though black yet comely to the view,
I tore him helpless from their side
    And gave him to a ruffian crew,
        To fiends that Afric's coast annoy
        I sold the hapless negro boy.

From country, friends and parents torn,
    His tender limbs in chains confined,
I saw him o'er the billows borne
    And marked his agony of mind:
        But still to gain this simple toy
        I gave the weeping negro boy.

In isles that deck the western wave
    I doomed the hapless youth to dwell,
A poor, forlorn, insulted slave,
    A beast – that Christians buy and sell,
        And in their cruel tasks employ
        The much enduring negro boy.

His wretched parents long shall mourn,
    Shall long explore the distant main
In hope to see the youth return,
    But all their hopes and sighs are vain:
        They never shall the sight enjoy
        Of their lamented negro boy.

RICHARD LLWYD

Beneath a tyrant's harsh command
  He wears away his youthful prime,
Far distant from his native land,
   A stranger in a foreign clime.
    No pleasing thoughts his mind employ:
    A poor dejected negro boy.

But He who walks upon the wind,
  Whose voice in thunder's heard on high,
Who doth the raging tempest bind
   And hurl the lightning through the sky,
    In his own time will sure destroy
    The oppressors of a negro boy.

RICHARD LLWYD
(1752 – 1835)

called The Bard of Snowdon

from *Beaumaris Bay*

Here, still sequestered, Penmon's sacred dome
Recalls to mind the inmates of the tomb
Who reared with pious zeal the massy pile
And filled with notes of praise the echoing aisle;
When Idwal, born of Cambria's regal race,
Beheld with guardian eye the happy place.
Alas! what is it now? the damp abode
Of slimy snails, the spider and the toad,
Where waking owls in screaming concert call
Their prowling mates when evening's shadows fall.

  We hie where Baron-Hill attracts the Muse,
The sunny glades, the brow, the varying views –
Isles, towns, the rising hills, the spreading bay,
The Muse, delighted, owns the grand display;
Here Flora smiles and flowers of every hue
Their glowing petals spread and drink the dew,
Luxuriant rise beneath her fostering care
And shed their fragrance on the ambient air;
Here warblers carol on the bending spray,
The Dryads gambol and the Satyrs play
Through wilds of foliage and the peaceful groves,
Haunts of the Muse, the leisure hour she loves:
For Art and Nature here their beauties blend,
And Taste and Bulkeley for the palm contend.

The landscape's various charms the Muse explores,
The druid haunts and Mona's hallowed shores,
High Arfon soaring o'er the humbler isle,
The winding Menai, Daniel's mitred pile;
Thy towers Caernarfon, triple summits Llŷn,
That distant close the vast and varied scene.
Below, amphibious man, as whim prevails,
Trims up his little bark and spreads his sails;
Or led by florid Health, descends to lave
And skims the surface of the bracing wave,
Or frets the liquid azure as he floats
Where sister nations crowd the busy boats.

Here glowed the patriot breast with public good
And urged a wish to stem th'obstructing flood,
Bade Genius form the potent pier that braves
Impeding tempests and the war of waves;
Beheld the embryo arch with fostering smile
Entice the infant to the parent isle.

Now Nature softening from the Carnedd bends
And gently to the humbler dale descends,
Alternate spreads the saline sheet or sands
And checks the waves with Aber's lengthened strands;
Here looks at Claude with eye benign and mild,
There stares at Rosa like a maniac wild.

Now day's bright beams to western waves retire
And Thetis hails again light's radiant sire.
We leave the isle and homeward point the prow,
And now the bark proceeds serene and slow,
While babbling Echo from the caverned shores
Repeats the dashing of the labouring oars
And, pleased with Arfon's mimic voice, prolongs
The laugh-approving and repeated songs.
And now, alternate, on distended sails
The breathing air or genial breeze prevails –
Plays on the surface, and at eve restores
The mirthful group to Mona's greeting shores:
The day is closed, the fluttering sails are furled,
And night in shade and stillness folds the world.

JULIA ANN HATTON
(1764 – 1838)

called Ann of Swansea

Swansea Bay

In vain by various griefs oppressed
I vagrant roam devoid of rest,
With aching heart, still lingering stray
Around the shores of Swansea Bay.

The restless waves that lave the shore,
Joining the tide's tumultuous roar,
In hollow murmurs seem to say –
Peace is not found at Swansea Bay.

The meek-eyed morning's lucid beam,
The pensive moon's pale shadowy gleam,
Still ceaseless urge – why this delay?
Go, hapless wretch, from Swansea Bay.

'Tis not for me the snowy sail
Swells joyous in the balmy gale,
Nor cuts the boat with frolic play
For me the waves of Swansea Bay.

The glow of health that tints each cheek,
The eyes that sweet contentment speak,
To mock my woes their charms display
And bid me fly from Swansea Bay.

Haste, smiling nymphs, your beauties lave
And sport beneath the sparkling wave,
While I pursue my lonely way
Along the shores of Swansea Bay.

The frowning mountain's awful sweep,
The rocks that beetle o'er the deep,
The winds that round their summits play,
All bid me fly from Swansea Bay.

Then, Kilvey hill, a long adieu,
I drag my sorrows hence from you:
Misfortune with imperious sway
Impels me far from Swansea Bay.

TALIESIN WILLIAMS

(1787 – 1847)

called Taliesin ab Iolo

from *Cardiff Castle*

The tourist, as he views the place,
Rebuilds the fane of other days
And hears the Whitefriars' vesper song
To heaven's high King; but ages long
Have held their course and passed away
Since there the priest was wont to pray:
Now Power reports a different creed –
Such are the changes that succeed
Beneath the sun; yet still we see
Man claims infallibility.

Yon stately pile whose ramparts frown
    O'er Taff's impetuous wave,
Whose keep, to ruin's grandeur grown,
All ivy-robed around, looks down
On Ratostabius' ancient town
    Like guardian sternly grave,
And high on central mound appears
Mouldered beneath the tread of years,
Recalls with warning voice to mind
The transient might of humankind.

Yon stately pile in ages past
Has known the hostile trumpet's blast,
Destruction's every hue and form –
The lengthened siege, th'impending storm:
Known each appalling deed of war –
The battered wall's tremendous jar,
    Its masses thundering down;
The reeking breach – an awful post
In quick succession won and lost,
The frenzy of the sallying host
    In conflict desperate grown:
The drawbridge gained by deadliest foe,
The corse encumbered moat below,
    Still fed by gushing wounds;
The onset at the outward gate,
Where carnage reigned in gory state
    And vengeance knew no bounds;

Where serf and chief of high renown,
Pinned by the barbed porcullis down,
Convulsive drew their struggling breath
And writhed in all the pangs of death.

JOHN JONES
(1788 – 1858)

called Poet Jones

from *Holywell*

Now slowly winding from the mountain's head,
Deep pits I witness, where the ore of lead
Is raised by miners from the stubborn soil,
To be transformed to various things by toil...
Industry's children are the sons of Wales,
No real starvation through their land prevails:
Their hills, though sterile, and their portion scant –
They ask no affluence and they know no want;
No bounds they crave for but their native sod,
With leave to labour and to worship God.
Yet will they not oppression bear too long,
But burst their fetters – a resistless throng,
And prove that spirit not extinguished quite
Which shone conspicuous on the. fields of fight,
And thinned the ranks of Saxons and of Danes
When thronging down they poured on British plains.

From yon high prospect now I've ventured down
And stand delighted in my native town;
But whence the noises that assail mine ear?
What crowds before me with their goods appear?
'Tis market day – loud dealers strain their lungs
And High Street echoes with two different tongues:
The Welsh and English there alternate cry
'Rhai'n, rhai'n, yw pethau rhad' – 'Come. buy, come buy!'
Now strangers hail raw natives as they meet,
Who cry "Dim Saesneg", wanting power to greet.
Some few with signs their various bargains end,
Some curse the tongue they cannot comprehend.
But such as landlords more perfection reach –
They know each language and converse in each:
What should be foreign they pronounce quite well –
Scarce aught were better save the drink they sell.

JOHN L. THOMAS
(1795 – 1871)

called Ieuan Ddu

from *Harry Vaughan*

His father did intend that Harry should
  Some time see Oxford University;
But now his prospects are beneath a cloud,
  And Lady Vaughan's attested piety
Did so much dread th'example of that crowd
  Which go for learning to find revelry,
    Her prayer both night and day was that her son
    Might end his schooling where he had begun.

That was in Wales, and now this son we see
  Pursued his studies at Carmarthen town:
A place that once could boast, saith history,
  A prophet whose great name's in part her own;
A castle proud which kept the *Llyfr Du**,
  A corporation stiff as the Mayor's gown;
    A little trade which at that time was growing,
    And civic records some may deem worth knowing.

O'er Towy stands this town of ancient fame,
  To ken her walls reflected mass on mass,
And there the river, hitherto more tame,
  Its pleasures gently lisps as it doth pass:
And though the tides there mingle with the same,
  Till acres scores are hid of meadow grass,
    High raised o'er fresh and salt – as from a throne –
    This town sees both reflect her ivied zone.

Yea, from Llansteffan, on whose towering height
  A son of song may gaze himself stone blind,
Up to its origin this vale is dight
  With all that can enchant poetic mind;
So many scenes – dark, gloomy, fresh, and bright –
  You see where'er the fairy stream doth wind;
    From Towy's wave-washed sands up to Llandovery
    Each mile you move is one of sweet discovery.

**Black Book*

– 111 –

Well, at Carmarthen in his nineteenth year
   Pored Harry o'er his Virgil and his Horace,
And to old Homer too attuned his ear,
   As all must do who pry through learning's
storehouse:
And by degrees, from willingness or fear
   Of the disgrace, the memory he did harass,
      So much acquired that what he understood
      Of Troy's hot contests oft could rouse his blood.

And though the humming of dead languages
   Was what his mind did with disgust oft move,
Yet when he met mellifluous passages
   Wherein's embalmed the Old World's Art of Love,
And understood that Virgil's sheep and bees
   Are things we meet by every hill and grove,
      He felt refreshed and had indeed a mind
      To know what more they taught of the same kind.

The *amo, amas, amat* had at first
   Done much to prepossess him for the Latin;
But Virgil's Eclogues first did raise a thirst
   That made him wish deep draughts, and as he sat in
The place prescribed, he was not thought the worst
   Of all the parrots whose incessant prating
      If it taught not what Greeks and Romans sung,
      Made them at least forget their mother tongue.

But Harry, being of rank, was never taught
   The melodies that owned his native land;
He little knew what lays with genius fraught
   In Ivor's days had cheered the festive band;
Ap Gwilym's fervid strains had never caught
   His ear, and had they, such to understand,
      He like the rest of Cambria's well-taught gentry
      Deemed the distinction of some bygone century.

Some say the Welsh doth nurse our native vices
   And cause rebellion, riots and what not;
And oft the landlord whose small farm's high price is
   So shameful, knows of Welsh – no, not one jot.
If Welshmen have a fault, 'tis that their slices
   Of their right's loaf to a mere crumb is brought;
      And but infers at last the English tongue
      Alone can save our skins from English wrong.

JOHN LLOYD
(1797 – 1875)

from *Thoughts of Boyhood*

Well I remember in my boyish hours
 Gazing with rapture on the fantailed kite
As hovering full o'er Brecknock's ivied towers
 Slowly he wheeled his solitary flight.

Now low, as though within the mirror clear
 Of Usk's fair bosom he his form admired;
Now like the tenant of some loftier sphere,
 A speck amid the far-off clouds retired.

And often in our blithest, noisiest mood,
 When yet unseen his shrill cry told him near,
Up-gazing that mysterious form we viewed
 With a long look of wonderment and fear.

Now 'mid the landscape is he seen no more
 Fanning his broad wings in the noontide sun,
Scared from his circuit on that 'customed shore
 By prowling keeper armed with trap and gun.

In lone Cwmserri where the thunder clouds,
 For so its name implies, delight to rest,
In the dark bosom of the Vunglas woods,
 Alike the spoilers robbed him of his nest.

Nor his alone they seek: the bustling jay
 And playful squirrel too they vermin call;
Each harmless, helpless thing alike they slay
 To make a show along their kennel wall.

Hence with each year more dull our woods become,
 The tapping woodpecker, the chattering pie,
Now rarely heard; the whooping owl is dumb,
 The raven calls not to his mate on high.

The Kingfisher

The kingfisher is a glorious thing
When the sun shines bright on his rainbow wing;
Oh! he is indeed the fisher's king.

For motionless all through the livelong hours
He sits like a dream in his osier bowers,
Taking his prey with a craft not ours.

His very beauty becomes a snare
To lure the young fry to the spoiler there,
As the salmon is caught by the torches' glare.

Nor is he alone of fishers the best:
How skillfully built is his sloping nest
High up in the bank where no waves molest.

His nest in the season of floods is dry:
Like him let us build, let us build on high;
We may not on earth, let us build in the sky.

JOHN JONES
(1810 – 1869)

called Talhaiarn

Glyndwr's War Song

Air – 'March of the Men of Harlech.'

Glyndwr, see thy comet flaming,
Hear a heavenly voice declaiming,
To the world below proclaiming,
   Cambria shall be free:
While thy star on high is beaming,
Soldiers from the mountains teeming,
With their spears and lances gleaming,
   Come to follow thee:
Hear the trumpet sounding,
While the steeds are bounding,
   On the gale from hill and dale,
The warcry is resounding:
Warriors famed in song and story,
Coming from the mountains hoary,
Rushing to the field of glory,
   Eager for the fray:
To the valley wending
Hearths and homes defending,
   With their proud and valiant Prince

From ancient kings descending;
See the mighty host advancing,
Sunbeams on their helmets dancing;
On his gallant charger prancing
   Glyndwr leads the way.

Now to battle they are going,
Every heart with courage glowing,
Pride and passion overflowing
   In the furious strife:
Lo! the din of war enrages,
Vengeance crowns the hate of ages,
Sternly foe with foe engages,
   Feeding Death with Life:
Hear the trumpets braying,
And the horses neighing,
   Hot the strife while fiery foes
Are one another slaying;
Arrows fly as swift as lightning,
Shout on shout the tumult height'ning,
Conquest's ruddy wing is bright'ning
   Helmet, sword, and shield:
With their lances flashing,
Warriors wild are crashing,
   Through the tyrant's serried ranks,
Whilst onward they are dashing:
Now the enemy is flying,
Trampling on the dead and dying;
Victory aloft is crying,
   Cambria wins the field.

Watching the Wheat

Air – 'Gwenith Gwyn.'

   While I watch the yellow wheat
      I wander by the river,
   To dream a day-dream of my love,
      For I must love her ever:
   I see her in the glassy stream,
      Her eyes with sweetness beaming:
   Oh, how delicious 'tis to me
      To be thus ever dreaming.

I see her when I close my eyes,
  Ah, do not deem me silly;
I sometimes dream she is a rose,
  At other times a lily:
And in the yellow wheat her face
  And form are ever present:
These daily visions cling to me,
  Though dreams are evanescent.

While the ocean ebbs and flows,
  And studded stars are shining,
And while the sun from East to West
  Is rising and declining,
With ardent joy I'll love my love,
  She steals my heart and fancy;
Of all the girls that grace the land,
  There's none like winsome Nansi.

FRANCIS HOMFRAY
(fl. 1817)

from *Thoughts on Happiness*

Severn and Vaga, each old Cambria's pride,
Take different channels down Pumlumon's side.
Destined they seem a separate course to keep
Through rough uneasy windings to the deep.
For if by chance one turns across the plain
In haste to meet its fellow stream again,
Some envious hill or rude projecting rock
Repels its ardour; the repulsive shock
Turns it aside, and with impetuous force
Sends the stream foaming down a different course.
But when no longer obstacles delay
And each impediment is moved away,
Nature in all her varied charms is seen
To hail the union of her river-queen.
Through riven rocks her sportive eddies foam,
Where blue-eyed Naiads keep their hallowed home;
Through blooming orchards winds her mazy flood,
Through deep low vales whose sides are crowned with wood.
Past Tintern's arches and its mouldering walls
In eager haste her rapid current falls;
Nor does she stay, so great her haste would seem,
To show their image in her rippling stream.

Severn advances in majestic pride
To meet his lost, his long deserted bride.
Vaga well pleased his summons to attend
At Striguil's towers meets her former friend;
Mixed with his wave she seeks his oozy reign
And flows with him to their last home, the main.

RICHARD HALL
(1817 – 1866)

Pontypool

P ontypool! thou dirtiest of dirty places;
O ften have I bewailed, when wandering through thee,
N ew garments which then bore the filthy traces
T hat those can ne'er escape who wish to view thee:
Y et thou dost show to us some wondrous phases;
P ouring forth their thick smokes curling to the skies,
O ut-belching scalding steam and scorching blazes,
O n every side huge furnaces arise;
L earn we from them man's skill and vigorous enterprise!

Crickhowel

C rowded with beauties is thy lovely vale,
R ich scenes and varied meet the wanderer's eye;
I n green-leaved groves the cushat tells its tale,   (*wood-pigeon*
C ooing a love-song to its mate close by:
K ept spellbound have our wandering footsteps been
H ere by Porthmawr, while we enchanted gazed
O n the luxuriant splendour of that scene
W here, winding down the dale, Usk's waters blazed
E ffulgent in the sun, like molten gold;
L ingered we there till evening mists across the
     landscape rolled.

from *Venni-Vach Revisited*

How oft, ere morning lit the eastern steep,
And flowers had scarcely wakened up from sleep
But drooping still hung down their perfumed heads
Heavy with pearl-drops which the night dew sheds,

We sought the river-side, elate, to try
The salmon catches with a new-made fly
In Pwll-y-gwaidd perchance – oh, happy luck!
A rushing plunge! the kingly fish was struck!
Sullenly to the bottom down he sailed;
There nosing, showed his brightsides, silver scaled.
Hoping to rub out thus the rankling barb,
The tackle strong his craftiness would curb;
Enraged he sprang to 'scape his dreaded doom
And lashed the surface into bubbling spume:
At last his strength being spent and struggles o'er,
The ready gaff-hook dragged him to the shore.

No joys like these the hungry poacher knows:
When night's shades thicken, stealthily he throws
His net across where shallows join the deep,
With practised hand then makes a murderous sweep;
And one dark midnight hour thus serves to clear
The trout-stream more than angling through the year.
When hoar-frosts first with dazzling beauty creep,
Crisping the earth and making clear the deep
Where rolls the river-monarch in his pride,
The poacher's eye soon spies his gleaming side;
The grappling-hooks are with precision thrown,
Fixed with a jerk – the fated fish dives down
The pool's dark depths, then darting out the tide
Tears forth the keen barbs from its wounded side
And seeks in watery caves a hiding lair,
But splashing stones the scaly victim scare:
The poacher, baffled once, keeps on pursuit.
In vain 'neath hollow rock or tangled root
The fish seeks refuge from the unequal strife –
The deadly spear or gaff there takes its life.
Thus poachers prowl the river night and day,
Nor does the sabbath keep them from their prey.

Yet for these lawless ones the thinking mind
In charity can some excuses find:
Ill-paid for labour, they but seek to have
A share of blessings which kind Nature gave
To all alike; and those who own the soil
Should yield a little to the sons of toil.
Be theirs the privilege of costlier sport,
The varied pleasures of another sort,

With gaze-hound swift to course the timid hare
Or rouse sly reynard from his rocky lair;
To seek the feathered game through wood and mead
Or round the race-course ride the rapid steed.
These are the rich man's joys; then let him give
A trifling part of what he doth receive,
And let the humble artisan enjoy
The angler's gentle craft without annoy.

ROWLAND WILLIAMS

(1817–1870)

Literature and Action

Wondrous, I grant, and caught from heaven the flame
 Of Grecian inspiration; cast in mould
 Of iron were the hands whose grasp could hold
Old Rome's dominion o'er the nations tame:
But shall our soul's great fabric to their fame
 Mere echoes render back, and not enfold
 And cradle in its depth things new and bold?
Who thus would ape the dead, but lives to shame.
Come, rather feed the flocks on Snowdon's side
 Or snatch fresh fields from rock or moor or wave;
Or risk the world's great strife; or patient bide,
 Warning, where Christ's flock tempt the greedy grave;
Or feed, or clothe, or heal: count better meed
Things to be sung than song of other's deed.

Lady Charlotte Guest

Oh, if my power might equal my desire,
 Imperishable melody thy name
 Should all enshrine; and I would woo great Fame
In her eternal dome to throne thee higher
Than fair Hypatia, who with mingled fire
 Of wisdom and of beauty free from blame
 The orient's saint and sage could melt and tame;
Or that inspired Corilla, on whose lyre
 All Rome the garland Capitolian hung.
For thee, of English birth but British heart,
 Our bardic harp neglected and unstrung
Moved to the soul, and at thy touch there start
 Old harmonies to life: our ancient tongue
Opens, its buried treasure to impart.

from *Education in Wales*

I saw a garden with a thousand rills
Which through the flowering shrubs, down sloping hills,
   Flowed pleasantly and merrily;
And as they went they murmured, not in tone
Inspired by breath of art, but nature's own,
   With free and living harmony.

But there were rocks which broke their eager course,
And heaving undulations which of force
   Made slow their passage to the sea;
There came a crowd of dark and deep-browed men
To smooth the hill, make straight the winding glen,
   That they might flow more easily.

Fain would they change the course the waters went,
Leave not a rippling stone nor winding bent,
   Nor let them speak their natural voice:
They loved not nature's music, and they strove
That not a rill from formal line should rove
   Nor, rippled by the wind, rejoice.

Teach you a hound with art his prey to trace,
Or steed to mock the tempest in his race?
   Let nature's instinct be your guide:
Would you a child should speak some foreign tongue?
First let him know the language which has rung
   Familiar by his own fireside.

Touch through the ear the heart; then not in vain
Invite your nurslings to some loftier strain,
   Then let them learn untrodden ways:
But force their ears to lore half-learnt, half-known,
Nor heart nor reason reached by alien tone,
   What can you hope save stranger's praise?

Children have conned with pain your English lore,
In dull toil sick of heart; and as of yore
   Have cherished still their father's tone.
How could such knowledge profit? how could ever
Their hearts, untouched, be grateful to the giver
   Of knowledge with its key unknown?

I pray you, deign to follow Nature's guiding;
Teach men their own tongue first; not there abiding
   But stretching thence your hands for more:
Who drinks the well of knowledge thirsts again,
Who understands a little not in vain
   Will come to learn your newer lore.

THOMAS HUGHES
(*fl.* 1818 – 1865)

A Cheese for the Archdeacon

Here's a good piece of cheese (I perhaps might have kept it)
But I hope the Archdeacon will kindly accept it
Nor suppose I deem wanting in bara a chaws –   *(bread and cheese*
A chroesaw – the Cloisters, a liberal house.   *(welcome*
To remain in my larder it's rather too nice
For a part has already been eaten by mice.
So my worthy Archdeacon (I once more repeat it)
You will do me a kindness to help me to eat it.
   It's moist and it's mild, and without too much boasting
I think it's a capital cheese for toasting.
It's not much decayed, nor strong in its savour:
Though for some it is rather too flat in its flavour.
And because it's too weak for to please every palate,
It perhaps may suit better when eaten with salad.
When cold or when toasted its taste is so mild
It will please the most delicate lady or child.
It will do when you dine, or perchance when you sup,
With a dainty swig of your Warden's cup.
Or else for a change, if you're in the habit
To eat of the same, it will make a Welsh rarebit.
When dining on mutton, and pastry, and fish,
It will make macaroni – a very good dish.
And should any remain when your appetite's sated,
With that let your mouse-traps be properly baited.
   To conclude, and no longer continue this rhyme
Or I fear I might trespass too long on your time,
These poor silly lines, Sir, I beg you'll excuse,
And accept the respects of your curate, T. Hughes.

THOMAS JEFFERY LLEWELYN PRICHARD
(fl. 1824 – 1861)

from *The Land Beneath the Sea*

What can you see in yonder bay
Save far-spread water at noonday
    Or boats, perchance, and ships beside?
But through the wave my glance is cast,
I see all as in ages past,
    The Lowland Hundred's pride –
The fair champaign, the growing grain,
    The royal park and smiling farms,
Each village neat and city great,
The plenteous harvest, boscage sweet,
    Both Art and Nature's charms.
Sixteen fair towns well fortified,
Surpassing all in Wales beside
    (Except Caerleon, the bright and proud),
All view I in their ancient dress,
Oh bright as song could e'er express,
    Where living souls do crowd;
All's clear to me as eye can see,
The vivid beauty of that land
Which you deem water, stone and sand,
    The Land beneath the Sea –
The deluged country song has hallowed,
In ancient days, Cantref y Gwaelod,
The vale at which the traveller wondered,
E'en Europe's gem: the Lowland Hundred.

JOHN MORGAN
(1827 – 1903)

from *My Welsh Home*

There might be found the flowing grace,
    The oratory prompt and bold,
    Of which Giraldus spoke of old
As native to the Celtic race.

The language too was surely made
    A handmaid meet for rhetoric –
    Sonorous, flexible, antique,
Which now could rouse and now persuade.

How often have I seen a crowd
 Entranced as by a wizard's pass,
 Or surging like a molten mass,
Around a voice that soft or loud

Could still enchain that throng of men
 And mould them to the speaker's will!
 Perchance beneath some grey-clad hill
Or by a brook that greened a glen,

And as unfettered as the breeze
 Arose that modulated strain;
 Or it was heard within a fane,
Amidst the yew and laurel trees;

Or else beneath the sea-cliffs hoar
 Where dwelt the hardy fisher-folk,
 And where the surf rushed in and broke
For ever on the shelving shore.

A growing shadow, seen to steal
 Across the loved sequestered land,
 Invests in gloom the sacred band
That burns with patriotic zeal –

The dread that with the newer day
 That sweeps along on iron roads,
 And all the changes it forebodes,
The language too must die away.

But love, old love, cries shame on me
 To hail the death-throes of the tongue
 In which my muse its earliest sung –
And sung too at my mother's knee.

SIR LEWIS MORRIS
(1833 – 1907)

from *St. David's Head*

Salt sprays deluge it, wild waves buffet it, hurricanes rave;
Summer and winter, the depths of the ocean girdle it round;
In leaden dawns, in golden noon-tides, in silvery moonlight
Never it ceases to hear the old sea's mystical sound.
 Surges vex it evermore
 By gray cave and sounding shore.

Think of the numberless far-away centuries, long before man,
When the hot earth with monsters teemed, and with monsters
   the deep,
And the red sun loomed faint, and the moon was caught fast in
   the motionless air,
And the warm waves seethed through the haze in a secular sleep.
      Rock was here and headland then,
      Ere the little lives of men.

Over it long the mastodons crashed through the tropical forest,
And the great bats swooped overhead through the half-defined
   blue;
Then they passed, and the hideous ape-man, speechless and half-
   erect,
Through weary ages of time tore and gibbered and slew.
      Grayer skies and chiller air,
      But the self-same rock was there.

So shall it be when the tide of our greatness has ebbed to the
   shallows;
So when there floats not a ship on this storm-tossed westerly
   main,
Hard by, the minster crumbles, the city has shrunk to a village;
Thus shall we shrink one day, and our forests be pathless again;
      And the headland stern shall stand,
      Guarding an undiscovered land.

from *Lydstep Caverns*

Here in these fretted caverns whence the sea
Ebbs only once in all the circling year,
Fresh from the deep I lie, and dreamily
Await the refluent current stealing near.
Not yet the furtive wavelets lip the shore,
Not yet Life's too brief interlude is o'er.

A child might play where late the embattled deep
Hurled serried squadrons on the rock-fanged shore,
Where now the creaming filmy shallows creep
White-horsed battalions dashed with ceaseless roar:
Stirred by no breath, the tiny rock-pools lie
Glassing in calm the blue September sky.

ERNEST RHYS

Today the many-hued anemone,
Waving, expands within the rock-pools green,
And swift transparent creatures of the sea
Dart through the feathery sea-fronds, scarcely seen:
Here all today is peaceful, calm and still,
Here where in storm the thundering breakers fill.

Here where the charging ocean squadrons rave
And seethe and shatter on the sounding shore,
And smite this high-arched roof, and wave on wave
Fall baffled backward with despairing roar,
Or fling against the sheer cliffs overhead
And sow these vaults with wreckage and the dead,

Now all is still. Yet ere today is done,
Where now these fairy runnels thread the sand,
Five fathoms deep the swelling tides shall run
Round the blind cave and swallow rock and strand,
And this discovered breast on which I lie
Shall clothe itself again with mystery.

ERNEST RHYS
(1859 – 1946)

Wales England Wed

Wales England wed, so I was bred.
    'twas merry London gave me breath.
I dreamt of love, – and fame. I strove:
    but Ireland taught me love was best.
And Irish eyes, and London cries,
    and streams of Wales, may tell the rest,
What more than these I asked of life,
    I am content to have from Death.

The Ballad of the Homing Man

He saw the sun, the Light-giver, step down behind the oak,
And send a tawny arrow-shaft along the engine-smoke.

He saw the last brown harvester lift up from mother earth
The sheaf that holds a mystery – the seed of death and birth;

And like a place in Paradise, the empty stubble-field
Waited, to watch the hock-cart go, with children she did yield.

He saw far-off the homing crows sail into mottled sky, –
Saw horse and horseman flag and tire, and trees like men go by.

He saw a woman close a door upon the warm fire-light, –
That, open, is the brow of day, and, closed, the shade of night.

He saw above the sallows the first lamps, lemon-hued,
Lead out the painted suburb into the hazel wood.

He saw the bob-tailed rabbits above the stoneman's pit
Where the years went, as the trains go, all unawares of it.

Another mile, the roofs begin; the rigid wilderness,
The smoke, the murky omens, upon his heart-beat press.

The night-reek of the townsfolk, the ferment of the place
Work like sharp ichor in his blood and strike him in the face.

But where the fields are fragrant, and where the town is passed,
There is a house, an open door; a face, a fire at last.

'Three voices in a doorway,' he says – 'a woman's form,
And a lighted hearth behind her can make a desert warm:

And what is Heaven but a house, like any other one,
Where the homing man finds harbour and the hundred roads
    are done?'

W. H. DAVIES
(1871 – 1940)

The Kingfisher

It was the Rainbow gave thee birth,
    And left thee all her lovely hues;
And, as her mother's name was Tears,
    So runs it in my blood to choose
For haunts the lonely pools, and keep
In company with trees that weep.

Go you and, with such glorious hues,
　Live with proud Peacocks in green parks;
On lawns as smooth as shining glass,
　Let every feather show its marks;
Get thee on boughs and clap thy wings
Before the windows of proud kings.

Nay, lovely Bird, thou are not vain;
　Thou hast no proud, ambitious mind;
I also love a quiet place
　That's green, away from all mankind;
A lonely pool, and let a tree
Sigh with her bosom over me.

Days that have Been

Can I forget the sweet days that have been,
　When poetry first began to warm my blood;
When from the hills of Gwent I saw the earth
　Burned into two by Severn's silver flood:

When I would go alone at night to see
　The moonlight, like a big white butterfly,
Dreaming on that old castle near Caerleon,
　While at its side the Usk went softly by:

When I would stare at lovely clouds in Heaven,
　Or watch them when reported by deep streams;
When feeling pressed like thunder, but would not
　Break into that grand music of my dreams?

Can I forget the sweet days that have been,
　The villages so green I have been in;
Llantarnam, Magor, Malpas, and Llanwern,
　Liswery, old Caerleon, and Alteryn?

Can I forget the banks of Malpas Brook,
　Or Ebbw's voice in such a wild delight,
As on he dashed with pebbles in his throat,
　Gurgling towards the sea with all his might?

Ah, when I see a leafy village now,
　I sigh and ask it for Llantarnam's green;
I ask each river where is Ebbw's voice –
　In memory of the sweet days that have been.

Leisure

What is this life if, full of care,
We have no time to stand and stare

No time to stand beneath the boughs
And stare as long as sheep or cows.

No time to see, when woods we pass,
Where squirrels hide their nuts in grass.

No time to see, in broad daylight,
Streams full of stars like skies at night.

No time to turn at Beauty's glance,
And watch her feet, how they can dance.

No time to wait till her mouth can
Enrich that smile her eyes began.

A poor life this if, full of care,
We have no time to stand and stare.

A Great Time

Sweet Chance, that led my steps abroad,
    Beyond the town, where wild flowers grow –
A rainbow and a cuckoo, Lord,
    How rich and great the times are now!
        Know, all ye sheep
        And cows, that keep

On staring that I stand so long
    In grass that's wet from heavy rain –
A rainbow and a cuckoo's song
    May never come together again;
        May never come
        This side the tomb.

The Inquest

I took my oath I would inquire,
    Without affection, hate or wrath,
Into the death of Ada Wright –
    So help me God! I took that oath.

When I went out to see the corpse,
    The four months' babe that died so young,
I judged it was seven pounds in weight,
    And little more than one foot long.

One eye, that had a yellow lid,
    Was shut – so was the mouth, that smiled;
The left eye open, shining bright –
    It seemed a knowing little child.

For as I looked at that one eye,
    It seemed to laugh, and say with glee:
'What caused my death you'll never know –
    Perhaps my mother murdered me.'

When I went into court again,
    To hear the mother's evidence –
It was a love-child, she explained.
    And smiled, for our intelligence.

'Now, Gentlemen of the Jury,' said
    The coroner – 'this woman's child
By misadventure met its death.'
    'Aye, aye,' said we. The mother smiled.

And I could see that child's one eye
    Which seemed to laugh, and say with glee:
'What caused my death you'll never know –
    Perhaps my mother murdered me.'

The Villain

While joy gave clouds the light of stars,
        That beamed where'er they looked;
And calves and lambs had tottering knees,
        Excited, while they sucked;
While every bird enjoyed his song,
Without one thought of harm or wrong –
I turned my head and saw the wind,
        Nor far from where I stood,
Dragging the corn by her golden hair,
        Into a dark and lonely wood.

E. HOWARD HARRIES
(1876 – 1961)

The Bone Prison

They say that in some Gower glen,
Below the bracken bushes deep,
All hidden from the eyes of men
Old Gwydion keeps his land of sleep.

Its pillars are the skulls of men
With eyeless socket, blue-veined bone,
And life is stagnant as a fen,
With music in a monotone.

There Gwydion's magic, like a vice,
Detains you in his house of bone.
There Feeling dies, and cold as ice
The heart grows to a pulseless stone.

The bard whose soul is void of fire
Is captive from the fields above,
The blinded mouth, the tuneless choir,
The lover who has lost his love,

Are captive there, and raptures old,
That cynic age delights to scorn,
Are in the icy silence cold,
And hope is all forlorn.

But glad am I that secret keeps,
Where lies old Gwydion's house of bone,
And in my heart no echo creeps
Of music of its monotone.

OLIVER DAVIES
(1881 – 1960)

Urban

Among tired men
    I labour far
From blackbird, wren,
      Night-owl, night-jar.

Here no one cares
    For tall green trees,
Foxes and hares
    That race the breeze.

Townspeople buy
    And sell, grow old
Quickly, and die
    Of too much gold.

But countrymen
    Whose friendships are
With blackbird, wren,
    Night-owl, night-jar,

Neighbourly give
    And take, whereby
Carefree they live,
    Carefree they die.

HUW MENAI
(1887 – 1961)

Pieces of Coal

Pieces of coal, hewn from the deeps of earth,
    Here in my hand, spectra of lights retain;
Crystal on crystal knit, back in its birth –
    Sun meeting sun again.

Shall I, when finished with this worldly pain –
    When of the sleep of death I am partaker –
Shall I ascend from earth, a soul again,
    To meet my Maker?

To One Who Died in a Garret in Cardiff

Friend, now for ever gone;
    Soul that was dear to me;
No more to see a fretting sun
    Set o'er an angry sea.

Lying now, silent, low,
    The long night covers thee;
As I await north winds do blow
    Musk of thy grave to me.

No more to quote Mynyddog, or the wise
   Khayyam, around the cup....
Asleep beneath the Odes of Arvon skies,
   The wine all frozen up...

Shouldering through this strife,
   I know not thou from me;
I seem to live a dual life -
   One half are thoughts of thee.

No more!—It seems so futile to make friends,
   Futile to love, O Lord!
Dreaming to live for aye, Death pulls, and rends,
   And then—the broken chord....

Dafydd fy Nhafydd bach
   Trwm yw fy nghalon i;
Ond hidia ddim, mae'r nef yn iach -
   Rhiw niwl yw d'angau di.

Rooks

(December)

Gleaners of grain they did not sow
Four rooks are standing in a row
Upon a rusty, upturned plough,
Whose blunted shares now wear a cloak
As brown as the brown earth they broke,
Far too well-fed to know unrest -
Each beak reclining on each breast,
When every bulging gizzard hath
Known surfeit of the aftermath,
Mute, living monuments are these
Of even darker mysteries,
In solemn conclave here, alone,
When Nature's fasting to the bone,
And I'd give much to understand
What quiet business they've in hand,
Perhaps a search might in them find
Spirits of Plato and his kind
Flown from Elysian fields to gaze
On frosted stubble and lean days;
Might know regret for shots which took
Old Pythagoras for a rook.

And on this Winter day so fine
How brilliantly their black coats shine –
Four lovely stars whose lustre strewn
A midnight maketh of blue noon,
And sensing some foul brute in man,
(Not the divinity in his plan)
They give to sturdy wings their span,
And fly away, as stars would fly,
If they had wings when man goes by!

A. G. PRYS-JONES
(b. 1888)

The Ploughman
(In Welsh Uplands)

Here did his fathers live and pass
  To slumber after ceaseless toil,
Sealing beneath the springing grass
  Their silent epic of the soil.

For here they tilled and hardly won
  From out the slow and stubborn weald
In murk and mist and kindlier sun
  These acres and their scanty yield.

And here he stands, as oft they stood,
  Untutored in the Saxon speech,
Driving his furrows from the wood
  Down to the long, low river-reach.

His words are few and few his needs
  He seeks no quarrel with his kind,
And silence deeper silence breeds
  Within the mazes of his mind.

Yet men have seen at one loved name
  His quiet face suffuse with fire,
A word that wakes within his frame
  The pulse of some Silurian sire,

Who, in this place and by this home,
  Heard from afar the tramping feet,
And knew the awful arm of Rome
  Had groped to find his green retreat,

Then swiftly to the onset came,
   Like some avenger of the years,
Swept on the cohorts like a flame,
   And burned and died amid the spears.

Henry Morgan's March on Panama

Morgan's curls are matted,
His lips are cracked and dry,
His tawny beard is tangled,
And his plumed hat hangs awry:
But his voice still booms like thunder
Through the foetid jungle glade
As he marches, bold as Lucifer,
Leading his gaunt brigade.

Twelve hundred famished buccaneers
Blistered, bitten and bled,
A stricken mob of men accursed
By the monstrous sun o'erhead:
Twelve hundred starveling scarecrows
Without a crumb to eat,
And not a drink for tortured throats
In that grim, festering heat.
Twelve hundred threadbare musketeers
Rotting in tropic mud
Where the reeking, fevered mangroves
Wake havoc in their blood:
Twelve hundred febrile wretches,
A legion of the dead:
But Morgan in his blue brocade
Goes striding on ahead.

Twelve hundred tatterdemalions,
The sorriest, maddest crew
That ever the green savannahs saw
When the Spanish bugles blew:
Twelve hundred rattling skeletons
Who sprang to life, and then
Like a wild wave took Panama,
For they were Morgan's men.

A. G. PRYS-JONES

Cors-y-Gwaed
(Fenland of Blood)

Heirs to these marshy lowlands
Willows and reeds remain;
This was no place for pasture,
These are no fields for grain.

Yet here in feuding foray
Young peasants fought and died,
Not knowing why their princes
Drew swords that Eastertide
Drenching with blood these acres,
Stagnant, useless and sour,
Acres that never nourished
Cattle nor crops nor flower.

So Easter after Easter,
Dumb as the soil and deep,
Two hundred men of Meirion
Unshriven, lie asleep.

Symbols, these barren marshes,
Of continents and seas
Wherein our lords and masters
Still cannot live at ease.
Symbols, these men of Meirion,
They learnt, not knowing why,
When rulers ride in anger
Who are the first to die.

Unfortunate Occurrence at Cwm-Cadno
(for Gwyn Thomas)

Pusey Hughes, a low-grade voter,
Partook of aniseed and bloater
Before proceeding down the street
To watch the muster at the Meet
Outside the Lion, where the bar
Knew Pusey as a regular
Who took his normal morning measure
Without emotion, yet with pleasure.

But due to fatal gaps in knowledge
(Pusey had never been to College)
Alas, on this supreme occasion,
He never reached this last potation:
In consequence of his repast
Things moved too quickly, much too fast,
For Pusey, on quite obvious grounds,
Surrounded by demented hounds,
Was pounced upon and torn apart:
This nearly broke the huntsman's heart,
The show was finished at the start.

We hope that Pusey, gone to bliss
Through ignorance, has now grown wiser:
Though all regret he had to miss
The story in ''The Advertiser''.

WYN GRIFFITH
(1890 – 1977)

Exile
(Welsh Service from Daventry)

Bethel, Horeb, Engedi, Soar:
Dark-roofed beneath a winter sky blown taut
From Manod to the sea, grey, cold in the mountain rain;
Dim lamps within pour yellow stain
Upon the stippled walls. I had forgotten naught
The eye can hold across the desert years.
But these slow-moving tunes are ghosts
Remembered not within the day: wind-waves
From crag to scree-footed rock rebounding, hissing staves
Of melancholy anger through the night,
And all in sadness, sadness, falling; I had forgotten naught
Save longing. I am a child, strong in the light
That nurtured me: I had forgotten naught.

Office Window

Beyond the waste of commerce there are hills
and a cool evening caught in the uplands
where ledger lines hold up the clouds.
No figures but the ciphers of the tarns,
no balance but a hawk poised waiting its profit
where small creatures scurry in the grass.

It is time to think sadly
but not despondently,
skirmish amongst the merchandise where doubt lies
but not without hope. No broken thought
heart cannot mend, no lack of grace
where folly laughs the market into wisdom.

Look to the end, then,
Let the coiled bracken be pattern of the will.

DUDLEY G. DAVIES
(1891 – 1981)

At Branwen's Grave

Bedd petrual a wnaed i Fronwen ferch Lyr ar lan Alaw,
ac yno a gladdwyd hi. (Mabinogion)

Branwen was buried here, so long ago
Time lies upon her like the drifted snow.

By Alaw bank, in Môn, her grave was found,
Four-sided, lonely, in the surge's sound.

Branwen who was most lovely, child of Llyr,
King of this isle, long since, was buried here –

She that went oversea, Matholwch's bride,
To Ireland, and was driven from his side,

And saw the slaying of Gwern her son, and came
To Môn again, and died, for sorrow and shame.

*   *   *

Far in the silver night a dog barks on,
Faint as a cry from those dim centuries gone.

As faint, as far, a voice within the wave,
Like vanished beauty crying from the grave

'Alas!' and 'Never more, O never more!',
Makes sorrowful song upon the ocean shore.

Lovers unloved, lost children far from home,
Weep and grieve on, there in the moonshot foam.

Here Branwen broke her heart, so long ago
Time lies upon her like the drifted snow.

Carmarthenshire

Carmarthen hills are green and low,
And therealong the small sheep go
Whose voices to the valley come
At eve, when all things else are dumb.

Carmarthen hills within their arms
Hold many quiet white-walled farms;
The cattle feed by Towy banks,
Silken, sleek, with dapple flanks.

The roads between the villages
Are shy and shadowy with trees,
And every turn to left or right
Brings a new picture of delight,

And hazel boughs are everywhere,
So that in autumn, walking there
On any roadside hedge you'll find
The brown nuts nodding to the wind.

DAVID JONES
(1895 – 1974)

from *In Parenthesis*

This Dai adjusts his slipping shoulder-straps, wraps close his
misfit outsize greatcoat – he articulates his English with an
alien care.
   My fathers were with the Black Prinse of Wales
at the passion of
the blind Bohemian king.
They served in these fields,
it is in the histories that you can read it, Corporal – boys
Gower, they were – it is writ down – yes.

DAVID JONES

Wot about Methusalum, Taffy?
I was with Abel when his brother found him,
under the green tree.
I built a shit-house for Artaxerxes.
I was the spear in Balin's hand
                    that made waste King Pellam's land.
I took the smooth stones of the brook,
I was with Saul
playing before him.
I saw him armed like Derfel Gatheren.
I the fox-run fire
            consuming in the wheatlands;
and in the standing wheat in Cantium made some attempt to
form – (between dun August oaks their pied bodies darting)
And I the south air, tossed from high projections by his Oli-
fant; (the arid marcher-slopes echoing –
should they lose
Clere Espaigne la bele).
    I am '62 Socrates, my feet are colder than you think
on this
Potidaean duck-board.
    I the adder in the little bush
whose hibernation-end
undid,
unmade victorious toil:
In ostium fluminis.
At the four actions in regione Linnuis
                    by the black waters.
At Bassas in the shallows.
At Cat Coit Celidon.
At Guinnion redoubt, where he carried the Image.
In urbe Legionis.
By the vallum Antonini, at the place of boundaries, at the toil-
ing estuary and strong flow called Tribruit.
By Agned mountain.
On Badon hill, where he bore the Tree.
    I am the Loricated Legions.
Helen Camulodunum is ours;
she's the toast of the Rig'ment,
she is in an especial way our Mediatrix.
    She's clement and loving, she's Friday's child, she's lov-
ing and giving;

– 139 –

O dulcis
imperatrix.
   Her ample bosom holds:
Pontifex maximus,
Comes Litoris Saxonici,
Comes Britanniarum,
Gwledig,
Bretwalda, as these square-heads say.
   She's the girl with the sparkling eyes,
she's the Bracelet Giver,
she's a regular draw with the labour companies,
whereby
the paved army-paths are hers that grid the island which is
   her dower.
Elen Lluyddawc she is – more she is than
Helen Argive.
   My mob digged the outer vallum,
we furnished picquets;
we staked trip-wire as a precaution at
Troy Novaunt.
   I saw the blessèd head set under
               that kept the narrow sea inviolate.
To keep the Land,
to give the yield:
   under the White Tower
          I trowelled the inhuming mortar.
   They learned me well the proportions due –
by water
by sand
by slacked lime.
   I drest the cist –
the beneficent artisans knew well how to keep
the king's head to keep
the land inviolate.
   The Bear of the Island: he broke it in his huge pride, and
over-reach of his imperium.
The Island Dragon.
The Bull of Battle
      (this is the third woeful uncovering).
Let maimed kings lie – let be
O let the guardian head
keep back – bind savage sails, lock the shield-wall, nourish
the sowing.

The War Duke
The Director of Toil –
   he burst the balm-cloth, unbricked the barrow
(cruel feet march because of this
                     ungainly men sprawl over us).
O Land! – O Brân lie under.
The chrism'd eye that watches the French-men
that wards under
that keeps us
that brings the furrow-fruit,
keep the land, keep us
keep the islands adjacent.

I marched, sixty thousand and one thousand marched, because
of the brightness of Flur, because of the keeper of promises
      (we came no more again)
who depleted the Island,
      (and this is the first emigrant host)
and the land was bare for our going.
   O blessèd head hold the striplings from the narrow sea.
   I marched, sixty thousand marched who marched for Kynan
and Elen because of foreign machinations,
      (we came no more again)
who left the land without harness
      (and this is the second emigrant host).
O Brân confound the counsel of the councillors, O blessèd
head, hold the striplings from the narrow sea.
   In the baized chamber confuse his tongue:
that Lord Agravaine.
He urges with repulsive lips, he counsels: he nets us into
expeditionary war.
   O blessèd head hold the striplings from the narrow sea.
   I knew the smart on Branwen's cheek and the turbulence
in Ireland
      (and this was the third grievous blow).
   I served Longinus that Dux bat-blind and bent;
the Dandy Xth are my regiment;
who diced
Crown and Mud-hook
under the Tree,
whose Five Sufficient Blossoms
yield for us.

I kept the boding raven
> from the Dish.
With my long pilum
I beat the crow
from that heavy bough.
   But I held the tunics of these –
I watched them work the terrible embroidery that He put on
I heard there sighing for the Feet so shod.
I saw cock-robin gain
> his rosy breast.
I heard Him cry:
> *Apples ben ripe in my gardayne*
I saw Him die.
   I was in Michael's trench when bright Lucifer bulged his
primal salient out.
That caused it,
that upset the joy-cart,
and three parts waste.
   You ought to ask: Why,
what is this,
what's the meaning of this.
Because you don't ask,
although the spear-shaft
drips,
there's neither steading – not a roof-tree.
   I am the Single Horn thrusting
by night-stream margin
in Helyon.
   Cripes-a-mighty-strike-me-stone-cold – you don't say.
   Where's that birth-mark, young 'un.
   Wot the Melchizzydix! – and still fading – jump to it
Rotherhithe.

> Never die never die
> Never die never die
> Old soljers never die
> Never die never die
> Old soljers never die they never die
> Never die
> Old soljers never die they
> Simply fade away.

DAVID JONES

from *The Anathemata*

Section V, 'The Lady of the Pool':

(The scene is London and the speaker a Britannia who first appears as a
lavender-seller.)

                    At each adytum over
where under the fathering figures rest that do keep us all.
                    So it's fabled
in Taffy's historias and gests of Brut the Conditor –
romans o' Belins, 'Wallons an' Wortipors
                    agéd viriles buried under
that from Lud's clay have ward of us that be his townies –
and certain THIS BOROUGH WERE NEVER FORCED,
cap-tin!!
                    And making to bear
bean-stalks, cherry gardens, tended 'lotments, conservatories and
stews of fish, pent fowl, moo-cows and all manner o' living
stock, such as, like us women, be quickened of kind: so God will.
                    Strong binders also
to make our loam the surer stereobate for so great a weight
of bonded courses,
                    so it is said.
Though there's a deal of subsidence hereabouts even so:
                    gravels, marls, alluviums
here all's alluvial, cap'n, and as unstable as these old annals
that do gravel us all. For, captain:
                    even immolated kings
be scarce a match for the deep fluvial doings of the mother.
                    But leastways
best let sleepers lie
                    and these slumberers
was great captains, cap'n:
tyrannoi come in keels from Old Troy
                    requiescant.
For, these fabliaux say, of one other such quondam king
rexque futurus.

                    And you never know, captain
you never know, not with what you might call metaphysical
certainty, captain: our phenomenology is but limited,
captain.

So of these let's say *requiescant*
till the Sejunction Day!
For should these stir, then would our Engle-Raum in this
Brut's Albion be like to come to some confusion!

You never know, captain:
What's under works up.

I will not say it shall be so
but, captain, rather I would say:

You never know!

from *The Tutelar of the Place*

Queen of the differentiated sites, administratrix of the
demarcations, let our cry come unto you.

In all times of imperium save us when the *mercatores*
come save us

from the guile of the *negotiatores* save us from the *missi,*
from the agents

who think no shame
by inquest to audit what is shameful to tell

deliver us.
When they check their capitularies in their curias

confuse their reckonings.
When they narrowly assess the *trefydd*

by hide and rod
by *pentan* and pent

by impost and fee on beast-head
and roof-tree
and number the souls of men

notch their tallies false
disorder what they have collated.
When they proscribe the diverse uses and impose the
rootless uniformities, pray for us.

When they sit in *Consilium*
to liquidate the holy diversities

mother of particular perfections
queen of otherness
mistress of asymmetry
patroness of things counter, parti, pied, several

protectress of things known and handled
help of things familiar and small
                   wardress of the secret crevices
                   of things wrapped and hidden
mediatrix of all the deposits
                   margravine of the troia
empress of the labyrinth
           receive our prayers.
When they escheat to the Ram
                      in the Ram's curia
the seisin where the naiad sings
             above where the forked rod bends
or where the dark outcrop
             tells on the hidden seam
pray for the green valley.
When they come with writs of oyer and terminer
                   to hear the false and
                   determine the evil
according to the advices of the Ram's magnates who serve the
Ram's wife, who write in the Ram's book of Death.
In the bland megalopolitan light
        where no shadow is by day or by night
be our shadow.
Remember the mound-kin, the kith of the *tarren* gone from this
mountain because of the exorbitance of the Ram...remember
them in the rectangular tenements, in the houses of the engines
that fabricate the ingenuities of the Ram...Mother of Flowers
save them then where no flower blows.
              Though they shall not come again because of
the requirements of the Ram with respect to the world plan,
remember them where the dead forms multiply, where no
stamen leans, where the carried pollen falls to the adamant
surfaces, where is no crevice.
In all times of *Gleichschaltung,* in the days of the central
economies, set up the hedges of illusion round some remnant of
us, twine the wattles of mist, white-web a Gwydion-hedge
           like fog on the *bryniau*
           against the commissioners
and assessors bearing the writs of the Ram to square the world-
floor and number the tribes and write down the secret things
and take away the diversities by which we are, by which we call
on your name...

EILUNED LEWIS
(1900 – 1979)

The Birthright

We who were born
In country places,
Far from cities
And shifting faces,
We have a birthright
No man can sell,
And a secret joy
No man can tell.

For we are kindred
To lordly things,
The wild duck's flight
And the white owl's wings;
To pike and salmon,
To bull and horse,
The curlew's cry
And the smell of gorse.

Pride of trees,
Swiftness of streams,
Magic of frost
Have shaped our dreams:
No baser vision
Their spirit fills
Who walk by right
On the naked hills.

THEODORE NICHOLL
(1902 – 1973)

His Friend's Last Battle

Loosing their feverish clutch
as if they had been spray-drenched watchers on a shore,
the men fell back, a white-faced eager band;
the Squadron-Leader let his hand stream
like a plume of chivalry.
They met the tide in grand array,
beaked viking vessels of foray,

EVAN J. THOMAS

and left the harboured landing-ground;
all that my watching heart could do,
was beat more furiously, too,
in rapid acclamation.
But heavy farewell in my soul
drew it to earth lumberingly,
smarting, to lie furrowed, in security.
Was he remembering how we flew
wing-tip to wing-tip through the blue
empyrean, shouting the hours down,
stripping the air, of the thin fair
webs of light, to make a cover for delight?
O that I were him, blown
by the wild wind's gust,
and he, the trumpet in its mouth
assembling my defiant dust!

EVAN J. THOMAS
(1903 – 1930)

The Spectator

When I was young, a questing child,
The dead came past these walls;
I saw them carried shoulder-high,
And women came with shawls,
The nodding hamlet women came
To watch those funerals.

The dead were brought here week by week;
And through the chapel-yard
The mourners followed two by two,
With a downcast regard;
The bearers' tread was muffled like
The marching of a guard.

It was my weekly spectacle,
Recurrence without change;
A routine so familiar
I never thought it strange,
A pleasure prized! I would not have
A wedding in exchange.

The window was my balcony;
My cheeks touched the cold glass;
I stood in marble posture there,
Waiting to sight the hearse,
Drawn by black horses up the road,
Where death had its egress.

Draughty the house was at all times,
Draughtier out-of-doors;
And when the mourning file had gone,
I sat and mused for hours
Of those who lay out in the cold,
When winds blew down the moors.

The Return

Like a prowling wolf, I padded from door to door
Of the dark, empty house, crying for entry there;
To the narrow stone-flagged hall, and the dingy stair,
And the room overhead, where I should sleep no more.

The cold, implacable windows were shuttered fast;
And gloomily high above me the chimneys soared
Into a stony sky; everything round ignored
That I was a child shut out from the house of the past.

GWYN WILLIAMS
(b. 1904)

City under Snow

Mosques into snow-palaces; banks, bagnios
party headquarters and apartment blocks
acquire an innocence; L. S. Lowry figures
lean into flocked air;

spittle, pigeon-dung, dogshit and broken
glass, the layer of soot all iced over and
a new fall powders the cleaned crotches
of cobbled alleys.

Super, Gwydion says, and over the surface
boys skim and tumble where wheels can't turn
for these few unsmutched days. The ferry boats
are icinged toys

on rumpled silk of shoreless water. It's
a world for ideal children. Positive nastiness
surely can't be. Until the squeezed snowball
is made stone-hard,

the wind switches, cats make a sortie, coats
lose their ermine, birds are here, the dimension
of whiteness drips into slush and grime.
Back comes our dirty world.

Saint Ursula of Llangwyryfon

Picked offhand by the angels to demonstrate
for Christ; little she-bear Ursula, saint
perhaps of some monstrous forgotten faith,
mother-goddess turned virgin or just a girl

afraid to marry a handsome pagan?
In Claude's picture you are already crowned
in thin gold, you stand calm, your girls
shoulder each other eagerly out of church

down the stone steps (what are those bows and arrows
for if not to foretell your martyrdom
by a brute's arrow in splendid Cologne?)
to the fine-sparred ships, the unregarding

stevedores, to the classic water and
the trip to death. Your bones lie abroad
and here where I think you lisped Latin
where you feared marriage and rough Saxon ways

where my forebears trimmed stone in your honour
and an arch by one of them is a local wonder,
does anyone else think of you as the cracked peal
of the bell of your Church of the Virgins

twists and dies up the pilgrim route through the still
Sunday air past the abandoned houses
to a ridge that looks over to Enlli
from old stones over the bear-god's valley?

Wild Night at Treweithan

The evening's late November, clouds hump and streak,
the starlings are swept off-course in a black spray,
the gale howls and rattles in my wide chimney,
whistles in a nasty searching hurry.

The ponies can hardly believe it and face it
instead of turning their backsides as they usually do.
Is it drink makes me silly enough to think there's a force
that wants to get rid of something here before day?

The mountain's still black, the great chimneys
aren't rocked, the singing wires hold, we're
still linked to those others, I think of the farmhouse
as a hill-fort of stone with lines out over the moor.

No, there's no power to fear out there in the darkness,
only the idiot unpathed swirl of air belting
over this earth's face as we swing through hidden
stars. I have confidence in my grandfather's building.

Pelagius

Tough traveller with your Celtic view
of Christ more as man than god,
rough, bearded and trousered,
did they scoff at you in Rome
when you found the centre of your world

soft, cruel, rotten and doomed
and told them so? Jewelled
reliquaries already in the churches
whilst the togaed or tattered mob
howled for blood over the arches

of the Colosseum. So you left the city
to the cleansing Goths and went
your way, arguing your humane sign
of man's responsibility, denying
the equality of evil, original sin,

to towered Jerusalem, to be
condemned at shining Ephesus
and ruined Carthage, though no doctrine
of yours ever presumed to order
your clear sight of man's condition.

Celtic monk who never took holy
orders, I, a heretic
in every faith I've been tempted by,
fifteen centuries after your stand
now greet you and your heresy.

IDRIS DAVIES
(1905 – 1953)

Capel Calvin

There's holy holy people
They are in capel bach –
They don't like surpliced choirs,
They don't like Sospan Fach.

They don't like Sunday concerts,
Or women playing ball,
They don't like Williams Parry much
Or Shakespeare at all.

They don't like beer or bishops,
Or pictures without texts,
They don't like any other
Of the nonconformist sects.

And when they go to Heaven,
They won't like that too well,
For the music will be sweeter
Than the music played in Hell.

Gwalia Deserta VIII

Do you remember 1926? That summer of soups and speeches,
The sunlight on the idle wheels and the deserted crossings,
And the laughter and the cursing in the moonlit streets?
Do you remember 1926? The slogans and the penny concerts,
The jazz-bands and the moorland picnics,
And the slanderous tongues of famous cities?
Do you remember 1926? The great dream and the swift disaster,
The fanatic and the traitor, and more than all,
The bravery of the simple, faithful folk?
'Ay, ay, we remember 1926,' said Dai and Shinkin,
As they stood on the kerb in Charing Cross Road,
'And we shall remember 1926 until our blood is dry.'

Gwalia Deserta XV

O what can you give me?
Say the sad bells of Rhymney.

Is there hope for the future?
Cry the brown bells of Merthyr.

Who made the mineowner?
Say the black bells of Rhondda.

And who robbed the miner?
Cry the grim bells of Blaina.

They will plunder willy-nilly,
Say the bells of Caerphilly.

They have fangs, they have teeth!
Shout the loud bells of Neath.

To the south, things are sullen,
Say the pink bells of Brecon.

Even God is uneasy,
Say the moist bells of Swansea.

Put the vandals in court!
Cry the bells of Newport.

All would be well if – if – if –
Say the green bells of Cardiff.

Why so worried, sisters, why?
Sing the silver bells of Wye.

IDRIS DAVIES

Gwalia Deserta XXII

I stood in the ruins of Dowlais
And sighed for the lovers destroyed
And the landscape of Gwalia stained for all time
By the bloody hands of progress.
I saw the ghosts of the slaves of The Successful Century
Marching on the ridges of the sunset
And wandering among derelict furnaces,
And they had not forgotten their humiliation,
For their mouths were full of curses.
And I cried aloud, O what shall I do for my fathers
And the land of my fathers?
But they cursed and cursed and would not answer
For they could not forget their humiliation.

Gwalia Deserta XXVI

The village of Fochriw grunts among the higher hills;
The dwellings of miners and pigeons and pigs
Cluster round the little grey war memorial.
The sun brings glitter to the long street roofs
And the crawling promontories of slag,
The sun makes the pitwheels to shine,
And praise be to the sun, the great unselfish sun,
The sun that shone on Plato's shoulders,
That dazzles with light the Taj Mahal.
The same sun shone on the first mineowner,
On the vigorous builder of this brown village,
And praise be to the impartial sun.
He had no hand in the bruising of valleys,
He had no line in the vigorous builder's plans,
He had no voice in the fixing of wages,
He was the blameless one.
And he smiles on the village this morning,
He smiles on the far-off grave of the vigorous builder,
On the ivied mansion of the first mineowner,
On the pigeon lofts and the Labour Exchange,
And he smiles as only the innocent can.

Hywel and Blodwen

Where are you going to, Hywel and Blodwen,
With your eyes as sad as your shoes?
We are going to learn a nimble language
By the waters of the Ouse.

We are tramping through Gloucester and through Leicester,
We hope we shall not drop,
And we talk as we go of the Merthyr streets
And a house at Dowlais Top.

We have triads and englyns from pagan Dyfed
To brace us in the fight,
And three or four hundred Methodist hymns
To sing on a starless night.

We shall grumble and laugh and trudge together
Till we reach the stark North Sea
And talk till we die of Pantycelyn
And the eighteenth century.

We shall try to forget the Sunday squabbles,
And the foreign magistrate,
And the stupid head of the preacher's wife,
And the broken iron gate.

So here we say farewell and wish you
Less trouble and less pain,
And we trust you to breed a happier people
Ere our blood flows back again.

The Angry Summer: 2

From Abertillery and Aberdare
   And Rhondda Fach and Rhondda Fawr
And Ogmore Vale and Nine Mile Point
   And Bargoed and Brynmawr,
The delegates come in morning trains
   To meet in Cardiff City,
And some have tongues and some have brains
   And some pretend they're witty,
And some have come with hearts aflame
   To plead and plan and fight
For those who toil without a name
   And pass into the night.

The Angry Summer: 7

Mrs. Evans fach, you want butter again.
How will you pay for it now, little woman
With your husband out on strike, and full
Of the fiery language? Ay, I know him,
His head is full of fire and brimstone
And a lot of palaver about communism,
And me, little Dan the grocer
Depending so much on private enterprise.

What, depending on the miners and their
Money too? O yes, in a way, Mrs. Evans,
Yes, in a way I do, mind you.
Come tomorrow, little woman, and I'll tell you then
What I have decided overnight.
Go home now and tell that rash red husband of yours
That your grocer cannot afford to go on strike
Or what would happen to the butter from Carmarthen?
Good day for now, Mrs. Evans fach.

In Gardens in the Rhondda

In gardens in the Rhondda
  The daffodils dance and shine
When tired men trudge homeward
  From factory and mine.

The daffodils dance in gardens
  Behind the grim brown row
Built among the slagheaps
  In a hurry long ago.

They dance as though in passion
  To shame and to indict
The brutes who built so basely
  In the long Victorian night.

GLYN JONES
(b. 1905)

Esyllt

As he climbs down our hill my kestrel rises,
Steering in silence up from five empty fields,
A smooth sun brushed brown across his shoulders,
Floating in wide circles, his warm wings stiff.
Their shadows cut; in new soft orange hunting boots
My lover crashes through the snapping bracken.

The still, gorse-hissing hill burns, brags gold broom's
Outcropping quartz; each touched bush spills dew.
Strangely, last moment's parting was never sad,
But unreal, like my promised years; less felt
Than this intense and silver snail calligraphy
Scrawled here in the sun across these stones.

Why have I often wanted to cry out
More against his going when he has left my flesh
Only for the night? When he has gone out
Hot from my mother's kitchen, and my combs
Were on the table under the lamp, and the wind
Was banging the doors of the shed in the yard.

Merthyr

Lord, when they kill me, let the job be thorough
And carried out behind that county borough
Known as Merthyr, in Glamorganshire.
It would be best if it could happen, Sir,
Upon some great green roof, some Beacon slope
Those monstrous clouds of childhood slid their soap
Snouts over, into the valley. The season,
Sir, for shooting, summer; and love the reason.
On that hill, varnished in the glazing tide
Of evening, stand me, with the petrified
Plantations, the long blue spoonful of the lake,
The gold stook-tufted acres without break
Below me, and the distant corduroy
Glass of the river – which, a mitching boy,
I fished – flowing as though to quench
The smouldering coalfield in its open trench
Of steamy valley, fifteen miles away.

Here, Sir, are more arrangements for that day:-
Lay me, lead-loaded, below the mourning satin
Of some burnt-out oak; the skylark's chirpy Latin
Be my *Daeth yr awr;* gather the black
Flocks for bleaters – sweet grass their ham – upon the back
Of lonely Fan Gihirych; let night's branchy tree
Glow with silver-coated planets over me.

And yet, some times, I can't help wondering;
Is this rather posh poetic death the thing,
After all, for somebody like me? I realize
I have a knack for telling bardic lies,
To say I see in some protean hill
A green roof, ship's prow or an eagle's bill,
To claim the mountain stream for me's as clear
As flowing gin, and yet as brown as beer.
I fancy words, some critics praise me for
A talent copious in metaphor.
But this my gift for logopoeic dance
Brothers, I know, a certain arrogance
Of spirit, a love of grandeur, style and dash,
Even vain-glory, the gaudiest *panache,*
Which might impel to great rascality
A heedless heart. This glorying in all
Created things, the golden sun, the small
Rain riding in the wind, the silvery shiver
Of the dawn-touched birches, and the chromium river,
Innocent itself, has yet calamitous
And wilful pride for child and famulus.
And thus I see the point when puritan
Or mystic poet harried under ban
Sensual nature, earth, sea and firmament;
I apprehend some strain of what they meant,
And look at nature with a wary eye.
Sir, that death I sought was pure effrontery.

Lord, when they kill me, let the job be thorough
And carried out *inside* that county borough
Known as Merthyr, in Glamorganshire,
A town easy enough to cast a slur
Upon, I grant. Some cyclopean ball
Or barn-dance, some gigantic free-for-all,
You'd guess, had caused her ruins, and those slums –
Frightening enough, I've heard, to daunt the bums –

Seem battered wreckage in some ghastly myth,
Some nightmare of the busting aerolith.
In short, were she a horse, so her attackers
Claim, her kindest destination were the knackers.
Yet, though I've been in Dublin, Paris, Brussels,
London, of course, too, I find what rustles
Oftest and scentiest through the torpid trees
Of my brain-pan, is some Merthyr-mothered breeze,
Not dreams of them – a zephyr at its best
Acting on arrogance like the alkahest.

An object has significance or meaning
Only to the extent that human feeling
And intellect bestow them. All that sensational news
The heart hears, before she starts to bruise
Herself against the universe's rocky rind,
Is what she treasures most – the sight of wind
Fretting a great beech like an anchored breaker;
The vale, pink-roofed at sunset, a heavenly acre
Of tufted and irradiated toothpaste; the moon
Glistening sticky as snail-slime in the afternoon;
Street-papers hurdling, like some frantic foal,
The crystal barriers of squalls; the liquid coal
Of rivers; the hooter's loud liturgic boom;
Pit-clothes and rosin fragrant in a warm room –
Such sensations deck a ruinous scene
(To strangers) with tinsel, scarlet, spangles, green,
Gold, ribbons, and the glare of pantomime's
Brilliancy in full floods, foots and limes.

But far more than the scene, the legendary
Walkers and actors of it, the memory
Of neighbours, worthies, relatives,
Their free tripudiation, is what gives
That lump of coal that Shelley talks about
Oftenest a puff before it quite goes out.
My grandfather's fantastic friends, old Sion
O Ferthyr, occultist, meddler with the unknown –
(The spirits in malevolence one night
Nigh strangled him, but sobered Sion showed fight!)
My grandfather himself, musician, bard,
Pit-sinker, joker, whom the Paddys starred
As basser for their choir – so broken out!
My undersized great granny, that devout

Calvinist, with mind and tongue like knives;
The tall boys from Incline Top, and those boys' wives;
The tailor we believed a Mexican,
A rider of the prairies; Dr. Pan
Jones (he it was who gave my father
The snowy barn-owl) Bishop – *soi-disant* rather;
Refined Miss Rees; Miss Thomas ditto; Evan
Davies, and the Williamses from Cefn.
Sir, where memories, dense as elephant
Grass, of these swarm round, in some common *pant*
Or hilltop lay me down; may the ghostly breeze
Of their presence be all my obsequies;
Not sheep and birds about me, but lively men,
And dead men's histories, O Lord. Amen.

Morning

On the night beach, quiet beside the blue
Bivouac of sea-wood, and fresh loaves, and the
Fish baking, the broken ghost, whose flesh burns
Blessing the dark bay and the still mast-light,
Shouts, 'Come'.
        A naked man on deck who heard
Also cockcrow, turning to the pebbles, sees
A dawn explode among the golden boats,
Pulls on his sea-plaid, leaps into the sea.

Wading the hoarfrost meadows of that fiord's
Daybreak, he, hungering fisherman, forgets
Cockcrow tears, dark noon, dead god, empty cave,
All those mountains of miraculous green
Light that swamped the landing-punt, and kneels,
Shivering, in a soaked blouse, eating by the
Blue blaze the sweet breakfast of forgiveness.

Swifts

Shut-winged fish, brown as mushroom,
The sweet, hedge-hurdling swifts, zoom
Over waterfalls of wind.
I salute all those lick-finned,
Dusky-bladed air-cutters.
Could you weave words as taut, sirs,
As those swifts', great *cywydd* kings,
Swart basketry of swoopings?

GLYN JONES

The Common Path

On one side the hedge, on the other the brook:
  Each afternoon I, unnoticed, passed
The middle-aged schoolmistress, grey-haired,
  Gay, loving, who went home along the path.

That spring she walked briskly, carrying her bag
  With the long ledger, the ruler, the catkin twigs,
Two excited little girls from her class
  Chattering around their smiling teacher.

Summer returned, each day then she approached slowly,
  Alone, wholly absorbed, as though in defeat
Between water and hazels, her eyes heedless,
  Her grey face deeply cast down. Could it be
Grief at the great universal agony had begun
  To feed upon her heart – war, imbecility,
Old age, starving, children's deaths, deformities?
  I, free, white, gentile, born neither
Dwarf nor idiot, passed her by, drawing in
  The skirts of my satisfaction, on the other side.

One day, at the last instant of our passing,
  She became, suddenly, aware of me
And, as her withdrawn glance met my eyes,
  Her whole face kindled into life, I heard
From large brown eyes a blare of terror, anguished
  Supplication, her cry of doom, death, despair.
And in the warmth of that path's sunshine
  And of my small and manageable success
I felt at once repelled, affronted by her suffering,
  The naked shamelessness of that wild despair.

Troubled, I avoided the common until I heard
  Soon, very soon, the schoolmistress, not from
Any agony of remote and universal suffering
  Or unendurable grief for others, but
Private, middle-aged, rectal cancer, was dead.

What I remember, and in twenty years have
  Never expiated, is that my impatience,
That one glance of my intolerance,
  Rejected her, and so rejected all
The sufferings of wars, imprisonments,
  Deformities, starvation, idiocy, old age –
Because fortune, sunlight, meaningless success,
  Comforted an instant what must not be comforted.

VERNON WATKINS
(1906 – 1967)

Foal

Darkness is not dark, nor sunlight the light of the sun
But a double journey of insistent silver hooves.
Light wakes in the foal's blind eyes as lightning illuminates corn
With a rustle of fine-eared grass, where a starling shivers.

And whoever watches a foal sees two images,
Delicate, circling, born, the spirit with blind eyes leaping
And the left spirit, vanished, yet here, the vessel of ages
Clay-cold, blue, laid low by her great wide belly the hill.

See him break that circle, stooping to drink, to suck
His mother, vaulted with a beautiful hero's back
Arched under the singing mane,
Shaped to her shining, pricked into awareness
By the swinging dug, amazed by the movement of suns;
His blue fellow has run again down into grass,
And he slips from that mother to the boundless horizons of air,
Looking for that other, the foal no longer there.

But perhaps
In the darkness under the tufted thyme and the downtrodden
    winds,
In the darkness under the violet's roots, in the darkness of the
    pitcher's music,
In the uttermost darkness of a vase
There is still the print of fingers, the shadow of waters.
And under the dry, curled parchment of the soil there is always
    a little foal
Asleep.

So the whole morning he runs here, fulfilling the track
Of so many suns; vanishing the mole's way, moving
Into mole's mysteries under the zodiac,
Racing, stopping in the circle. Startled he stands
Dazzled, where darkness is green, where the sunlight is black,
While his mother, grazing, is moving away
From the lagging star of those stars, the unrisen wonder
In the path of the dead, fallen from the sun in her hooves,
And eluding the dead hands, begging him to play.

Returning to Goleufryn

Returning to my grandfather's house, after this exile
From the coracle-river, long left with a coin to be good,
Returning with husks of those venturing ears for food
To lovely Carmarthen, I touch and remember the turnstile
Of this death-bound river. Fresh grass. Here I find that crown
In the shadow of dripping river-wood; then look up to the
   burning mile
Of windows. It is Goleufryn, the house on the hill;
And picking a child's path in a turn of the Towy I meet the
   prodigal town.

Sing, little house, clap hands: shut, like a book of the Psalms,
On the leaves and pressed flowers of a journey. All is sunny
In the garden behind you. The soil is alive with blind-petalled
   blooms
Plundered by bees. Gooseberries and currants are gay
With tranquil, unsettled light. Breathless light begging alms
Of the breathing grasses bent over the river of tombs
Flashes. A salmon has swallowed the tribute-money
Of the path. On the farther bank I see ragged urchins play

With thread and pin. O lead me that I may drown
In those earlier cobbles, reflected; a street that is strewn with
   palms,
Rustling with blouses and velvet. Yet I alone
By the light in the sunflower deepening, here stand, my eyes
   cast down
To the footprint of accusations, and hear the faint, leavening
Music of first Welsh words; that gust of plumes
'They shall mount up like eagles', dark-throated assumes,
Cold-sunned, low thunder and gentleness of the authentic
   Throne.

Yet now I am lost, lost in the water-wound looms
Where brief, square windows break on a garden's decay.
Gold butter is shining, the tablecloth speckled with crumbs.
The kettle throbs. In the calendar harvest is shown,
Standing in sheaves. Which way would I do you wrong?
Low, crumbling doorway of the infirm to the mansions of
   evening,
And poor, shrunken furrow where the potatoes are sown,
I shall not unnumber one soul I have stood with and known
To regain your stars struck by horses, your sons of God
   breaking in song.

Crowds

Why should the living need my oil?
I see them, and their eyes are blest.
No. For those others I must toil:
I toil to set the dead at rest.

Yet when I watch in solemn tides
The drifting crowds, each life a ghost,
I mourn them, for their truth abides;
Nor is one loved, till he is lost.

Music of Colours – White Blossom

White blossom, white, white shell; the Nazarene
Walking in the ear; white touched by souls
Who know the music by which white is seen,
Blinding white, from strings and aureoles,
Until that is not white, seen at the two poles,
Nor white the Scythian hills, nor Marlowe's queen.

The spray looked white until this snowfall.
Now the foam is grey, the wave is dull.
Call nothing white again, we were deceived.
The flood of Noah dies, the rainbow is lived.
Yet from the deluge of illusions an unknown colour is saved.

White must die black, to be born white again
From the womb of sounds, the inscrutable grain,
From the crushed, dark fibre, breaking in pain.

The bud of the apple is already forming there.
The cherry-bud, too, is firm, and behind it the pear
Conspires with the racing cloud. I shall not look.
The rainbow is diving through the wide-open book
Past the rustling paper of birch, the sorceries of bark.

Buds in April, on the waiting branch,
Starrily opening, light raindrops drench,
Swinging from world to world when starlings sweep,
Where they alight in air, are white asleep.
They will not break, not break, until you say
White is not white again, nor may may.

White flowers die soonest, die into that chaste
Bride-bed of the moon, their lives laid waste.
Lilies of Solomon, taken by the gust,
Sigh, make way. And the dark forest
Haunts the lowly crib near Solomon's dust,
Rocked to the end of majesty, warmed by the low beast,
Locked in the liberty of his tremendous rest.

If there is white, or has been white, it must have been
When His eyes looked down and made the leper clean.
White will not be, apart, though the trees try
Spirals of blossom, their green conspiracy.
She who touched His garment saw no white tree.

Lovers speak of Venus, and the white doves,
Jubilant, the white girl, myth's whiteness, Jove's,
Of Leda, the swan, whitest of his loves.
Lust imagines him, web-footed Jupiter, great down
Of thundering light; love's yearning pulls him down
On the white swan-breast, the magical lawn,
Involved in plumage, mastered by the veins of dawn.

In the churchyard the yew is neither green nor black.
I know nothing of Earth or colour until I know I lack
Original white, by which the ravishing bird looks wan.
The mound of dust is nearer, white of mute dust that dies
In the soundfall's great light, the music in the eyes,
Transfiguring whiteness into shadows gone,
Utterly secret. I know you, black swan.

Music of Colours: The Blossom Scattered

O, but how white is white, white from shadows come,
Sailing white of clouds, not seen before
On any snowfield, any shore;
Or this dense blue, delivered from the tomb,
White of the risen body, fiery blue of sky,
Light the saints teach us, light we learn to adore;
Not space revealed it, but the needle's eye
Love's dark thread holding, when we began to die.
It was the leper's, not the bird's cry,
Gave back that glory, made that glory more.

I cannot sound the nature of that spray
Lifted on wind, the blossoms falling away,
A death, a birth, an earthy mystery,
As though each petal stirring held the whole tree
That grew, created on the Lord's day.
There is no falling now. Yet for time's sake
These blossoms are scattered. They fall. How still they are.
They drop, they vanish, where all blossoms break.
Who touches one dead blossom touches every star.

So the green Earth is first no colour and then green.
Spirits who walk, who know
All is untouchable, and, knowing this, touch so,
Who know the music by which white is seen,
See the world's colours in flashes come and go.
The marguerite's petal is white, is wet with rain,
Is white, then loses white, and then is white again
Not from time's course, but from the living spring,
Miraculous whiteness, a petal, a wing,
Like light, like lightning, soft thunder, white as jet,
Ageing on ageless breaths. The ages are not yet.

Is there a tree, a bud, that knows not this:
White breaks from darkness, breaks from such a kiss
No mind can measure? Locked in the branching knot,
Conception shudders; that interior shade
Makes light in darkness, light where light was not;
Then the white petal, of whitest darkness made,
Breaks, and is silent. Immaculate they break,
Consuming vision, blinding eyes awake,
Dazzling the eyes with music, light's unspoken sound,
White born of bride and bridegroom, when they take
Love's path through Hades, engendered of dark ground.

Leda remembers. The rush of wings cast wide.
Sheer lightning, godhead, descending on the flood.
Night, the late, hidden waters on the moon's dark side.
Her virgin secrecy, doomed against time to run. .
Morning. The visitation. All colours hurled in one.
Struggling with night, with radiance! That smothering
    glory cried:
'Heavenborn am I. White-plumaged heart, you beat
    against the sun!'
All recollection sinking from the dazzled blood.

She woke, and her awakened wings were fire,
Darkened with light; O blinding white was she
With white's bewildering darkness. So that secret choir
Know, in the thicket, and witness more than we,
Listening to early day, dew's voice, the lightest feet,
As though Saint Francis passing, told who they were,
Fledged of pure spirit, though upheld by air.
I think one living is already there,
So sound asleep she is, her breath so faint,
She knows, she welcomes the footstep of the saint,
So still, so moving, joy sprung of despair,
And the two feasts, where light and darkness meet.

The Heron

The cloud-backed heron will not move:
He stares into the stream.
He stands unfaltering while the gulls
And oyster-catchers scream.
He does not hear, he cannot see
The great white horses of the sea,
But fixes eyes on stillness
Below their flying team.

How long will he remain, how long
Have the grey woods been green?
The sky and the reflected sky,
Their glass he has not seen,
But silent as a speck of sand
Interpreting the sea and land,
His fall pulls down the fabric
Of all that windy scene.

Sailing with clouds and woods behind,
Pausing in leisured flight,
He stepped, alighting on a stone,
Dropped from the stars of night.
He stood there unconcerned with day,
Deaf to the tumult of the bay,
Watching a stone in water,
A fish's hidden light.

Sharp rocks drive back the breaking waves,
Confusing sea with air.
Bundles of spray blown mountain-high
Have left the shingle bare.
A shipwrecked anchor wedged by rocks,
Loosed by the thundering equinox,
Divides the herded waters,
The stallion and his mare.

Yet no distraction breaks the watch
Of that time-killing bird.
He stands unmoving on the stone;
Since dawn he has not stirred.
Calamity about him cries,
But he has fixed his golden eyes
On water's crooked tablet,
On light's reflected word.

The Replica

Once more the perfect pattern falls asleep,
And in the dark of sleep the replica
Springs to awareness. Light is born of dark
As the young foal beside his mother steps,
Closer than her own shadow. All runs down
To agile youth, born of laborious age.
She feels his presence in the pulse of earth,
Entranced above her pasture, how his eyes
From that new darkness at the end of time
In wonder stare, astonished by her world.
Each pristine, airy venture is prescribed
By weight of the maternal shade he left,
The circle ending where his race began.

The waterfall by falling is renewed
And still is falling. All its countless changes
Accumulate to nothing but itself.
The voice of many mountains or of one,
The dissipation of unnumbered drops
Vanishing in a dark that finds itself
In a perpetual music, and gives light
In fading always from the measuring mind:

VERNON WATKINS

Such is the waterfall; and though we watch it
Falling from rock to rock and always changing,
Cast to a whirlpool, pent by rock, pursuing
A reckless path, headlong in radiant mist
Leaping within the roar of its own chains,
We know it lives by being consumed, we know
Its voice is new and ancient, and its force
Flies from a single impulse that believes
Nothing is vain, though all is cast for sorrow.
There hangs the image of our life, there flies
The image of our transience. If you ask
Where may divinity or love find rest
When all moves forward to a new beginning
And each obeys one constant law of change,
I cannot answer.
                    Yet to man alone,
Moving in time, birth gives a timeless movement,
To taste the secret of the honeycomb
And pluck from night that blessing which outweighs
All the calamities and griefs of time.
There shines the one scene worthy of his tears,
For in that dark the greatest light was born
Which, if man sees, then time is overthrown,
And afterwards all acts are qualified
By knowledge of that interval of glory:
Music from heaven, the incomparable gift
Of God to man, in every infant's eyes
That vision which is ichor to the soul
Transmitted there by lightning majesty,
The replica, reborn, of Christian love.

Taliesin and the Mockers

Before men walked
I was in these places.
I was here
When the mountains were laid.

I am as light
To eyes long blind,
I, the stone
Upon every grave.

I saw black night
Flung wide like a curtain.
I looked up
At the making of stars.

I stood erect
At the birth of rivers.
I observed
The designing of flowers.

Who has discerned
The voice of lightning,
Or traced the music
Behind the eyes?

My Lord prescribed
The paths of the planets.
His fingers scattered
The distant stars.

He shaped the grave shore's
Ringing stones
And gave to the rocks
An echoing core.

He bound great mountains
With snow and ice
And bathed in glory
The lesser hills.

He made the sun
Of sulphurous fire.
From secret darkness
He called the moon.

Under her voice
And moving light
He chained the tides
Of the great seas rolling.

Still upon Earth
Was no live creature.
Barren still
Was the womb of the sea.

Mute the features
Slept in the rock,
Limbs and the soul
Inert, unbeckoned.

Marrowed with air
He made the birds.
Fish He sowed
In the restless wave.

Antelope, horse
And bull He made.
From caves of ice
He released the stormwinds.

He numbered the meadow's
Drops of rain
Caught in the cloud
And the teeming rose-bush.

Lions He made
Like fallen suns,
Fiery sand
And the beasts of burden.

He gave to the trees
Mysterious fruits
And twined in the husk
Miraculous corn.

Where lizards breathed
On the pathless desert
He gave each atom
A hidden sun.

Last, all labour
He bent on dust.
Out of the red dust
Made He Man.

Ancient music
Of silence born:
All things born
At the touch of God.

He built for him
His eternal garden,
Timeless, moving,
And yet in time.

He cast on him
Dark veils of sleep.
Out of his side
He took the Female.

Ask my age:
You shall have no answer.
I saw the building
Of Babel's Tower.

I was a lamp
In Solomon's temple;
I, the reed
Of an auguring wind.

What do you seek
In the salmon river,
Caught in the net
What living gold?

What do you seek
In the weir, O Elphin?
You must know
That the sun is mine.

I have a gift
For I have nothing.
I have love
Which excels all treasures.

Certain there were
Who touched, who knew Him.
Blind men knew
On the road their God.

Mock me they will
Those hired musicians,
They at Court
Who command the schools.

Mock though they do,
My music stands
Before and after
Accusing silence.

LYNETTE ROBERTS

(*b.* 1909)

Poem From Llanybri

If you come my way that is...
Between now and then, I will offer you
A fist full of rock cress fresh from the bank
The valley tips of garlic red with dew
Cooler than shallots, a breath you can swank

In the village when you come. At noon-day
I will offer you a choice bowl of cawl
Served with a 'lover's' spoon and a chopped spray
Of leeks or savori fach, not used now,

In the old way you'll understand. The din
Of children singing through the eyelet sheds
Ringing 'smith hoops, chasing the butt of hens;
Or I can offer you Cwmcelyn spread

With quartz stones from the wild scratchings of men:
You will have to go carefully with clogs
Or thick shoes for it's treacherous the fen,
The East and West Marshes also have bogs.

Then I'll do the lights, fill the lamp with oil,
Get coal from the shed, water from the well;
Pluck and draw pigeon with crop of green foil
This your good supper from the lime-tree fell.

A sit by the hearth with blue flames rising,
No talk. Just a stare at 'Time' gathering
Healed thoughts, pool insight, like swan sailing
Peace and sound around the home, offering

You a night's rest and my day's energy.
You must come – start this pilgrimage
Can you come? – send an ode or elegy
In the old way and raise our heritage.

JEAN EARLE
(b. 1909)

A Saturday in the '20s

The child came to the dark library,
Afraid. Feeling the darkness of the men
Sitting so silently – not reading –
On the tilted chairs.

The steps to go in were loaded with darkness.
Men stood hinged on their heavy arms.
A smell of cloth-pudding boiling on a winter day –
The child knew this smell
Damp caps over embittered minds, they smell the same.
Men's gear stricken, like the ancient smoke
Above the table. No one was smoking,
Yet there it hung.

Then the lame man stumped with his keys,
Opening cases,
Muttering. What was a child doing here,
Among darkened men? Wanting locked books?
The child snatched and fled

While the books bloomed in a fire between the covers,
Waiting to burst for her – Saturday's great new rose.
The men lolled silent, holding their empty hands
On their dark knees. She was afraid.
Yet above fear, she wanted their books
That they did not read.

What the dark men wanted
She was too young and well cared for to understand.

Village

In this old village now, at night,
Towering above, the strange neons point their flares high,
Blanching the street: all shadows fled
Back, back, under these potent organs,
Into our doorways, making them dark hoods
From which emerge mauve faces of our dead.

When we lie down, the neons burn through the curtains
Into the rooms, scorching our oldfashioned sleep.
Great tankers fly
Corrosive liquids, the simple milk
Frightened in loud drums, enormous decks of sheep,
Hurtling down the Roman road.

We think we hear the sheep cry –
It is the memory of a sound, we have not really heard it
For some years, so hard and swift they roar now
To their morning deaths. And we seldom cross the road
Into their fields.

The sun rises. But the neons take over
Sunset. Woods, and the village tree,
Glare as in pantomimes. When the river breathes
Into our evenings its familiar mist
Scented with grass and sewin, all those homely vapours
Suddenly turn a sickening red.

Around this time, the mauve dead patiently peer and gossip
Under the hoods.

KEN ETHERIDGE
(1911 – 1981)

Annunciation

I have seen rare sunshine held in the first birch leaves
    And the wind rearing to smell the blood of the tree,
And He has marched athwart with trumpets in the air
    And cymbals of celandine beating about his feet.

In Summer He has thrust arched breast through dark branches,
    His lips livid as campion, His breath the honeysuckle,
His golden mane live sunshine, His limbs a lion's
    Languorous with overstrength, then taut for the mating.

At the burning of autumn I have seen Him
    Crushing the vine in a wood of cypresses
And flinging a torch of disaster in bracken and heather,
    Treading proudly the corn-crop, roaring with delight.

TOM EARLEY

In winter I have seen Him on the black cross of a tree
  With crows under his armpits and about his chest
Pecking with cruel beaks and eating frost.
  He suffered silently. The air mimicked his agony.

My brain replies: 'Poor fool, this is your image.
  Nature is a mirror wherein we see ourselves.
The lonely man finds mountains, the shy man valleys:
  The powerful man loves oaks, the weak man reeds.

'You make men out of trees, women from flowers,
  Boys and innocent girls out of simple grasses,
Like the Druid who made a damsel out of broom-blossom
  And flowers of the oak and meadow-sweet gathered in
    dew.

'Life is a lasting chaos, the world a wilderness
  Confounding little orders in devastation.'
Deny yourself then, or find Him in this black husk,
  For I can tell you, only if you know.

TOM EARLEY
(*b.* 1911)

Lark

Helicopter of the hill,
with your vertical take-
off and controlled poise
as you climb, you make
the mountain shrill
with your noise.

Coming in to land,
you drop suddenly
straight as a stone
to meet the ground
but not directly
to your home.

You leave the air
through cold couch-grass
and wind-blown heather
so none know whether
you merely pass
or live there.

If put to the test
when I was young,
I could find the nest
of any species among
the birds of Wales
except yours.

ELWYN DAVIES
(b. 1912)

Portrait of Auntie Blodwen

Women who were mothers told us about it,
chicks hatching in Auntie Blodwen's,
go and watch, Auntie will be pleased.

Once we heard, Poor Blodwen, he
gives her hell, heard and did not hear,
but the silence after the warning nod
told of the acid dropped by mischance
in ears too young for such chemistry.
Uncomprehending, we sensed only
an image endangered, that Blodwen was different.

Her house still stands, roofed and occupied
by others in its sovereign now, mocking
the pitiful remnants of vanished rooms
and gestures and moments waiting under
memory's curtains for their last appearances.
At her house where the lino, the brass and the furniture
but never the faces shone, where we dared
not go round the side but knocked on the door,
were the eggs on a tray in front of the fire.
On our knees we laughed at the small explosions,
the fierce unseen thrusting in shells,
the pauses for rest or thought of life
the size of an egg-cup fighting into the light.

Aunt Blodwen stands there, stands for as long
as my ever will last, never did, never will
sit in her house, her lost fingers
plucking the tablecloth, watching us
newly broken from darkness laugh
at the chicks, and her drowned smile floats
in the waters of her face, hurt by the light.

BRENDA CHAMBERLAIN
(1912 – 1971)

Islandman

Full of years and seasoned like a salt timber
The island fisherman has come to terms with death.
His crabbed fingers are coldly afire with phosphorus
From the night-sea he fishes for bright-armoured herring.

Lifting his lobster pots at sunrise,
He is not surprised when drowned sailors
Wearing ropes of pearl round green throats
Nod their heads at him from underwater forests.

His black-browed wife who sits at home
Before the red hearth, does not guess
That only a fishscale breastplate protects him
When he sets out across ranges of winter sea.

R. S. THOMAS
(*b.* 1913)

A Peasant

Iago Prytherch his name, though, be it allowed,
Just an ordinary man of the bald Welsh hills,
Who pens a few sheep in a gap of cloud.
Docking mangels, chipping the green skin
From the yellow bones with a half-witted grin
Of satisfaction, or churning the crude earth
To a stiff sea of clods that glint in the wind –
So are his days spent, his spittled mirth
Rarer than the sun that cracks the cheeks
Of the gaunt sky perhaps once in a week.
And then at night see him fixed in his chair
Motionless, except when he leans to gob in the fire.

There is something frightening in the vacancy of his mind.
His clothes, sour with years of sweat
And animal contact, shock the refined,
But affected, sense with their stark naturalness.
Yet this is your prototype, who, season by season
Against siege of rain and the wind's attrition,
Preserves his stock, an impregnable fortress
Not to be stormed even in death's confusion.
Remember him, then, for he, too, is a winner of wars,
Enduring like a tree under the curious stars.

The Welsh Hill Country

Too far for you to see
The fluke and the foot-rot and the fat maggot
Gnawing the skin from the small bones,
The sheep are grazing at Bwlch-y-Fedwen,
Arranged romantically in the usual manner
On a bleak background of bald stone.

Too far for you to see
The moss and the mould on the cold chimneys,
The nettles growing through the cracked doors,
The houses stand empty at Nant-yr-Eira,
There are holes in the roofs that are thatched with sunlight,
And the fields are reverting to the bare moor.

Too far, too far to see
The set of his eyes and the slow pthisis
Wasting his frame under the ripped coat,
There's a man still farming at Ty'n-y-Fawnog,
Contributing grimly to the accepted pattern,
The embryo music dead in his throat.

Cynddylan on a Tractor

Ah, you should see Cynddylan on a tractor.
Gone the old look that yoked him to the soil;
He's a new man now, part of the machine,
His nerves of metal and his blood oil.
The clutch curses, but the gears obey
His least bidding, and lo, he's away
Out of the farmyard, scattering hens.

R. S. THOMAS

Riding to work now as a great man should,
He is the knight at arms breaking the fields'
Mirror of silence, emptying the wood
Of foxes and squirrels and bright jays.
The sun comes over the tall trees
Kindling all the hedges, but not for him
Who runs his engine on a different fuel.
And all the birds are singing, bills wide in vain,
As Cynddylan passes proudly up the lane.

Welsh History

We were a people taut for war; the hills
Were no harder, the thin grass
Clothed them more warmly than the coarse
Shirts our small bones.
We fought, and were always in retreat,
Like snow thawing upon the slopes
Of Mynydd Mawr; and yet the stranger
Never found our ultimate stand
In the thick woods, declaiming verse
To the sharp prompting of the harp.

Our kings died, or they were slain
By the old treachery at the ford.
Our bards perished, driven from the halls
Of nobles by the thorn and bramble.

We were a people bred on legends,
Warming our hands at the red past.
The great were ashamed of our loose rags
Clinging stubbornly to the proud tree
Of blood and birth, our lean bellies
And mud houses were a proof
Of our ineptitude for life.

We were a people wasting ourselves
In fruitless battles for our masters,
In lands to which we had no claim,
With men for whom we felt no hatred.

We were a people, and are so yet.
When we have finished quarrelling for crumbs
Under the table, or gnawing the bones
Of a dead culture, we will arise,
Armed, but not in the old way.

Expatriates

Not British; certainly
Not English. Welsh
With all the associations,
Black hair and black heart
Under a smooth skin,
Sallow as vellum; sharp
Of bone and wit that is turned
As a knife against us.
Four centuries now
We have been leaving
The hills and the high moors
For the jewelled pavements
Easing our veins of their dark peat
By slow transfusions.
In the drab streets
That never knew
The cold stream's sibilants
Our tongues are coated with
A dustier speech.
With the year's passing
We have forgotten
The far lakes,
Aled and Eiddwen, whose blue litmus
Alone could detect
The mind's acid.

A Line From St. David's

I am sending you this letter,
Something for neo-Edwardians
Of a test-tube age to grow glum about
In their conditioned libraries.
As I came here by way of Plwmp,
There were hawkweeds in the hedges;
Nature had invested all her gold
In the industry of the soil.
There were larks, too, like a fresh chorus
Of dew, and I thought, remembering Dewi
The water-drinker, the way back
Is not so far as the way forward.
Here the cathedral's bubble of stone
Is still unpricked by the mind's needle,

And the wall lettuce in the crevices
Is as green now as when Giraldus
Altered the colour of his thought
By drinking from the Welsh fountain...

I ramble; what I wanted to say
Was that the day has a blue lining
Partly of sky, partly of sea;
That the old currents are in the grass,
Though rust has becalmed the plough.
Somewhere a man sharpens a scythe;
A child watches him from the brink
Of his own speech, and this is of more
Importance than all the visitors keeping
A spry saint asleep in his tomb.

Sir Gelli Meurig
(Elizabethan)

I imagine it, a land
Rain-soaked, far away
In the west, in time;
The sea folded too rough
On the shingle, with hard
Breakers and steep
To climb; but game-ridden
And lining his small table
Too thickly – Gelli Meurig,
Squire of a few
Acres, but swollen-headed
With dreaming of a return
To incense, to the confections
Of worship; a Welsh fly
Caught in a web spun
For a hornet.
    Don't blame him.
Others have turned their backs,
As he did, and do so still,
On our land. Leaves light
The autumn, but not for them.
Emptily the sea's cradle
Rocks. They want the town
And its baubles; the fine clothes

They dress one in, who manage
The strings. Helplessly they dance
To a mad tune, who at home
In the bracken could have remained
Humble but free.

A Welshman at St. James' Park

I am invited to enter these gardens
As one of the public, and to conduct myself
In accordance with the regulations;
To keep off the grass and sample flowers
Without touching them; to admire birds
That have been seduced from wildness by
Bread they are pelted with.
                                        I am not one
Of the public; I have come a long way
To realise it. Under the sun's
Feathers are the sinews of stone,
The curved claws.
                                        I think of a Welsh hill
That is without fencing, and the men,
Bosworth blind, who left the heather
And the high pastures of the heart. I fumble
In the pocket's emptiness; my ticket
Was in two pieces. I kept half.

Llanrhaeadr Ym Mochnant

This is where he sought God.
And found him? The centuries
Have been content to follow
Down passages of serene prose.

There is no portrait of him
But in the gallery of
The imagination: a brow
With the hair's feathers
Spilled on it? a cheek
Too hollow? rows of teeth
Broken on the unmanageable bone

Of language? In this small room
By the river expiating the sin
Of his namesake?
                        The smooth words
Over which his mind flowed
Have become an heirloom. Beauty
Is how you say it, and the truth,
Like this mountain-born torrent,
Is content to hurry
Not too furiously by.

Reservoirs

There are places in Wales I don't go:
Reservoirs that are the subconscious
Of a people, troubled far down
With gravestones, chapels, villages even;
The serenity of their expression
Revolts me, it is a pose
For strangers, a watercolour's appeal
To the mass, instead of the poem's
Harsher conditions. There are the hills,
Too; gardens gone under the scum
Of the forests; and the smashed faces
Of the farms with the stone trickle
Of their tears down the hills' side.

Where can I go, then, from the smell
Of decay, from the putrefying of a dead
Nation? I have walked the shore
For an hour and seen the English
Scavenging among the remains
Of our culture, covering the sand
Like the tide and, with the roughness
Of the tide, elbowing our language
Into the grave that we have dug for it.

Other

It was perfect. He could do
Nothing about it. Its waters
Were as clear as his own eye. The grass
Was his breath. The mystery

Of the dark earth was what went on
In himself. He loved and
Hated it with a parent's
Conceit, admiring his own
Work, resenting its
Independence. There were trysts
In the greenwood at which
He was not welcome. Youths and girls,
Fondling the pages of
A strange book, awakened
His envy. The mind achieved
What the heart could not. He began planning
The destruction of the long peace
Of the place. The machine appeared
In the distance, singing to itself
Of money. Its song was the web
They were caught in, men and women
Together. The villages were as flies
To be sucked empty.
              God secreted
A tear. Enough, enough,
He commanded, but the machine
Looked at him and went on singing.

The Bright Field

I have seen the sun break through
to illuminate a small field
for a while, and gone my way
and forgotten it. But that was the pearl
of great price, the one field that had
the treasure in it. I realize now
that I must give all that I have
to possess it. Life is not hurrying

on to a receding future, nor hankering after
an imagined past. It is the turning
aside like Moses to the miracle
of the lit bush, to a brightness
that seemed as transitory as your youth
once, but is the eternity that awaits you.

The Empty Church

They laid this stone trap
for him, enticing him with candles,
as though he would come like some huge moth
out of the darkness to beat there.
Ah, he had burned himself
before in the human flame
and escaped, leaving the reason
torn. He will not come any more

to our lure. Why, then, do I kneel still
striking my prayers on a stone
heart? Is it in hope one
of them will ignite yet and throw
on its illumined walls the shadow
of someone greater than I can understand?

The White Tiger

It was beautiful as God
must be beautiful; glacial
eyes that had looked on
violence and come to terms

with it; a body too huge
and majestic for the cage in which
it had been put; up
and down in the shadow

of its own bulk it went,
lifting, as it turned,
the crumpled flower of its face
to look into my own

face without seeing me. It
was the colour of the moonlight
on snow and as quiet
as moonlight, but breathing

as you can imagine that
God breathes within the confines
of our definition of him, agonising
over immensities that will not return.

DYLAN THOMAS
(1914 – 1953)

Especially when the October wind

Especially when the October wind
With frosty fingers punishes my hair,
Caught by the crabbing sun I walk on fire
And cast a shadow crab upon the land,
By the sea's side, hearing the noise of birds,
Hearing the raven cough in winter sticks,
My busy heart who shudders as she talks
Sheds the syllabic blood and drains her words.

Shut, too, in a tower of words, I mark
On the horizon walking like the trees
The wordy shapes of women, and the rows
Of the star-gestured children in the park.
Some let me make you of the vowelled beeches,
Some of the oaken voices, from the roots
Of many a thorny shire tell you notes,
Some let me make you of the water's speeches.

Behind a pot of ferns the wagging clock
Tells me the hour's word, the neural meaning
Flies on the shafted disk, declaims the morning
And tells the windy weather in the cock.
Some let me make you of the meadow's signs;
The signal grass that tells me all I know
Breaks with the wormy winter through the eye.
Some let me tell you of the raven's sins.

Especially when the October wind
(Some let me make you of autumnal spells,
The spider-tongued, and the loud hill of Wales)
With fists of turnips punishes the land,
Some let me make you of the heartless words.
The heart is drained that, spelling in the scurry
Of chemic blood, warned of the coming fury.
By the sea's side hear the dark-vowelled birds.

DYLAN THOMAS

After the Funeral
(In memory of Ann Jones)

After the funeral, mule praises, brays,
Windshake of sailshaped ears, muffle-toed tap
Tap happily of one peg in the thick
Grave's foot, blinds down the lids, the teeth in black,
The spittled eyes, the salt ponds in the sleeves,
Morning smack of the spade that wakes up sleep,
Shakes a desolate boy who slits his throat
In the dark of the coffin and sheds dry leaves,
That breaks one bone to light with a judgment clout,
After the feast of tear-stuffed time and thistles
In a room with a stuffed fox and a stale fern,
I stand, for this memorial's sake, alone
In the snivelling hours with dead, humped Ann
Whose hooded, fountain heart once fell in puddles
Round the parched worlds of Wales and drowned each sun
(Though this for her is a monstrous image blindly
Magnified out of praise; her death was a still drop;
She would not have me sinking in the holy
Flood of her heart's fame; she would lie dumb and deep
And need no druid of her broken body).
But I, Ann's bard on a raised hearth, call all
The seas to service that her wood-tongued virtue
Babble like a bellbuoy over the hymning heads,
Bow down the walls of the ferned and foxy woods
That her love sing and swing through a brown chapel,
Bless her bent spirit with four, crossing birds.
Her flesh was meek as milk, but this skyward statue
With the wild breast and blessed and giant skull
Is carved from her in a room with a wet window
In a fiercely mourning house in a crooked year.
I know her scrubbed and sour humble hands
Lie with religion in their cramp, her threadbare
Whisper in a damp word, her wits drilled hollow,
Her fist of a face died clenched on a round pain; .
And sculptured Ann is seventy years of stone.
These cloud-sopped, marble hands, this monumental
Argument of the hewn voice, gesture and psalm,
Storm me forever over her grave until
The stuffed lung of the fox twitch and cry Love
And the strutting fern lay seeds on the black sill.

– 187 –

Poem in October

It was my thirtieth year to heaven
Woke to my hearing from harbour and neighbour wood
    And the mussel pooled and the heron
        Priested shore
      The morning beckon
With water praying and call of seagull and rook
And the knock of sailing boats on the net webbed wall
        Myself to set foot
        That second
    In the still sleeping town and set forth.

    My birthday began with the water-
Birds and the birds of the winged trees flying my name
    Above the farms and the white horses
        And I rose
      In rainy autumn
And walked abroad in a shower of all my days.
High tide and the heron dived when I took the road
        Over the border
        And the gates
    Of the town closed as the town awoke.

    A springful of larks in a rolling
Cloud and the roadside bushes brimming with whistling
    Blackbirds and the sun of October
        Summery
      On the hill's shoulder,
Here were fond climates and sweet singers suddenly
Come in the morning where I wandered and listened
        To the rain wringing
        Wind blow cold
    In the wood faraway under me.

    Pale rain over the dwindling harbour
And over the sea wet church the size of a snail
    With its horns through mist and the castle
        Brown as owls
      But all the gardens
Of spring and summer were blooming in the tall tales
Beyond the border and under the lark full cloud.
        There could I marvel
        My birthday
    Away but the weather turned around.

It turned away from the blithe country
And down the other air and the blue altered sky
Streamed again a wonder of summer
With apples
Pears and red currants
And I saw in the turning so clearly a child's
Forgotten mornings when he walked with his mother
Through the parables
Of sun light
And the legends of the green chapels

And the twice told fields of infancy
That his tears burned my cheeks and his heart moved in mine.
These were the woods the river and sea
Where a boy
In the listening
Summertime of the dead whispered the truth of his joy
To the trees and the stones and the fish in the tide.
And the mystery
Sang alive
Still in the water and singingbirds.

And there could I marvel my birthday
Away but the weather turned around. And the true
Joy of the long dead child sang burning
In the sun.
It was my thirtieth
Year to heaven stood there then in the summer noon
Though the town below lay leaved with October blood.
O may my heart's truth
Still be sung
On this high hill in a year's turning.

The Hunchback in the Park

The hunchback in the park
A solitary mister
Propped between trees and water
From the opening of the garden lock
That lets the trees and water enter
Until the Sunday sombre bell at dark

Eating bread from a newspaper
Drinking water from the chained cup
That the children filled with gravel
In the fountain basin where I sailed my ship
Slept at night in a dog kennel
But nobody chained him up.

Like the park birds he came early
Like the water he sat down
And Mister they called Hey mister
The truant boys from the town
Running when he had heard them clearly
On out of sound

Past lake and rockery
Laughing when he shook his paper
Hunchbacked in mockery
Through the loud zoo of the willow groves
Dodging the park keeper
With his stick that picked up leaves.

And the old dog sleeper
Alone between nurses and swans
While the boys among willows
Made the tigers jump out of their eyes
To roar on the rockery stones
And the groves were blue with sailors

Made all day until bell time
A woman figure without fault
Straight as a young elm
Straight and tall from his crooked bones
That she might stand in the night
After the locks and chains

All night in the unmade park
After the railings and shrubberies
The birds the grass the trees the lake
And the wild boys innocent as strawberries
Had followed the hunchback
To his kennel in the dark.

DYLAN THOMAS

In my Craft or Sullen Art

In my craft or sullen art
Exercised in the still night
When only the moon rages
And the lovers lie abed
With all their griefs in their arms,
I labour by singing light
Not for ambition or bread
Or the strut and trade of charms
On the ivory stages
But for the common wages
Of their most secret heart.

Not for the proud man apart
From the raging moon I write
On these spindrift pages
Nor for the towering dead
With their nightingales and psalms
But for the lovers, their arms
Round the griefs of the ages,
Who pay no praise or wages
Nor heed my craft or art.

Fern Hill

Now as I was young and easy under the apple boughs
About the lilting house and happy as the grass was green,
        The night above the dingle starry,
            Time let me hail and climb
        Golden in the heydays of his eyes,
And honoured among wagons I was prince of the apple towns
And once below a time I lordly had the trees and leaves
            Trail with daisies and barley
        Down the rivers of the windfall light.

And as I was green and carefree, famous among the barns
About the happy yard and singing as the farm was home,
        In the sun that is young once only,
            Time let me play and be
        Golden in the mercy of his means,
And green and golden I was huntsman and herdsman, the calves
Sang to my horn, the foxes on the hills barked clear and cold,
            And the sabbath rang slowly
        In the pebbles of the holy streams.

All the sun long it was running, it was lovely, the hay
Fields high as the house, the tunes from the chimneys, it was air
    And playing, lovely and watery
        And fire green as grass.
    And nightly under the simple stars
As I rode to sleep the owls were bearing the farm away,
All the moon long I heard, blessed among stables, the nightjars
    Flying with the ricks, and the horses
        Flashing into the dark.

And then to awake, and the farm, like a wanderer white
With the dew, come back, the cock on his shoulder: it was all
    Shining, it was Adam and maiden,
        The sky gathered again
    And the sun grew round that very day.
So it must have been after the birth of the simple light
In the first, spinning place, the spellbound horses walking warm
    Out of the whinnying green stable
        On to the fields of praise.

And honoured among foxes and pheasants by the gay house
Under the new made clouds and happy as the heart was long,
    In the sun born over and over,
        I ran my heedless ways,
    My wishes raced through the house high hay
And nothing I cared, at my sky blue trades, that time allows
In all his tuneful turning so few and such morning songs
    Before the children green and golden
        Follow him out of grace,

Nothing I cared, in the lamb white days, that time would take me
Up to the swallow thronged loft by the shadow of my hand,
    In the moon that is always rising,
        Nor that riding to sleep
    I should hear him fly with the high fields
And wake to the farm forever fled from the childless land.
Oh as I was young and easy in the mercy of his means,
        Time held me green and dying
    Though I sang in my chains like the sea.

Over Sir John's hill

    Over Sir John's hill,
    The hawk on fire hangs still;
    In a hoisted cloud, at drop of dusk, he pulls to his claws
    And gallows, up the rays of his eyes the small birds of the bay

And the shrill child's play
Wars
Of the sparrows and such who swansing, dusk, in wrangling
    hedges.
And blithely they squawk
To fiery tyburn over the wrestle of elms until
The flashed the noosed hawk
Crashes, and slowly the fishing holy stalking heron
In the river Towy below bows his tilted headstone.

Flash, and the plumes crack,
And a black cap of jack-
Daws Sir John's just hill dons, and again the gulled birds hare
To the hawk on fire, the halter height, over Towy's fins,
In a whack of wind.
There
Where the elegiac fisherbird stabs and paddles
In the pebbly dab-filled
Shallow and sedge, and 'dilly dilly,' calls the loft hawk,
'Come and be killed,'
I open the leaves of the water at a passage
Of psalms and shadows among the pincered sandcrabs prancing

And read, in a shell,
Death clear as a buoy's bell:
All praise of the hawk on fire in hawk-eyed dusk be sung,
When his viperish fuse hangs looped with flames under the brand
Wing, and blest shall
Young
Green chickens of the bay and bushes cluck, 'dilly dilly,
Come let us die.'
We grieve as the blithe birds, never again, leave shingle and elm,
The heron and I,
I young Aesop fabling to the near night by the dingle
Of eels, saint heron hymning in the shell-hung distant

Crystal harbour vale
Where the sea cobbles sail,
And wharves of water where the walls dance and the white
    cranes stilt.
It is the heron and I, under judging Sir John's elmed
Hill, tell-tale the knelled

Guilt
Of the led-astray birds whom God, for their breast of whistles,
Have mercy on,
God in his whirlwind silence save, who marks the sparrows hail,
For their souls' song.
Now the heron grieves in the weeded verge. Through windows
Of dusk and water I see the tilting whispering

Heron, mirrored, go,
As the snapt feathers snow,
Fishing in the tear of the Towy. Only a hoot owl
Hollows, a grassblade blown in cupped hands, in the looted elms
And no green cocks or hens
Shout
Now on Sir John's hill. The heron, ankling the scaly
Lowlands of the waves,
Makes all the music; and I who hear the tune of the slow,
Wear-willow river, grave,
Before the lunge of the night, the notes on this time-shaken
Stone for the sake of the souls of the slain birds sailing.

Prologue to The Collected Poems

This day winding down now
At God speeded summer's end
In the torrent salmon sun,
In my seashaken house
On a breakneck of rocks
Tangled with chirrup and fruit,
Froth, flute, fin and quill
At a wood's dancing hoof,
By scummed, starfish sands
With their fishwife cross
Gulls, pipers, cockles, and sails,
Out there, crow black, men
Tackled with clouds, who kneel
To the sunset nets,
Geese nearly in heaven, boys
Stabbing, and herons, and shells
That speak seven seas,
Eternal waters away
From the cities of nine
Day's night whose towers will catch

In the religious wind
Like stalks of tall, dry straw,
At poor peace I sing
To you strangers (though song
Is a burning and crested act,
The fire of birds in
The world's turning wood,
For my sawn, splay sounds),
Out of these seathumbed leaves
That will fly and fall
Like leaves of trees and as soon
Crumble and undie
Into the dogdayed night.
Seaward the salmon, sucked sun slips,
And the dumb swans drub blue
My dabbed bay's dusk, as I hack
This rumpus of shapes
For you to know
How I, a spinning man,
Glory also this star, bird
Roared, sea born, man torn, blood blest.
Hark: I trumpet the place,
From fish to jumping hill! Look:
I build my bellowing ark
To the best of my love
As the flood begins,
Out of the fountainhead
Of fear, rage red, manalive,
Molten and mountainous to stream
Over the wound asleep
Sheep white hollow farms

To Wales in my arms.
Hoo, there, in castle keep,
You king singsong owls, who moonbeam
The flickering runs and dive
The dingle furred deer dead!
Huloo, on plumbed bryns,
O my ruffled ring dove
In the hooting, nearly dark
With Welsh and reverent rook,
Coo rooing the woods' praise,

Who moons her blue notes from her nest
Down to the curlew herd!
Ho, hullaballoing clan
Agape, with woe
In your beaks, on the gabbing capes!
Heigh, on horseback hill, jack
Whisking hare! who
Hears, there, this fox light, my flood ship's
Clangour as I hew and smite
(A clash of anvils for my
Hubbub and fiddle, this tune
On a tongued puffball)
But animals thick as thieves
On God's rough tumbling grounds
(Hail to His beasthood).
Beasts who sleep good and thin,
Hist, in hogsback woods! The haystacked
Hollow farms in a throng
Of waters cluck and cling,
And barnroofs cockcrow war!
O kingdom of neighbours, finned
Felled and quilled, flash to my patch
Work ark and the moonshine
Drinking Noah of the bay,
With pelt, and scale, and fleece:
Only the drowned deep bells
Of sheep and churches noise
Poor peace as the sun sets
And dark shoals every holy field.
We will ride out alone, and then,
Under the stars of Wales,
Cry, Multitudes of arks! Across
The water lidded lands,
Manned with their loves they'll move,
Like wooden islands, hill to hill.
Huloo, my prowed dove with a flute!
Ahoy, old, sea-legged fox,
Tom tit and Dai mouse!
My ark sings in the sun
At God speeded summer's end
And the flood flowers now.

CLIFFORD DYMENT
(1914 – 1970)

'Derbyshire Born, Monmouth is My Home'

Derbyshire born, Monmouth is my home,
Monmouth I call Wales, for the voices there
Speak in the songs of Welshmen, and the names
Used every day there – Llantarnum, Pontypool,
Tyn Barlwyn, Ebbw Vale –
Are letters from Wales wherever I see them in print.
Caerleon, my youthful home, was a green hill,
A Buddha's belly smiling in a flat field,
Its rondure assimilating for a future age
The marvels of Rome – villas, baths, a bracelet;
And the bridge, too, grey over the yellow Usk,
A thick wide river reminding me of Tiber
In later memory, Tiber unseen,
For Caerleon is all romance and Rome to me –
Brachets and palfreys, the tourney, the hart in the woods,
Imperial roads, the caves of Mithra, fortresses,
And the salt of the ships at Newport and Barry.

Derbyshire born, Monmouth is my home,
Monmouth I call Wales despite cartographers,
My home for a few young years and now,
In spite of Leicestershire that schooled and fought me
And fights me still insisting in my blood.
Yes, Leicester got into my blood and made my bone –
Leicestershire loved me, its stubborn son
Who hated the no man's land, the elbower-out
Of northern and southern culture, possessing none,
I declared in my youthful arrogance:
I saw the cinder paths of mining villages –
Ibstock, Moira, Ellistown –
The chip shop and the corner shop that sold
Racing tips and shameful novelettes;
I saw the dirty pub that loved the colliery
Like its fat and dirtier purse;
And I saw the migrations of miners moving
Across the coalfields from shift to shift
In the red Midland buses they called Red Emmas,
Men's faces black, with rubber-dinghy lips
And floating eyes like nightmare Christy minstrels –
And as I saw I shuddered and cycled on,
Homeless and sick in the towns my home;

Cycled to Charnwood for its hobo roads,
Pre-Cambrian rocks and lonely lapwings,
Rock rose and oak and prairies of fern –
Cycled in solitude to meet a monk
Who stared from a long way off and did not speak.
Charnwood to me was a shape of fear:
Square Teutons of granite, blue jowls
Of bullying slate: I shuddered and ran
To the railway wagons with their owners' names
Painted along their sides like Yankee athletes',
And I was homeless again in Leicestershire.

But Leicester is in my eyes and mind: the Trappist
Tall in the mist, the crags like fangs,
The ruined abbeys, the smell of coal
Have mined in me like secret workings. Monmouth
I choose, but Leicestershire has chosen,
And lucky I am, reluctant, having a home
Today when the world is homeless.

ALUN LEWIS
(1915 – 1944)

Raiders' Dawn

Softly the civilized
Centuries fall,
Paper on paper,
Peter on Paul.

And lovers waking
From the night –
Eternity's masters,
Slaves of Time –
Recognize only
The drifting white
Fall of small faces
In pits of lime.

Blue necklace left
On a charred chair
Tells that Beauty
Was startled there.

All Day it has Rained...

All day it has rained, and we on the edge of the moors
Have sprawled in our bell-tents, moody and dull as boors,
Groundsheets and blankets spread on the muddy ground
And from the first grey wakening we have found
No refuge from the skirmishing fine rain
And the wind that made the canvas heave and flap
And the taut wet guy-ropes ravel out and snap.
All day the rain has glided, wave and mist and dream,
Drenching the gorse and heather, a gossamer stream
Too light to stir the acorns that suddenly
Snatched from their cups by the wild south-westerly
Pattered against the tent and our upturned dreaming faces.
And we stretched out, unbuttoning our braces,
Smoking a Woodbine, darning dirty socks,
Reading the Sunday papers – I saw a fox
And mentioned it in the note I scribbled home; –
And we talked of girls, and dropping bombs on Rome,
And thought of the quiet dead and the loud celebrities
Exhorting us to slaughter, and the herded refugees;
 – Yet thought softly, morosely of them, and as indifferently
As of ourselves or those whom we
For years have loved, and will again
Tomorrow maybe love; but now it is the rain
Possesses us entirely, the twilight and the rain.

And I can remember nothing dearer or more to my heart
Than the children I watched in the woods on Saturday
Shaking down burning chestnuts for the schoolyard's merry play,
Or the shaggy patient dog who followed me
By Sheet and Steep and up the wooded scree
To the Shoulder O' Mutton where Edward Thomas brooded
    long
On death and beauty – till a bullet stopped his song.

Post-script: for Gweno

If I should go away,
Beloved, do not say
'He has forgotten me'.
For you abide,
A singing rib within my dreaming side;
You always stay.

And in the mad tormented valley
Where blood and hunger rally
And Death the wild beast is uncaught, untamed,
Our soul withstands the terror
And has its quiet honour
Among the glittering stars your voices named.

The Sentry

I have begun to die.
For now at last I know
That there is no escape
From Night. Not any dream
Nor breathless images of sleep
Touch my bat's-eyes. I hang
Leathery-arid from the hidden roof
Of Night, and sleeplessly
I watch within Sleep's province.

I have left
The lovely bodies of the boy and girl
Deep in each other's placid arms;
And I have left
The beautiful lanes of sleep
That barefoot lovers follow to this last
Cold shore of thought I guard.
I have begun to die
And the guns' implacable silence
Is my black interim, my youth and age,
In the flower of fury, the folded poppy,
Night.

The Mountain over Aberdare

From this high quarried ledge I see
The place for which the Quakers once
Collected clothes, my father's home,
Our stubborn bankrupt village sprawled
In jaded dusk beneath its nameless hills;
The drab streets strung across the cwm,
Derelict workings, tips of slag
The gospellers and gamblers use
And children scrutting for the coal
That winter dole cannot purvey;

Allotments where the collier digs
While engines hack the coal within his brain;
Grey Hebron in a rigid cramp,
White cheap-jack cinema, the church
Stretched like a sow beside the stream;
And mourners in their Sunday best
Holding a tiny funeral, singing hymns
That drift insidious as the rain
Which rises from the steaming fields
And swathes about the skyline crags
Till all the upland gorse is drenched
And all the creaking mountain gates
Drip brittle tears of crystal peace;
And in a curtained parlour women hug
Huge grief, and anger against God.

But now the dusk, more charitable than Quakers,
Veils the cracked cottages with drifting may
And rubs the hard day off the slate.
The colliers squatting on the ashtip
Listen to one who holds them still with tales,
While that white frock that floats down the dark alley
Looks just like Christ; and in the lane
The clink of coins among the gamblers
Suggests the thirty pieces of silver.

I watch the clouded years
Rune the rough foreheads of these moody hills,
This wet evening, in a lost age.

Goodbye

So we must say Goodbye, my darling,
And go, as lovers go, for ever;
Tonight remains, to pack and fix on labels
And make an end of lying down together.

I put a final shilling in the gas,
And watch you slip your dress below your knees
And lie so still I hear your rustling comb
Modulate the autumn in the trees.

And all the countless things I shall remember
Lay mummy-cloths of silence round my head;
I fill the carafe with a drink of water;
You say 'We paid a guinea for this bed,'

And then, 'We'll leave some gas, a little warmth
For the next resident, and these dry flowers,'
And turn your face away, afraid to speak
The big word, that Eternity is ours.

Your kisses close my eyes and yet you stare
As though God struck a child with nameless fears;
Perhaps the water glitters and discloses
Time's chalice and its limpid useless tears.

Everything we renounce except our selves;
Selfishness is the last of all to go;
Our sighs are exhalations of the earth,
Our footprints leave a track across the snow.

We made the universe to be our home,
Our nostrils took the wind to be our breath,
Our hearts are massive towers of delight,
We stride across the seven seas of death.

Yet when all's done you'll keep the emerald
I placed upon your finger in the street;
And I will keep the patches that you sewed
On my old battledress tonight, my sweet.

The Mahratta Ghats

The valleys crack and burn, the exhausted plains
Sink their black teeth into the horny veins
Straggling the hills' red thighs, the bleating goats
– Dry bents and bitter thistles in their throats –
Thread the loose rocks by immemorial tracks.
Dark peasants drag the sun upon their backs.

High on the ghat the new turned soil is red,
The sun has ground it to the finest red,
It lies like gold within each horny hand.
Siva has spilt his seed upon this land.

Will she who burns and withers on the plain
Leave, ere too late, her scraggy herds of pain,
The cow-dung fire and the trembling beasts,
The little wicked gods, the grinning priests,
And climb, before a thousand years have fled,
High as the eagle to her mountain bed
Whose soil is fine as flour and blood-red?

But no! She cannot move. Each arid patch
Owns the lean folk who plough and scythe and thatch
Its grudging yield and scratch its stubborn stones.
The small gods suck the marrow from their bones.

Who is it climbs the summit of the road?
Only the beggar bumming his dark load.
Who was it cried to see the falling star?
Only the landless soldier lost in war.

And did a thousand years go by in vain?
And does another thousand start again?

In Hospital: Poona (1)

Last night I did not fight for sleep
But lay awake from midnight while the world
Turned its slow features to the moving deep
Of darkness, till I knew that you were furled,

Beloved, in the same dark watch as I.
And sixty degrees of longitude beside
Vanished as though a swan in ecstasy
Had spanned the distance from your sleeping side.

And like to swan or moon the whole of Wales
Glided within the parish of my care:
I saw the green tide leap on Cardigan,
Your red yacht riding like a legend there,

And the great mountains, Dafydd and Llewelyn,
Plynlimmon, Cader Idris and Eryri
Threshing the darkness back from head and fin,
And also the small nameless mining valley

Whose slopes are scratched with streets and sprawling graves
Dark in the lap of firwoods and great boulders
Where you lay waiting, listening to the waves –
My hot hands touched your white despondent shoulders

 – And then ten thousand miles of daylight grew
Between us, and I heard the wild daws crake
In India's starving throat; whereat I knew
That Time upon the heart can break
But love survives the venom of the snake.

The Jungle

I

In mole-blue indolence the sun
Plays idly on the stagnant pool
In whose grey bed black swollen leaf
Holds Autumn rotting like an unfrocked priest.
The crocodile slides from the ochre sand
And drives the great translucent fish
Under the boughs across the running gravel.
Windfalls of brittle mast crunch as we come
To quench more than our thirst – our selves –
Beneath this bamboo bridge, this mantled pool
Where sleep exudes a sinister content
As though all strength of mind and limb must pass
And all fidelities and doubts dissolve,
The weighted world a bubble in each head,
The warm pacts of the flesh betrayed
By the nonchalance of a laugh,
The green indifference of this sleep.

II

Wandering and fortuitous the paths
We followed to this rendezvous today
Out of the mines and offices and dives,
The sidestreets of anxiety and want,
Huge cities known and distant as the stars,
Wheeling beyond our destiny and hope.
We did not notice how the accent changed
As shadows ride from precipice to plain
Closing the parks and cordoning the roads,
Clouding the humming cultures of the West –
The weekly bribe we paid the man in black,
The day shift sinking from the sun,
The blinding arc of rivets blown through steel,
The patient queues, headlines and slogans flung
Across a frightened continent, the town
Sullen and out of work, the little home
Semi-detached, suburban, transient
As fever or the anger of the old,
The best ones on some specious pretext gone.

But we who dream beside this jungle pool
Prefer the instinctive rightness of the poised
Pied kingfisher deep darting for a fish
To all the banal rectitude of states,
The dew-bright diamonds on a viper's back
To the slow poison of a meaning lost
And the vituperations of the just.

III

The banyan's branching clerestories close
The noon's harsh splendour to a head of light.
The black spot in the focus grows and grows:
The vagueness of the child, the lover's deep
And inarticulate bewilderment,
The willingness to please that made a wound,
The kneeling darkness and the hungry prayer;
Cargoes of anguish in the holds of joy,
The smooth deceitful stranger in the heart,
The tangled wrack of motives drifting down
An oceanic tide of Wrong.
And though the state has enemies we know
The greater enmity within ourselves.

Some things we cleaned like knives in earth,
Kept from the dew and rust of Time
Instinctive truths and elemental love,
Knowing the force that brings the teal and quail
From Turkestan across the Himalayan snows
To Kashmir and the South alone can guide
That winging wildness home again.

Oh you who want us for ourselves,
Whose love can start the snow-rush in the woods
And melt the glacier in the dark coulisse,
Forgive this strange inconstancy of soul,
The face distorted in a jungle pool
That drowns its image in a mort of leaves.

IV

Grey monkeys gibber, ignorant and wise.
We are the ghosts, and they the denizens;
We are like them anonymous, unknown,
Avoiding what is human, near,

Skirting the villages, the paddy fields
Where boys sit timelessly to scare the crows
On bamboo platforms raised above their lives.

A trackless wilderness divides
Joy from its cause, the motive from the act:
The killing arm uncurls, strokes the soft moss;
The distant world is an obituary,
We do not hear the tappings of its dread.
The act sustains; there is no consequence.
Only aloneness, swinging slowly
Down the cold orbit of an older world
Than any they predicted in the schools,
Stirs the cold forest with a starry wind,
And sudden as the flashing of a sword
The dream exalts the bowed and golden head
And time is swept with a great turbulence,
The old temptation to remould the world.

The bamboos creak like an uneasy house;
The night is shrill with crickets, cold with space.
And if the mute pads on the sand should lift
Annihilating paws and strike us down
Then would some unimportant death resound
With the imprisoned music of the soul?
And we become the world we could not change?
Or does the will's long struggle end
With the last kindness of a foe or friend?

CYRIL HODGES
(1915-1974)

Naturalised

My father was a Cornish customs officer,
My mother a Scottish butcher's daughter.

He knew the art of rummage,
She the essential parts of animals.

I have inherited nothing of their arts.
I stroll down echoing corridors
From the proud aristrocracy of pure Welsh words,
Shoulder to shoulder with the arrogant bards,
Secured in my deed to Welshness.

Being born in a traditional mystery
Is the vital claim...there is no line of blood
Dictating name, clan, or tribal continuity.

These are my chosen ones, the nation
Of the heart. Port Isaac is a myth of Cornwall;
Fife the mere hint, the sentiment of Scotland.
Trelawney moves only an ache of memory:
My clan is stoneless at Culloden.

I was born in this climate, this air:
The very breath of Wales was my first breath,
The luminous earth of Wales my first hard challenge.

Hence I am Welsh from the lungs outward,
From hands and feet upward, aggressively Welsh
With great grievances and deprivations.
My tongue, naturally insolent and hard,
Avoiding Cornish slur and Scottish burr,
Is the one crooked satire of identity,
The personal name-gift to my foster-kin.

Voice was an inessential animal part:
My mother would not have known it.
There is no rummage to unearth illegal
Secretions of Welsh in unlikely shipboard places:
Of this my father could have known nothing.

For them I have no blame, only a chemical
Love, and hope their native wisdom can forgive
Bedding of family roots in new congenial soil.

All that come after me must be transformed
Into concordance with reality,
Hands levering the body into more intimate
Relationship with good Welsh mud, the levering mind
Revealing the treasure of strange inheritance,
All touched, all changed, muted into agreement
With my inspired and arbitrary choice.

Asked now of my ancestry, I claim Aneirin,
Wholesale Northumbrian-butcher, as my father:
Creirwy, the customary invocation
Of medieval loveliness, for my mother.

- 207 -

Half-history, half-legend, the whole tight-woven
Into acceptance, none can dispute my right
Within the nine essential parts of family
To be the equal of the arrogant bards,
Parodied out of sheer insolence of love.

KEIDRYCH RHYS
(*b.* 1915)

Interlude

Simply I would sing for the time being
Of the wayward hills I must make my feeling
The rickety bicycle, the language of birds
Caught fishing up the church street for preaching words,
The deacon hawking swedes, the gyppos clapping on
Their way to vans over common's crushed sandstone
And the milk stands so handy to sit upon!
The roadmen laying pipes of local cement
The Italian's chip shop and the village comment
'No reserve; all they know on the tip of their tongue.'
That educated tramp from the lodging-house league.

The lady, the lake, both sleeping, the cattle
Called back through stories, bells silent, a deep down rattle,
Comics, rivers well-named, dense gorse floodlights the valley's
Gurgling. Grief in a mailbag; drama on trolleys.
Less and less shoeing for smith and farming's polite dying
'Messiah' in the chapel – but a warning, gulls crying
Up at Easter miners off the race's soothing colour.
Oh simply simply I sing down the masterly contour.

ROLAND MATHIAS
(*b.* 1915)

The Flooded Valley

My house is empty but for a pair of boots:
The reservoir slaps at the privet hedge and uncovers the roots
And afterwards pats them up with a slack good will:
The sheep that I market once are not again to sell.
I am no waterman, and who of the others will live
Here, feeling the ripple spreading, hearing the timbers grieve?
The house I was born in has not long to stand:
My pounds are slipping away and will not wait for the end.

I will pick up my boots and run round the shire
To raise an echo louder than my fear.
Listen, Caerfanell, who gave me a fish for my stone,
Listen, I am alone, alone.
And Grwyney, both your rivers are one in the end
And are loved. If I command
You to remember me, will you, will you,
Because I was once at noon by your painted church of Patricio?
You did not despise me once, Senni, or run so fast
From your lovers. And O I jumped over your waist
Before sunrise or the flower was warm on the gorse.
You would do well to listen, Senni. There is money in my
    purse.

So you are quiet, all of you, and your current set away
Cautiously from the chapel ground in which my people lie...
Am I not Kedward, Prosser, Morgan, whose long stones
Name me despairingly and set me chains?
If I must quarrel and scuff in the weeds of another shire
When my pounds are gone, swear to me now in my weakness,
    swear
To me poor you will plant a stone more in this tightening field
And name there your latest dead, alas your unweaned feeblest
    child.

Testament

I cannot be sure what
I remember, but it was
Not a heroic escape, a grave
Hypocrisy strangled, the cortège
Of deacons stunned by one
Honest stroke. I was the child
Of belief, aching pitifully
In the unready hours
At the wounds I must suffer
When I walked out weaponless
And grown.

They were all heroes then,
All bullyboys kicking the pews
In, stirring their history up
In a pint-pot, jeering

The shabby unmuscled parades
Of the old Model Army.
But I was a little trembling
Fellow who had known love
And saw only greed
And false heart in such great
Drunken tales.

Porth Cwyfan

June, but the morning's cold, the wind
Bluffing occasional rain. I am clear
What brings me here across the stone
Spit to the island, but not what I shall find
When the dried fribbles of seaweed
Are passed, the black worked into the sandgrains
By the tide's mouthing. I can call nothing my own.

A closed-in, comfortless bay, the branchy
Shifts of voyage everywhere. On a slope
Of sand reaching up to the hidden
Field or stretch of marram, a tipwhite, paunchy
Terrier sits pat on his marker, yapping me
Bodily out of range. What in God's name is he
Guarding that he thinks I want of a sudden?

To the left is the island, granite-hulled
Against froth, the chapel's roof acute
As Cwyfan put it when the finer
Passions ruled, convergent answers belled
Wetherlike towards God. Ahead is the cliff
Eaten by sand. On the quaking field beyond
Low huts, ordered and menacing. Porth China.

Once on the island those last shingle
Feet I came by seem in threat.
Can you, like Beuno, knit me back severed
Heads, Cwyfan, bond men to single
Living? Your nave has a few wild settles
And phantasmagoric dust. And Roger Parry,
Agent to Owen Bold, has a stone skew-whiff in the yard.

Doubling back again is a small
Inevitable tragedy, the umpteenth
In a sinuous month. Now I avoid
The violent pitch of the dog, with all
And nothing to guard, remark his croup,
The hysteric note in the bark. Two dunlin,
Huffing on long legs, pick in and out of the tide.

A man on the beach, a woman
And child with a red woollen cap,
Hummock and stop within earshot,
Eyeing my blundering walk. 'Can
We get to the island?' he asks, Lancashire
Accent humble, dark curls broad. And I
Am suddenly angry. But how is my tripright sounder,
Save that I know Roger Parry and he does not?

Sir Gelli to R.S.

Even the worst intelligence must needs ride
Some years to reach me where I am, and hardihood
Bids me to leave yours lie. But that I cannot bear
To be held innocent and frail, a touch
For baubles and fine clothes. As well regret
Your verse for simpering at women. All
That I cherished, all, lay in the head –
The secret webs of a Gladestry morning, sun
Lofting at Wigmore or my other house
Of Llanelwedd, the clustered recusants, puritans
And Essex captains waiting on black-browed
Judgment. There was my Wales in thrall, delivered,
Dumb, to the cause. As for the town, man, London,
When was I there more happentimes than you?
I was at Cadiz, sure enough, with the spoils
To divide for my master, I the black pinnace
Roped to the heaving flagship, provisioner
For the extravagant wars. But London's a place
To pass through for a Welshman, always was. And I
Was no Penfro squireling with a perch of squill
On the cliff-top, idling it out in a city
Of coneys. I diced and ran with the Devereux, he
And I at Lamphey, boys of the dangerous covert. My
Black looks defended his bright ones. I

Clothed him with darkness, saturnine, setting the meats
For the rout, pricking him dumb men for sheriffs
Throughout the March, bribing the Assizes' scratch
To a lazy quill for the papists' sake. The magic
Silence there and before my Lord Pembroke's notaries
Was like the spell of Llwyd son of Cil Coed that Manawydan
Knew when he came from plying his trade in Lloegr.

I was always a man of silence. Even at Tyburn
When Cuffe, my cumbersome scaffold fellow, pleaded
To make his peace, I cut him short. It
Was no time for wheedling. The Devereux
Was my master, in treason or out. Why demean
His title a moment for such alien grace?
'Set the axe to', I said. Yet you aver
I cried for the baubles. Man, when we meet
I'll blood you sharply an you'll not declare
Which of us left an innocence in Wales.

Memling

What was it brought you, Seligenstadter,
Ambition cursed with smiles, the escalins
All counted and fingered, asking to be taken for
Bourgeois in the staid halls of Brugge?
And why did the Dom of Köln so fret your sky
That Ursula, that little bear of the Celts,
Stepped out of it, a boatload of priests
And maidens fast to her skirts, the white trim
Of innocence to their fold and the flower
Of death? This was an old, preposterous
Story, not meant for your burgher ears. And
Were not the villain Huns the ancestors
You could hardly name without the revilements
Of history? What had you still to exorcise
In your fine stone house on the Vlamingdam?

The gold of this painted reliquary shines
In the poor pilgrims' dark of the Hospital
Of St. John, the long tables of poverty
Barely gone from under the arches. What
Is the paradox that has us all by the throat?

That auburn hair, the young girl's unformed
Face, the blue soft sleeves and tiny
Refusing hands, colour and deck our youth as
We like to think it was. And the Hunnish
Tents are elaborate, Burgundian, rigid
Pavilions for Charles the Rash and his
Knights, their arbalests and fluted knee-
Joints and epaulets, the sophisticate
Sheen on their full black armour. It is all
Safely transposed, the ravisher and ravished.
The history we choose speaks largely of ourselves.

Brechfa Chapel

Not a shank of the long lane upwards
Prepared our wits for the myth, the slimed
Substantiation of the elements. And the coot
With his off-white blaze and queasy paddle
Was an old alarm, the timid in flight
From the ignorant. The lowered shoulder
Of mountain it is, dabbled within the collar,
That shallows and darkens the eye, the first
Slack argent losing the light as bitterly
As the blackened water treads and nibbles
The reeds and bushes afloat in the new
Pool's centre. Beyond, a surviving ray
Points and fondles a reed-knot, the swan
That dreams on it taking no note of stumps
Or visitations. Nearer, however, and shifting
Like pillagers from weed to shore, settling
And starting raucously, hundreds of testy
Black-backs utter their true society, bankrupt
Hatred of strangers and bully unrest whichever
Marge they think themselves forced to. It
Is a militant brabble, staked out by wind
To the cropped-down pasture. Mud and the tricky
Green of the edge contrivingly clap it round
What's left of this latish day that began with love.

Opposite, to the west of the harsh lagoon,
Stands a chapel, shut in its kindred wall
With a score of graves. Legend on one
Cries a minister, dead of the heats in Newport

Before he came twenty-eight, his wife
Rambling on to her eighties. On another a woman
Loosens at thirty, her man afield on the mission
Ploughing till dark. O these stones trouble
The spirit, give look for look! A light from this
Tiny cell brisked in far corners once, the hand held
Steady. But now the black half-world comes at it,
Bleaks by its very doors. Is the old witness done?
The farmers, separate in their lands, hedge,
Ditch, no doubt, and keep tight pasture. Uphill
They trudge on seventh days, singly, putting
Their heads to the pews as habit bids them to,
And keep counsel. The books, in pyramid, sit tidy
On the pulpit. The back gallery looks
Swept. But the old iron gate to the common,
Rusted a little, affords not a glimpse
Of the swan in her dream on the reed-knot
Nor of the anxious coot enquiring of the grasses.
The hellish noise it is appals, the intolerable shilly-
Shally of birds quitting the nearer mud
For the farther, harrying the conversation
Of faith. Each on his own must stand and conjure
The strong remembered words, the unanswerable
Texts against chaos.

Laus Deo

(No. X of the sequence 'Tide-Reach')

The water is hard in the well
But it never fails:
The clifftop fields are infinite salt
When the gales flock and pummel
Roof and farmstack and holt:
But the worm speaks well
Of the earth, the pheasant
Is heavy with praise in the lane:
The sea-birds, for all their grieving,
Gamble and dive at the nape of the storm:
And man embroiders his tales.
Hard hands have not kept it, this puissant
And sacred endeavour, nor high
Heads either this old domain.

It is one engrossing work, this frail
Commerce of souls in a corner,
Its coming and going, and the mark
Of the temporal on it. It is one
Coherent work, this Wales
And the seaway of Wales, its Maker
As careful of strength as
Of weakness, its quirk and cognomen
And trumpet allowed for
The whole peninsula's length.
It is one affirmative work, this Wales
And the seaway of Wales.

EMYR HUMPHREYS
(b. 1919)

Ancestor Worship

1. The dead are horizontal and motionless
   They take less room
   Than the stones which mark the tomb

   But the words they spoke
   Grow like flowers in the cracked rock

   Their ghosts move easily between words
   As people move between trees
   Gathering days and sunlight
   Like fuel for an invisible fire.

2. Grandparents whose portraits hang
   Like ikons in our hearts
   Carved out acres drew up codicils
   To brace our lives
   But the new estates cover the fields
   All the names are changed and their will
   Is broken up by sewers and pylons.

3. Our remote ancestors knew better.
   They were all poets
   They all wove
   Syllabic love into their wooden homes

   They saw the first invaders come
   Pushing their boats through the water meadows
   Their teeth and their swords glittering in the stealthy light
   And they carved metrical systems out of their own flesh.

4.   The air is still committed to their speech
      Their voices live in the air
      Like leaves like clouds like rain
      Their words call out to be spoken
      Until the language dies
      Until the ocean changes.

From Father to Son

There is no limit to the number of times
Your father can come to life, and he is as tender as ever he was
And as poor, his overcoat buttoned to the throat,
His face blue from the wind that always blows in the outer
   darkness
He comes towards you, hesitant,
Unwilling to intrude and yet driven at the point of love
To this encounter.

You may think
That love is all that is left of him, but when he comes
He comes with all his winters and all his wounds.
He stands shivering in the empty street,
Cold and worn like a tramp at the end of a journey
And yet a shape of unquestioning love that you
Uneasy and hesitant of the cold touch of death
Must embrace.

Then, before you can touch him
He is gone, leaving on your fingers
A little more of his weariness
A little more of his love.

JOHN STUART WILLIAMS
(b. 1920)

In Duffryn Woods

      Where the path opened
      and the wild bramble drew back,
      I saw a red fox
      standing in the checkered light
      just watching me, bold as brass.

Stock still, I looked back:
insects and birds deafened me.
Then he broke the thread
and, lengthening casually,
shifted into shadows, went.

Many times since then
I have seen him, that old fox,
stand for a moment
in the stillness of crossing light;
looking when I least expect

down a turning path
to ask the same sharp question
I could not answer
that first green time, asserting
being beyond becoming.

River Walk

Walking by the river, the morning cold
thick between old trees
dimly spread in parkland ease,
he stops to watch a mess of small
boys, a muddy ruck of all-sorts,
playing at playing rugby, hurts
and triumphs muffled in the turf.
                                          The ball,
kicked true for once, hangs
in the lifting wind, gull without wings,
then drops dead in his unused hands.
The feel of it, the dubbined skin, sends old
signals through his fingers, cold
and clumsy, releases things long forgot,
the smell of wintergreen, the hot roar
of crowds, running in to score,
a snatch of rude song: a scene
that mocks the years in between, fall
of leaf, the cruel quickness of it all.

A clatter of startled rooks breaks
him free: he grins, wryly kicks
the ball back, resumes his steady walk.

HARRI WEBB
(b. 1920)

The Nightingales

Once there were none and the dark air was dumb
Over the treestumps, the bare deforested hills.
They were a legend that the old bards had sung,
Gone now, like so much, so much.
But once I heard them drilling away the dark,
Llandaff was loud with them all of a summer's night
And the great Garth rose like a rock from their storm.
This most of all I desire: to hear the nightingales
Not by Taff only but by all our streams,
Black Rhymni, sullen Ogwr, dirty Ebbw
Dishonoured Tawe and all our sewered drabs.
And others whose names are an unvisited music
(Wales, Wales, who can know all your rivers?)
The nightingales singing beyond the Teifi,
By Aeron, Ystwyth, Rheidol, and those secret waters
The Beacons hold: Rhiangoll, Tarrell, Crawnon,
By Hepste and Mellte outstanding Scwd Einion Gam
(But let them not sing by Elan, Claerwen, Fyrnwy
Or Tryweryn of the Shame.)
You who have outsung all our dead poets,
Sing for them again in Cwm Prysor and Dyffryn Ceiriog,
And humble Gwydderig and Creidiol, do not forget them.
And that good man, no poet, who gave us a song
Even sweeter than yours, sing for him at Llanrhaeadr,
And in Glyndyfrdwy, what need to tell you to sing?
Sing in the faded lands, Maelienydd and Elfael,
And in the plundered cantrefs that have no name.
Come back and sing to us, we have waited too long,
For too long have not been worth singing for.
The magic birds that sang for heroes in Harlech
And hushed to wonder the wild Ardudwy sea
And they of Safaddan that sing only for princes,
We cannot call them again, but come you
And fill our hearts like the hearts of other men.
Shall we hear you again soon, soon?

Epil y Filiast

Already something of a stranger now
A spry old man is walking his milgi out
Of a Sunday morning when the nineteenth century

Is in chapel and the twentieth is in bed.
But his morning is centuries younger than these
As he steps it out and the lean dog lopes beside him
To fields where it will flash and pounce and double
As once in Glyn Cuch Woods.
And the old man stands in his grubby mackintosh
With a jaunty set to his shoulders,
A clean white scarf around his withered throat
And his cap on one side – ticyn slic.
His whistle carries further than the rotting pitheads,
The grass-grown tips, the flashy, flimsy estates.
He is a gambler, a drinker, a doggy-boy,
Better at drawing the dole than earning a wage.
The supermarket rises where Calfaria stood,
To him it is all one, he is older than any of it.
Mark him well, he is the last of his kind,
The last heir of Cadwaladr, Caswallon
And all our dead princes.

Synopsis of the Great Welsh Novel

Dai K lives at the end of a valley. One is not quite sure
Whether it has been drowned or not. His Mam
Loves him too much and his Dada drinks.
As for his girlfriend Blodwen, she's pregnant. So
Are all the other girls in the village – there's been a Revival.
After a performance of Elijah, the mad preacher
Davies the Doom has burnt the chapel down.
One Saturday night after the dance at the Con Club,
With the Free Wales Army up to no good in the back lanes,
A stranger comes to the village; he is, of course,
God, the well known television personality. He succeeds
In confusing the issue, whatever it is, and departs
On the last train before the line is closed.
The colliery blows up, there is a financial scandal
Involving all the most respected citizens; the Choir
Wins at the National. It is all seen, naturally,
Through the eyes of a sensitive boy who never grows up.
The men emigrate to America, Cardiff and the moon. The girls
Find rich and foolish English husbands. Only daft Ianto
Is left to recite the Complete Works of Sir Lewis Morris
To puzzled sheep, before throwing himself over
The edge of the abandoned quarry. One is not quite sure
Whether it is fiction or not.

HARRI WEBB

Cywydd o Fawl
(yn null y gogogynfeirdd à gogo)

Flap we our lips, praise Big Man,
Bards religious shire Cardigan.
Not frogs croaking are we
Nor vain crows are bards tidy.
Wise is our speak, like Shadrach,
Hearken you now, people bach.
Mouth some, Cardiff ach y fi,
Not holy like Aberteifi.
Twp it is to speech so,
In Cardiff is gold yellow,
Truth it is and no fable,
All for bards respectable.
White Jesus bach, let no ill
Befall Big Heads Arts Council.
Pounds they have, many thousand,
Like full till shop draper grand.
Good is the work they are at,
Soaped they shall be in Seiat,
Reserved shall be for them
A place in Big Seat Salem.
Praised let them be for this thing,
Money they are distributing
Like Beibil Moses his manna,
Tongue we all, bards Welsh, Ta!

Thanks in Winter

The day that Eliot died I stood
By Dafydd's grave in Ystrad Fflur,
It was the depth of winter,
A day for an old man to die.
The dark memorial stone,
Chiselled in marble of Latin
And the soft intricate gold
Of the old language
Echoed the weather's colour
A slate vault over Ffair Rhos
Pontrhydfendigaid, Pumlumon,
The sheep runs, the rough pasture
And the lonely whitewashed houses

Scattered like frost, the dwellings
Of country poets, last inheritors
To the prince of song who lies
Among princes, among ruins.
A pilgrim under the yew at Ystrad Fflur
I kept my vow, prayed for my country,
Cursed England, came away

And home to the gas fire and television
News. Caught between two languages,
Both dying, I thanked the long-dead
Minstrel of May and the newly silent
Voice of the bad weather, the precise
Accent of our own time, taught
To the disinherited, offering
Iron for gold.

The Stone Face

(discovered at Deganwy, Spring 1966)

It may of course be John his father-in-law,
Their worst, our best not easily discernible
After so many buried centuries. The experts
Cannot be sure, that is why they are experts.
But this stone face under a broken crown
Is not an impersonal mask of sovereignty;
This is the portrait of a living man
And when his grandson burnt Deganwy down
So that no foreign army should hold its strength
I think they buried the head of Llywelyn Fawr
As primitive magic and for reasons of state.

No fortress was ever destroyed so utterly
As was Deganwy by Llywelyn the Last,
The thoroughness of despair, foreknown defeat,
Was in the burning and breaking of its walls.
But at some door or window a hand paused,
A raised crowbar halted by the stare
Of a stone face. The Prince is summoned
And the order given: bury it in the earth,
There will be other battles, we'll be back—
Spoken in the special Welsh tone of voice
Half banter, half blind fervour, the last look
Exchanged between the hunted living eyes
And dead majesty for whom there are no problems,

The burning of Deganwy, the throne and fortress
Of Llywelyn Fawr shattered, his principality
Gone in the black smoke drifting over Menai
And his last heir forced into endless retreat
To the banks of Irfon and the final lance-thrust.
There was no return, no reverent unearthing.
A stone face sleeps beneath the earth
With open eyes. All history is its dream.
The Great Orme shepherds the changing weather,
On Menai's shores the tides and generations
Ebb, grumble and flow; harps and hymns
Sound and fall silent; briefly the dream flares out of the eyes
Then darkness comes again.

Seven hundred and fifty years of darkness.
Now in a cold and stormy spring we stand
At the unearthing of the Sovereign head,
The human face under the chipped crown.
Belatedly, but not too late, the rendezvous is made.
The dream and the inheritors of the dream,
The founder and father, and those who must rebuild
The broken fortresses, re-establish the throne
Of eagles, here exchange the gaze of eagles
In the time of the cleansing of the eyes.

Abbey Cwmhir

Cowpasture and the ragged line
Of a ruined wall. A few more cartloads
Of dressed stone filched for a new farmhouse
Or sections of clustered column taken for a cheesepress
And there would be nothing, less even
Than these scrappy remains under the big trees.
The coffin-lid of an old abbot is propped up
Behind the door of the Victorian church,
That's all. Heavy with July the elms
Remember nothing.

Appropriately
There is no signpost, not even a fieldpath
To the place where they brought the hacked trunk,
Who were they, I wonder, who lugged him here,

All that was left of him, after the English
Had done their thing, what went on in their minds,
Conventional piety, simple human pity
Or the cosmic grief the Son of the Red Judge
Sang into the stormwind, as they urged the pony
Felted with its winter coat, and over the crupper
The bloody carcase, along the bad ways?

Centuries later, in high summer, I feel the cold.

ROBERT MORGAN
(b. 1920)

Shadow Valley

And in the evening the black river
Creeps on as though tired
Of its journey through valley and time.
And when the light falls from the mountains
The mist floats on the black water.
Windowless chapels glow over sleeping
Streets, pit gears vibrate
With a quiet song and inside the tremulous
Earth the night shift men, wet
With huge efforts, hammer and strain
In the semi-dark.
              In this broken earth
Under Wales time is the music of water
And pain where angular men imperfected
By work and dust fall away
From the tense trees in the grey stones.
And when the exhausted earth is childless and spent
The human scratches will crumble in the wilderness
To the echoes of the feet of strangers.

Blood Donor

The searching was easy and memory ripens
On the grey earth picture of Rees
In his grimy vest soaked in blood.
Forty-eight years under tense rock
Had stripped him like a tree with roots
In slag and marked him with texture of strain
And accident. But it was slow legs
And dust-worn eyes that were to blame.

LESLIE NORRIS

The iron rock-bar was still in his hands
Held like a spear of a fallen warrior.
The rocks had dyed his silver hair red
And the heavy bar was warm and worn.
Blind flies swarmed in the blood-sweat
Air and the tough men with bruised
Senses were gentle, using distorted
Hands like women arranging flowers.

On the way out through roads of rocky
Silence you could sense images of confusion
In the slack chain of shadows. Muscles
Were nerve-tight and thoughts infested
With wrath and sharp edges of fear.
Towards the sun's lamp we moved, taking
Home the dark prisoner in his shroud of coats.

LESLIE NORRIS
(b. 1921)

The Ballad of Billy Rose

Outside Bristol Rovers' Football Ground –
The date has gone from me, but not the day,
Nor how the dissenting flags in stiff array
Stuck bravely out against the sky's grey round –

Near the car park then, past Austin and Ford,
Lagonda, Bentley, and a colourful patch
Of country coaches come in for the match,
Was where I walked, having travelled the road

From Fishponds to watch Portsmouth in the Cup.
The Third Round, I believe. And I was filled
With the old excitement which had thrilled
Me so completely when, while growing up,

I went on Saturdays to match or fight.
Not only me; for thousands of us there
Strode forward eagerly, each man aware
Of tingling memory, anticipating delight.

We all marched forward, all except one man.
I saw him because he was paradoxically still,
A stone against the flood, face upright against us all,
Head bare, hoarse voice aloft, blind as a stone.

I knew him at once, despite his pathetic clothes;
Something in his stance, or his sturdy frame
Perhaps. I could even remember his name
Before I saw it on his blind man's tray. Billy Rose.

And twenty forgetful years fell away at the sight.
Bare-kneed, dismayed, memory fled to the hub
Of Saturday violence, with friends to the Labour Club,
Watching the boxing on a sawdust summer night.

The boys' enclosure close to the shabby ring
Was where we stood, clenched in a resin world,
Spoke in cool voices, lounged, were artificially bored
During minor bouts. We paid threepence to go in.

Billy Rose fought there. He was top of the bill.
So brisk a fighter, so gallant, so precise!
Trim as a tree he stood for the ceremonies,
Then turned to meet George Morgan of Tirphil.

He had no chance. Courage was not enough,
Nor tight defence. Donald Davies was sick
And we threatened his cowardice with an embarrassed kick.
Ripped across both his eyes was Rose, but we were tough

And clapped him as they wrapped his blindness up
In busy towels, applauded the wave
He gave his executioners, cheered the brave
Blind man as he cleared with a jaunty hop

The top rope. I had forgotten that day
As if it were dead for ever, yet now I saw
The flowers of punched blood on the ring floor,
As bright as his name. I do not know

How long I stood with ghosts of the wild fists
And the cries of shaken boys long dead around me,
For struck to act at last, in terror and pity
I threw some frantic money, three treacherous pence –

And I cry at the memory – into his tray, and ran,
Entering the waves of the stadium like a drowning man.
Poor Billy Rose. God, he could fight,
Before my three sharp coins knocked out his sight.

Water

On hot summer mornings my aunt set glasses
On a low wall outside the farmhouse,
With some jugs of cold water.
I would sit in the dark hall, or
                Behind the dairy window,
Waiting for children to come from the town.

They came in small groups, serious, steady,
And I could see them, black in the heat,
Long before they turned in at our gate
To march up the soft, dirt road.
                They would stand by the wall,
Drinking water with an engrossed thirst. The dog

Did not bother them, knowing them responsible
Travellers. They held in quiet hands their bags
Of jam sandwiches, and bottles of yellow fizz.
Sometimes they waved a gratitude to the house,
                But they never looked at us.
Their eyes were full of the mountain, lifting

Their measuring faces above our long hedge.
When they had gone I would climb the wall,
Looking for them among the thin sheep runs.
Their heads were a resolute darkness among ferns,
                They climbed with unsteady certainty.
I wondered what it was they knew the mountain had.

They would pass the last house, Lambert's, where
A violent gander, too old by many a Christmas,
Blared evil warning from his bitten moor,
Then it was open world, too high and clear
                For clouds even, where over heather
The free hare cleanly ran, and the summer sheep.

I knew this; and I knew all summer long
Those visionary gangs passed through our lanes,
Coming down at evening, their arms full
Of cowslips, moon daisies, whinberries, nuts,
                All fruits of the sliding seasons,
And the enormous experience of the mountain

That I who loved it did not understand.
In the summer, dust filled our winter ruts
With a level softness, and children walked
At evening through golden curtains scuffed
               From the road by their trailing feet.
They would drink tiredly at our wall, talking

Softly, leaning, their sleepy faces warm for home.
We would see them murmur slowly through our stiff
Gate, their shy heads gilded by the last sun.
One by one we would gather up the used jugs,
               The glasses. We would pour away
A little water. It would lie on the thick dust, gleaming.

Early Frost

We were warned about frost, yet all day the summer
Has wavered its heat above the empty stubble. Late
Bees hung their blunt weight,
Plump drops between those simplest wings, their leisure
An ignorance of frost.
My mind is full of the images of summer
And a liquid curlew calls from alps of air;

But the frost has come. Already under trees
Pockets of summer are dying, wide paths
Of the cold glow clean through the stricken thickets
And again I feel on my cheek the cut of winters
Dead. Once I awoke in a dark beyond moths
To a world still with freezing,
Hearing my father go to the yard for his ponies,

His hands full of frostnails to point their sliding
To a safe haul. I went to school,
Socks pulled over shoes for the streets' clear glass,
The early shops cautious, the tall
Classroom windows engraved by winter's chisel,
Fern, feather and flower that would not let the pale
Day through. We wrote in a cold fever for the morning

Play. Then boys in the exulting yard, ringing
Boots hard on winter, slapped with their polishing
Caps the arrows of their gliding, in steaming lines
Ran till they launched one by one
On the skills of ice their frail balance,
Sliding through life with not a fall in mind,
Their voices crying freely through such shouting

As the cold divided. I slid in the depth
Of the season till the swung bell sang us in.
Now insidious frost, its parched grains rubbing
At crannies, moved on our skin.
Our fingers died. Not the warmth
Of all my eight wide summers could keep me smiling.
The circle of the popping stove fell still
And we were early sped through the hurrying dark.

I ran through the bitterness on legs
That might have been brittle, my breath
Solid, grasping at stabs of bleak
Pain to gasp on. Winter branched in me, ice cracked
In my bleeding. When I fell through the teeth
Of the cold at my haven door I could not see

For locked tears, I could not feel the spent
Plenty of flames banked at the range,
Nor my father's hands as they roughed the blue
Of my knees. But I knew what he meant
With the love of his rueful laugh, and my true
World unfroze in a flood of happy crying,
As hot on my cheek as the sting of this present

Frost. I have stood too long in the orderly
Cold of the garden. I would not have again the death
Of that day come unasked as the comfortless dusk
Past the stakes of my fences. Yet these are my
Ghosts, they do not need to ask
For housing when the early frost comes down.
I take them in, all, to the settled warmth.

Stone and Fern

It is not that the sea lanes
Are too long, nor that I am not
Tempted by the birds' sightless

Roads, but that I have listened
Always to the voice of the stone,
Saying: Sit still, answer, say

Who you are. And I have answered
Always with the rooted fern,
Saying: We are the dying seed.

LESLIE NORRIS

Barn Owl

Ernie Morgan found him, a small
Fur mitten inexplicably upright,
And hissing like a treble kettle
Beneath the tree he'd fallen from.
His bright eye frightened Ernie,
Who popped a rusty bucket over him
And ran for us. We kept him
In a backyard shed, perched
On the rung of a broken deck-chair,
Its canvas faded to his down's biscuit.
Men from the pits, their own childhood
Spent waste in the crippling earth,
Held him gently, brought him mice
From the wealth of our riddled tenements,
Saw that we understood his tenderness,
His tiny body under its puffed quilt,
Then left us alone. We called him Snowy.

He was never clumsy. He flew
From the first like a skilled moth,
Sifting the air with feathers,
Floating it softly to the place he wanted.
At dusk he'd stir, preen, stand
At the window-ledge, fly. It was
A catching of the heart to see him go.
Six months we kept him, saw him
Grow beautiful in a way each thought
His own knowledge. One afternoon, home
With pretended illness, I watched him
Leave. It was daylight. He lifted slowly
Over the Hughes's roof, his cream face calm,
And never came back. I saw this;
And tell it for the first time,
Having wanted to keep his mystery.

And would not say it now, but that
This morning, walking in Slindon woods
Before the sun, I found a barn owl
Dead in the rusty bracken.
He was not clumsy in his death,
His wings folded decently to him,
His plumes, unruffled orange,
Bore flawlessly their delicate patterning.

LESLIE NORRIS

With a stick I turned him, not
Wishing to touch his feathery stiffness.
There was neither blood nor wound on him,
But for the savaged foot a scavenger
Had ripped. I saw the sinews.
I could have skewered them out
Like a common fowl's. Moving away
I was oppressed by him, thinking
Confusedly that down the generations
Of air this death was Snowy's
Emblematic messsenger, that I should know
The meaning of it, the dead barn owl.

Elegy for David Beynon

David, we must have looked comic, sitting
there at next desks; your legs stretched
half-way down the classroom, while
my feet hung a free inch above

the floor. I remember, too, down
at The Gwynne's Field, at the side
of the little Taff, dancing with
laughing fury as you caught

effortlessly at the line-out, sliding
the ball over my head direct to
the outside-half. That was Cyril
Theophilus, who died in his quiet

so long ago that only I, perhaps,
remember he'd hold the ball one-handed
on his thin stomach as he turned
to run. Even there you were careful

to miss us with your scattering
knees as you bumped through
for yet another try. Buffeted
we were, but cheered too by our

unhurt presumption in believing
we could ever have pulled you down.
I think those children, those who died
under your arms in the crushed school,

would understand that I make this
your elegy. I know the face you had,
have walked with you enough mornings
under the fallen leaves. Theirs is

the great anonymous tragedy one word
will summarise. Aberfan, I write it
for them here, knowing we've paid to it
our shabby pence, and now it can be stored

with whatever names there are where
children end their briefest pilgrimage.
I cannot find the words for you, David. These
are too long, too many; and not enough.

Ravenna Bridge

Thinking he walked on air, he
Thrust each step, stretched straight
His ankle. We saw him lift
On thinnest stone between him-
self and earth, and then dip on.

Such undulant progress! Stern
Herons walk like that; but he
Just rose again into his
Highest possible smiling air,
Stepped seriously by us,

And kept for all himself
The edges, even, of his happiness.
Passing, we caught the recognition
Of his transfiguring sweet
Smoke. And so he stepped, he

Skipped, the thin boy, on narrow
Ravenna Bridge, itself a height
Over pines and sycamores. He
Danced above their heads. If
He'd hopped the handrail, had

Swayed into flight, fallen
To stony death among wood-doves,
We should have watched him. I did
Not stand as I felt, hand
To mouth in a still gasp, but

Coldly and relaxed, and saw the boy
Perform his happy legs across
Ravenna Bridge and up the hill
To Fifty-Second. We walked home,
Thanking his god, and ours.

T. HARRI JONES
(1921 – 1965)

Rhiannon

My daughter of the Mabinogion name
Tells me Ayer's Rock is ten times higher than
A house, and she, being seven today,
Would like to see it, especially
To ride there on a camel from Alice Springs.
She also says she wants to be a poet –
Would the vision of that monolith
Stay in her mind and dominate her dreams
As in my mind and dreams these thirty years
There stands the small hill, Allt-y-clych,
The hill of bells, bedraggled with wet fern
And stained with sheep, and holding like a threat
The wild religion and the ancient tongue,
All the defeated centuries of Wales?

The Welshman in Exile Speaks

Being a boy from the hills, brought up
Believing that fornication is a sin,
Adultery abomination, what should I do
But fornicate until I'm caught, and then
Commit adultery in my dreams. *My* dreams
—You have to plough the furrows I have ploughed,
Or pick the stones off the bitter fields
Before they're fit for ploughing, all day, all day,
Or lift potatoes until your back is breaking,
And then go home to the grudged candlelight
And the green bacon – you want your childhood
Spent like that – and with the compensations:
An old man's voice like something out of Daniel
Making the Belshazzars of the tractors tremble,
Hills, like Mam's breasts, homely and tremendous,
Schooled wildness of sheepdogs, ponies stubborn

As myself, and each winter's killing snow.
And the capel, God in a little *bwthyn*
Once whitewashed – but God in the voices
Of the mean, the crippled, the green bacon eaters,
The lead me beside still waters buggers, the wild boys,
The sin-eaters, and the godly daughters,
All of them suddenly in unison
In the ugliest building I have ever seen
– Pisgah I shall never see again –
All suddenly bursting – not bursting,
All suddenly startled into song, to praise
The god of fornication and the world we lived in.

Boyo, if you come from a country like that
You can talk to me of sin and related matters.

Llanafan Unrevisited

I took for emblem the upland moors and the rocky
Slopes above them, bitter parishes
Of the buzzard striking from lonely circles
And the ragged fox hunting the lean
Rabbits, and the starved preacher nourishing
A little heat from a hell that once had meaning.
I had thought to be a proud man and isolated,
Inviolate as my hills even in defeat,
Not easily marked even by the incessant
Savagery of weather, God, and my relations.
Small, maybe, but tough I thought and unendearing
As feg and able to endure weather
That smashes the great oaks and makes mud
Of the good meadows and destroys good men.

And now I live in the good meadows, and I have
No emblem except your body, and I am
Still a member of a narrow chapel, and a boy
From a hungry parish, a spoiled preacher,
Greedily taking the surplus of your sunshine,
And still afraid of hell because I've been there.

My Grandmother Died in the Early Hours of the Morning

It was cold in that room, after the cold hours
Of keeping company with the big, shrunk man
Who had been her husband, my father's father.

Her sallow face seemed peaceful as ever,
Her straggle of hair blanched into the pillow
—You would not have guessed at a body under the bedclothes.
Past tiredness, I was a boy, incurious.
A little woman was dead, a little old woman
Who had long confused me with her youngest son.
I did not even think, How small she looks.
And certainly had no thoughts for her life of labour,
Nor wondered how she who had always been old to me
Had once been whatever beauty the world has
To the old man I now led out of the room,
Out of the house, up the narrow road,
In the dawn he could not see for tears, taking
My hand in his as he'd done when I was small,
Both of us wordless against the dawn and death.

Cwmchwefri

I have been walking above Cwmchwefri
Where the hills slant sharply into rock
And nothing, not even a kite, hopes to live.

Up there, above even the last sheepdroppings
And bits of rabbitfur and peewit feathers,
I could see sickeningly below me
The sideland farms precariously
Clinging among the bracken to an old
And often defeated hope.
                    You must believe
In some impossibly glorious promise
To mow meadows and milk cows in such
Unlikely places.
                    What will happen now
When they listen to the six o'clock news
Instead of bawling Alleluia
To their beautifully unjust God?

Back?

(to R. S. Thomas)

Back is the question
Carried to me on the curlew's wing
And the strong sides of the salmon.

Should I go back then
To the narrow path, the sheep turds,
And the birded language?

Back to an old, thin bitch
Fawning on my spit, writhing
Her lank belly with memories:

Back to the chapel, and a charade
Of the word of God made by a preacher
Without a tongue:

Back to the ingrowing quarrels,
The family where you have to remember
Who is not speaking to whom:

Back to the shamed memories of Glyn Dŵr
And Saunders Lewis's aerodrome
And a match at Swansea?

Of course I'd go back if somebody'd pay me
To live in my own country
Like a bloody Englishman.

But for now, lacking the money,
I must be content with the curlew's cry
And the salmon's taut belly

And the waves, of water and of fern
And words, that beat unendingly
On the rocks of my mind's country.

RUTH BIDGOOD
(b. 1922)

Chimneys

Far away, we saw three chimneys in the trees
across the valley, on a little hill
beyond the first hill's shoulder.

Shading our eyes from the sidelong evening sun,
we gazed and guessed till we could almost see
the roofs of beast-house, stable and barn.

No smoke rose from the chimneys, we said at first,
but soon we swore there was smoke, so alive the house
seemed in the dying sunlight.

And afterwards, alone, I searched on maps
to make the house more mine by knowing its name –
and found there is no farm on the hill,

no house of any kind, not even a ruin.
What trick of sun and shade put chimneys there
for us to find and talk about?

And is the evening more real than the house?
Now both are gone, it seems a fine distinction
that one was and the other was not.

Remembering, I build the evening again,
the plunging valley and the little hill,
and look! there are chimneys in the trees.

Burial Path

When we carried you, Siân, that winter day,
over four rivers and four mountains
to the burial place of your people,
it was not the dark rocks of Cwm-y-Benglog
dragged down my spirit,
it was not the steepness of Rhiw'r Ych
that cracked my heart.

Four by four, Siân, we carried you,
over the mountain wilderness of Dewi,
fording Pysgotwr and Doithie,
crossing Camddwr by Soar-y-Mynydd,
Tywi at Nant-y-Neuadd; every river passed
brought us the challenge of another hill beyond.

Again and again from his rough pony's back our leader
signalled with his hazel-staff of office
four, breathless, to lay down your coffin,
four, fresh in strength, to bear you
up the old sledge-ways, the sinew-straining tracks,
the steeps of Rhiw Gelynen and Rhiw'r Ych.

RUTH BIDGOOD

I with the rest, Siân, carried you.
The burial path is long – forty times and more
I put my shoulder to the coffin
before the weary journey was accomplished
and down at last through leafless oaks
singing we carried you to the crumbling church,
the ancient yews, at the burial place of your people.

It was not then my heart cracked, Siân,
nor my soul went into darkness.
Carrying you, there was great weariness,
and pride in an old ritual well performed –
our friend's firm leadership, smooth changes
from four to four, the coffin riding
effortlessly the surge of effort;
and at the grave, pride too in showing
churchmen how we of Soar knew well
ways of devotion, fit solemnity.

But with your grave whitened – the last ceremony –
and my neighbours, as I had urged them, gone ahead,
then it was I felt the weight of death
for the first time, Siân, and I knew
it would be always with me now
on the bitter journey that was not yet accomplished.

Now as I went down Rhiw'r Ych alone
and turned west over the ford of Nant-y-Neuadd,
I knew there was only darkness waiting
for me, beyond the crags of Cwm-y-Benglog.
It was then my heart cracked, Siân, my spirit
went into that darkness and was lost.

Dragon

West wind sets the dragon rippling over the flag,
launches a legend to whip its scaly tail
out through the trees, pad through Rhyd Goch
(splashes slithering off metallic flanks)
and pace Cefn Fanog at dusk, be glimpsed
as a dark sinuosity on the hill,
a distant puff of red-lit smoke.

Is it kin to the dragon, cast as villain,
that slants an unjudging eye upon
its unvindicative slayer, and coils
in elegant agony round the saint's
transfixing lance? Or are all dragons one
with the winged and convoluted image of life?
This perhaps is a maverick among dragons,
ill at ease in such portentous company.

West wind dies before dark tonight.
Last of light finds the flag hardly fluttered,
dragon hidden in folds. Whatever went plashing
through the ford, whatever slid along
the darkening hill, now rests again,
but is a light sleeper. That image it leaves
of antique and raffish splendour
is vigorous, if unclear; and likely to recur.

All Souls'

Shutting my gate, I walk away
from the small glow of my banked fire
into a black All Souls'. Presently
the sky slides back across the void
like a grey film. Then the hedges
are present, and the trees, which my mind
already knows, are no longer
strangers to my eyes.
The road curves. Further along,
a conversation of lights begins
from a few houses, invisible except as light,
calling to farms that higher in darkness
answer still, though each now speaks
for others that lie dumb.
Light at Tymawr above me, muted by trees,
is all the voice Brongwesyn has,
that once called clearly enough
into the upper valley's night.
From the hill Clyn ahead
Glangwesyn's lively shout of light
celebrates old Nant Henfron, will not let
Cenfaes and Blaennant be voiceless.

RUTH BIDGOOD

I am a latecomer, but offer
speech to the nameless, those
who are hardly a memory, those
whose words were always faint
against the deafening darkness
of remotest hills.
For them tonight when I go home
I will draw back my curtains, for them
my house shall sing with light.

Standing Stone

The stone stands among new firs,
still overtopping them. Soon
they will hide it. Their lower branches
will find its cold bulk
blocking their growth. After years,
lopped trunks will lie piled,
awaiting haulage. The stone will stand
in a cleared valley, and offer again
the ancient orientation.

The stone stores, transmits.
Against its almost-smoothness
I press my palms. I cannot ask,
having no word of power,
no question formed. Have I
anything to give? My hands offer
a dumb love, a hope towards
the day of the freed valley.
Flesh fits itself to the slow curve
of dominating stone, as prayer
takes the shape of a god's will.

A mindless ritual is not empty.
When the dark mind fails, faith lives
in the supplication of hands
on prayer-wheel, rosary, stone.
It is evening. I walk down-valley
on an old track. Behind me
the ephemeral trees darken.
Among them, the stone waits.

DANNIE ABSE
(b. 1923)

Social revolution in England

Insolent as waiters, they did not ring the bell.
    Some slid down banisters, stomped up again.
    We assumed they were agencies from hell
    but why they had come no one was certain.
Best to smile like landlords, offer a jargonelle.

Number Thirteen, we said distracted, is next door.
    Often cold politeness works quite neatly.
    They brushed us aside trying to ignore
    our hints, the nice way we coughed discreetly.
They just ran up and down the staircase as before.

Preternatural bailiffs, they stripped the house bare
    of properties. Light the oblong patches
    on walls where once our gouty fathers were.
    We heard them talking in dirty snatches
as heavy doors opened. Our eyes began to blur.

It was as if we weren't, like phantoms, there at all
    and they in some intimate, cruel game
    engaged – horrid, olid and medieval.
    Why ask why, from exactly where they came
when ergatocracies, too, in time must fall?

Who'd query such common, anonymous powers?
    By asking questions man becomes insane.
    In the empty hall now we've waited hours
    by the telephone for someone to explain,
to send some message, even if it's only flowers.

Return to Cardiff

'Hometown'; well, most admit an affection for a city:
grey, tangled streets I cycled on to school, my first cigarette
in the back lane, and, fool, my first botched love affair.
First everything. Faded torments; self-indulgent pity.

The journey to Cardiff seemed less a return than a raid
on mislaid identities. Of course the whole locus smaller:
the mile-wide Taff now a stream, the castle not as in some
    black,
gothic dream, but a decent sprawl, a joker's toy facade.

Unfocused voices in the wind, associations, clues,
odds and ends, fringes caught, as when, after the doctor quit,
a door opened and I glimpsed the white, enormous face
of my grandfather, suddenly aghast with certain news.

Unable to define anything I can hardly speak,
and still I love the place for what I wanted it to be
as much as for what it unashamedly is
now for me, a city of strangers, alien and bleak.

Unable to communicate I'm easily betrayed,
uneasily diverted by mere sense reflections
like those anchored waterscapes that wander, alter, in the Taff,
hour by hour, as light slants down a different shade.

Illusory, too, that lost dark playground after rain,
the noise of trams, gunshots in what they once called Tiger Bay.
Only real this smell of ripe, damp earth when the sun comes
    out,
a mixture of pungencies, half exquisite and half plain.

No sooner than I'd arrived the other Cardiff had gone,
smoke in the memory, these but tinned resemblances,
where the boy I was not and the man I am not
met, hesitated, left double footsteps, then walked on.

Peachstone

I do not visit his grave. He is not there.
Out of hearing, out of reach. I miss him here,
seeing hair grease at the back of a chair
near a firegrate where his spit sizzled,
or noting, in the cut-glass bowl, a peach.

For that night his wife brought him a peach,
his favourite fruit, while the sick light glowed,
and his slack, dry mouth sucked, sucked, sucked,
with dying eyes closed – perhaps for her sake –
till bright as blood the peachstone showed.

Not Adlestrop

Not Adlestrop, no – besides, the name
hardly matters. Nor did I languish in June heat.
Simply, I stood, too early, on the empty platform,
and the wrong train came in slowly, surprised, stopped.
Directly facing me, from a window,
a very, *very* pretty girl leaned out.

When I, all instinct,
stared at her, she, all instinct, inclined her head away
as if she'd divined the much married life in me,
or as if she might spot, up platform,
some unlikely familiar.
For my part, under the clock, I continued
my scrutiny with unmitigated pleasure.
And she knew it, she certainly knew it, and would not
glance at me in the silence of not Adlestrop.

Only when the train heaved noisily, only
when it jolted, when it slid away, only *then*,
daring and secure, she smiled back at my smile,
and I, daring and secure, waved back at her waving.
And so it was, all the way down the hurrying platform
as the train gathered atrocious speed
towards Oxfordshire or Gloucestershire.

A New Diary

This clerk-work, this first January chore
of who's in, who's out. A list to think about
when absences seem to shout, Scandal! Outrage!
So turning to the blank, prefatory page
I transfer most of the names and phone tags
from last year's diary. True, Meadway, Speedwell,
Mountview, are computer-changed into numbers,
and already their pretty names begin to fade
like Morwenna, Julie, Don't-Forget-Me-Kate,
grassy summer girls I once swore love to.
These, whispering others and time will date.

Cancelled, too, a couple someone else betrayed,
one man dying, another mind in rags.
And remembering them my clerk-work flags,
bitterly flags, for all lose, no-one wins,
those in, those out, *this* at the heart of things.
So I stop, ask: whom should I commemorate,
and who, perhaps, is crossing out my name now
from some future diary? Oh my God,
Morwenna, Julie, don't forget me, Kate.

Cousin Sidney

Dull as a bat, said my mother
of cousin Sidney in 1940 the time he tried
to break his garden swing, jumping on it,
size 12 shoes – at fifteen the tallest boy
in the class, taller than loping Dan Morgan
when Dan Morgan wore his father's top hat.

Duller than a bat, said my father
when hero Sidney lied about his age
to claim rough khaki, silly ass;
and soon, somewhere near Dunkirk,
some foreign corner was forever Sidney
though uncle would not believe it.

Missing not dead please God, please,
he said, and never bolted the front door,
never string taken from the letter box,
never the hall light off lest his one son
came home through a night of sleet
whistling, We'll meet again.

Aunt crying and raw in the onion air
of the garden (the unswinging empty swing)
her words on a stretched leash
while Uncle shouted, Bloody Germans.
And on November 11th, two howls
of silence even after three decades

till last year, their last year,
when uncle and aunt also went missing,
missing alas, so that now strangers
have bolted their door and cut the string
and no-one at all (the hall so dark)
waits up for Sidney, silly ass.

X-Ray

Some prowl sea-beds, some hurtle to a star
and, mother, some obsessed turn over every stone
or open graves to let that starlight in.
There are men who would open anything.

Harvey, the circulation of the blood,
and Freud, the circulation of our dreams,
pried honourably and honoured are
like all explorers. Men who'd open men.

And those others, mother, with diseases
like great streets named after them: Addison,
Parkinson, Hodgkin – physicians who'd arrive
fast and first on any sour death-bed scene.

I am their slowcoach colleague, half afraid,
incurious. As a boy it was so: you know how
my small hand never teased to pieces
an alarm clock or flensed a perished mouse.

And this larger hand's the same. It stretches now
out from a white sleeve to hold up, mother,
your X-ray to the glowing screen. My eyes look
but don't want to; I still don't want to know.

JOHN ORMOND
(b. 1923)

My Grandfather and his Apple-Tree

Life sometimes held such sweetness for him
As to engender guilt. From the night vein he'd come,
From working in water wrestling the coal,
Up the pit slant. Every morning hit him
Like a journey of trams between the eyes;
A wild and drinking farmboy sobered by love
Of a miller's daughter and a whitewashed cottage
Suddenly to pay rent for. So he'd left the farm
For dark under the fields six days a week
With mandrel and shovel and different stalls.
All light was beckoning. Soon his hands
Untangled a brown garden into neat greens.

JOHN ORMOND

There was an apple-tree he limed, made sturdy;
The fruit was sweet and crisp upon the tongue
Until it budded temptation in his mouth.
Now he had given up whistling on Sundays,
Attended prayer-meetings, added a concordance
To his wedding Bible and ten children
To the village population. He nudged the line,
Clean-pinafored and collared, glazed with soap,
Every seventh day of rest in Ebenezer;
Shaved on a Saturday night to escape the devil.

The sweetness of the apples worried him.
He took a branch of cooker from a neighbour
When he became a deacon, wanting
The best of both his worlds. Clay from the colliery
He thumbed about the bole one afternoon
Grafting the sour to sweetness, bound up
The bleeding white of junction with broad strips
Of working flannel-shirt and belly-bands
To join the two in union. For a time
After the wound healed the sweetness held,
The balance tilted towards an old delight.

But in the time that I remember him
(His wife had long since died, I never saw her)
The sour half took over. Every single apple
Grew – across twenty Augusts – bitter as wormwood.
He'd sit under the box-tree, his pink gums
(Between the white moustache and goatee beard)
Grinding thin slices that his jack-knife cut,
Sucking for sweetness vainly. It had gone,
Gone. I heard him mutter
Quiet Welsh oaths as he spat the gall-juice
Into the seeding onion-bed, watched him toss
The big core into the spreading nettles.

The Key

Its teeth worked doubtfully
At the worn wards of the lock,
Argued half-heartedly
With the lock's fixed dotage.
Between them they deferred decision.
One would persist, the other
Not relent. That lock and key

Were old when Linus Yale
Himself was born. Theirs
Was an ageless argument.

The key was as long as my hand,
The ring of it the size
Of a girl's bangle. The bit
Was inches square. A grandiose key
Fit for a castle, yet our terraced
House was two rooms up, two down;
Flung there by sullen pit-owners
In a spasm of petulance, discovering
That colliers could not live
On the bare Welsh mountain:

Like any other house in the domino
Row, except that our door
Was nearly always on the latch.
Most people just walked in, with
'Anybody home?' in greeting
To the kitchen. This room
Saw paths of generations cross;
This was the place to which we all came
Back to talk by the oven, on the white
Bench. This was the home patch.

And so, if we went out, we hid
The key – though the whole village
Knew where it was – under a stone
By the front door. We lifted up
The stone, deposited the key
Neatly into its own shape
In the damp earth. There, with liquid
Metal, we could have cast,
Using that master mould,
Another key, had we had need of it.

Sometimes we'd dip a sea-gull's
Feather in oil, corkscrew it
Far into the keyhole to ease
The acrimony there. The feather, askew
In the lock, would spray black
Droplets of oil on the threshold
And dandruff of feather-barb.
The deep armoreal stiffness, tensed
Against us, stayed. We'd put away
The oil, scrub down the front step.

The others have gone for the long
Night away. The evidence of grass
Re-growing insists on it. This time
I come back to dispose of what there is.
The knack's still with me. I plunge home
The key's great stem, insinuate
Something that was myself between
The two old litigants. The key
Engages and the bolt gives to me
Some walls enclosing furniture.

Certain Questions for Monsieur Renoir

Did you then celebrate
That grave discovered blue
With salt thrown on a fire
In honour of all blues?

I mean the dress of La Parisienne
(Humanly on the verge of the ceramic),
Blue of Delft, dream summary of blues,
Centre-piece of a fateful exhibition;

Whose dress-maker and, for that matter,
Stays-maker the critics scorned;
Who every day receives her visitors
In my country where the hard slate is blue.

She has been dead now nearly a century
Who wears that blue of smoke curling
Beyond a kiln, and blue of gentians,
Blue of lazurite, turquoise hauled

Over the blue waves, blue water, from Mount Sinai;
Clematis blue: she, Madame Henriot,
Whose papers fall to pieces in the files
In the vaults of the Registrar General.

Did you see in her garment the King of Illyria
Naming his person's flower in self-love?
And in the folds, part of polyphony
Of all colour, thunder blue,

Blue of blue slipper-clay, blue
Of the blue albatross? Blue sometimes
Without edge, blue liquified
By distance? Or did they start

Those ribbons at her wrists in blue
Of a sea-starwort? Or in verdigris, perhaps,
Blue on a Roman bead? Or in that regal blue
Of the Phœnicians, of boiled whelks;

That humbly-begun but conquering blue
Which, glowing, makes a god of man?
She who is always poised between appointments
For flirtation, what nuances of blue

Her bodice had, this blue you made
For your amusement, painter of fans and porcelain,
You set on gaiety; who saw, in the blue fog
Of the city, a candle burning blue

(Not heralding a death but) harbouring
A clear illusion, blue spot on the young salmon,
A greater blue in shadow; blue's calm
Insistence on a sense. Not for you

Indigo blue, or blue of mummy's cloth
Or the cold unction of mercury's blue ointment,
But the elect blue of love in constancy,
Blind, true blue; blue gage, blue plum,

Blue fibrils of a form, roundness
Absorbed by light, quintessence
Of blue beautiful. It was not blue
Tainted, taunted by dark. Confirm it.

The eyes are bells to blue
Inanimate pigment set alight
By gazing which was passionate.
So what is midnight to this midinette?

Ultramarine, deep-water blue?
Part of a pain and darkness never felt?
Assyrian crystal? Clouded blue malachite?

Blue of a blue dawn trusting light.

Ancient Monuments

(for Alexander Thom)

They bide their time off serpentine
Green lanes, in fields, with railings
Round them and black cows; tall, pocked
And pitted stones, grey, ochre-patched
With moss, lodgings for lost spirits.

Sometimes you have to ask their
Whereabouts. A bent figure, in a hamlet
Of three houses and a barn, will point
Towards the moor. You find them there,
Aloof lean markers, erect in mud.

Long Meg, Five Kings, Nine Maidens,
Twelve Apostles: with such familiar names
We make them part of ordinary lives.
On callow pasture-land
The Shearers and The Hurlers stand.

Sometimes they keep their privacy
In public places: nameless, slender slabs
Disguised as gate-posts in a hedge; and some,
For centuries on duty as scratching-posts,
Are screened by ponies on blank uplands.

Search out the farthest ones, slog on
Through bog, bracken, bramble: arrive
At short granite footings in a plan
Vaguely elliptical, alignments sunk
In turf strewn with sheep's droppings;

And wonder whether it was this shrunk place
The guide-book meant, or whether
Over the next ridge the real chamber,
Accurate by the stars, begins its secret
At once to those who find it.

Turn and look back. You'll see horizons
Much like the ones that they saw,
The tomb-builders, milleniums ago;
The channel scutched by rain, the same old
Sediment of dusk, winter returning.

Dolerite, porphyry, gabbro fired
At the earth's young heart: how those men
Handled them. Set on back-breaking
Geometry, the symmetries of solstice,
What they awaited we, too, still await.

Looking for something else, I came once
To a cromlech in a field of barley.
Whoever farmed that field had true
Priorities. He sowed good grain
To the tomb's doorstep. No path

Led to the ancient death. The capstone,
Set like a cauldron on three legs,
Was marooned by the swimming crop.
A gust and the cromlech floated,
Motionless at time's moorings.

Hissing dry sibilance, chafing
Loquacious thrust of seed
This way and that, in time and out
Of it, would have capsized
The tomb. It stayed becalmed.

The bearded foam, rummaged
By wind from the westerly sea-track,
Broke short not over it. Skirted
By squalls of that year's harvest,
That tomb belonged in that field.

The racing barley, erratically-bleached
Bronze, cross-hatched with gold
And yellow, did not stop short its tide
In deference. It was the barley's
World. Some monuments move.

Definition of a Waterfall

Not stitched to air or water but to both
A veil hangs broken in concealing truth

And flies in vague exactitude, a dove
Born diving between rivers out of love

In drums' crescendo beat its waters grow
Conceding thunder's pianissimo

Transfixing ancient time and legend where
A future ghost streams in the present air:

From ledge to pool breakneck across rocks
Wild calm, calm chaos skein their paradox

So that excited poise is fiercely dressed
In a long instant's constant flow of rest,

So that this bridegroom and his bride in white
Parting together headlong reunite

Among her trailing braids. The inconstancy
Is reconciled to fall, falls and falls free

Lament for a Leg

Near the yew tree under which the body of Dafydd ap Gwilym is buried in
Strata Florida, Cardiganshire, there stands a stone with the following
inscription: 'The left leg and part of the thigh of Henry Hughes, Cooper,
was cut off and interr'd here, June 18, 1756'. Later the rest of Henry
Hughes set off across the Atlantic in search of better fortune.

A short service, to be sure,
With scarcely half a hymn they held,
Over my lost limb, suitable curtailment.
Out-of-tune notes a crow cawed
By the yew tree, and me,
My stump still tourniqued,
Awkward on my new crutch,
Being snatched towards the snack
Of a funeral feast they made.
With seldom a dry eye, for laughter,
They jostled me over the ale
I'd cut the casks for, and the mead.
'Catch me falling under a coach',
Every voice jested, save mine,
Henry Hughes, cooper. A tasteless caper!
Soon with my only, my best, foot forward
I fled, quiet, to far America:

Where, with my two tried hands, I plied
My trade and, true, in time made good
Though grieving for Pontrhydfendigaid.
Sometimes, all at once, in my tall cups,
I'd cry in *hiraeth* for my remembered thigh
Left by the grand yew in Ystrad Fflur's
Bare ground, near the good bard.

Strangers, astonished at my high
Beer-flush, would stare, not guessing,
Above the bar-board, that I, of the starry eye,
Had one foot in the grave; thinking me,
No doubt, a drunken dolt in whom a whim
Warmed to madness, not knowing a tease
Of a Welsh worm was tickling my distant toes.

'So I bequeath my leg', I'd say and sigh,
Baffling them, 'my unexiled part, to Dafydd
The pure poet who, whole, lies near and far
From me, still pining for Morfudd's heart',
Giving him, generous to a fault
With what was no more mine to give,
Out of that curt plot, my quarter grav
Good help, I hope. What will the great God say
At Dafydd's wild-kicking-climbing extra leg,
Jammed hard in heaven's white doorway
(I'll limp unnimble round the narrow back)
Come the quick trumpet of the Judgement Day?

Design for a Quilt

First let there be a tree, roots taking ground
In bleached and soft blue fabric.
Into the well-aired sky branches extend
Only to bend away from the turned-back
Edge of linen where day's horizons end;

Branches symmetrical, not over-flaunting
Their leaves (let ordinary swansdown
Be their lining), which in the summertime
Will lie lightly upon her, the girl
This quilt's for, this object of designing;

But such too, when deep frosts veneer
Or winds prise at the slates above her,
Or snows lie in the yard in a black sulk,
That the embroidered cover, couched
And applied with pennants of green silk,

Will still be warm enough that should she stir
To draw a further foliage about her
The encouraged shoots will quicken
And, at her breathing, midnight's spring
Can know new season as they thicken.

Feather-stitch on every bough
A bird, one neat French-knot its eye,
To sing a silent night-long lullaby
And not disturb her or disbud her.
See that the entwining motives run

In and about themselves to bring
To bed the sheens and mossy lawns of Eden;
For I would have a perfect thing
To echo if not equal Paradise
As garden for her true temptation:

So that in future times, recalling
The pleasures of past falling, she'll bequeath it
To one or other of the line,
Bearing her name or mine,
With luck I'll help her make beneath it.

ALISON BIELSKI
(b. 1925)

Token

extract from (*'Journey through a Stone Landscape'*)

walking this winter beach alone
over cold arcs of barren sand
I will give him a white stone

small universe to hold and own
rounded as time, within his hand
walking this winter beach alone

caught between ebb-tide's sobbing moan
and cliff grass leaping on green land
I will give him a white stone

harder than truth, colder than bone
or flesh, then he shall understand
walking this winter beach alone

that destiny's salt wind has thrown
this token down dark pebbled strand
I will give him a white stone

there is no heart in monotone
grey sea, sky, rock make no demand
walking this winter beach alone
I will give him a white stone

Intruder

That ragged vagabond, snow, brings
for company a shambling softness
worrying at white silent heels.

Snow leaves crystal litter, coughs
cracked icicles. Feathering glass,
he sneaks up doors, intrudes at windows.

Out of fields, he steals thin cattle,
trapping sheep in a cotton quilt;
counts up his killings in a whisper.

Departing in spring, with a sack of bulbs
bursting over his blackened shoulder,
he hobbles off to northern hills.

RAYMOND GARLICK
(b. 1926)

Note on the Iliad

Why are epics
always about
the anti-life
of a noble lout?

I sing Lely
who burnt no tower
but brought the sea-floor
into flower.

RAYMOND GARLICK

Imagine it –
the moment when
out of the
architectured fen

the polder surfaced
sleek as a whale
and still awash.
Then the last veil

of standing water
slides away.
Glistening land
like a wet tray

serves up its past,
wreck upon wreck
glazed in the sand
of this smooth deck:

like Ararat,
the antique shores
ride up again
ready for Noahs.

Now wheat ripples
where schooner and barque
thrashed down the waters
to ultimate dark –

avenued Holland
waves over plains
which twenty years back
rocked fishing-seines.

Hard to imagine
the North Sea floor
was where we picnic –
and even more

to imagine this:
a people at grips
with genesis
not apocalypse.

RAYMOND GARLICK

Still Life

A piece of forest
suddenly crashed
out of its place,
and a thicket flashed

into the sunlight
dazing its rush.
There it halted,
a ton of brush,

like an old hearthrug
raised with a roar
of sinew and breath
from the gunroom floor.

Then the head swings,
huge as a knout –
the sly pig's eyes
and anteater snout

perceiving you.
And in the husks
of cerebellum
behind the tusks

the proto-brain
flares like a crumb
of phosphorus.
Within this drum

of bristle and bone,
matted and male,
the forest itself
approaches the pale

of consciousness.
Brushwood and bark
thrust through the boar
to gouge their mark.

Stillness alone
can hold the door
against their surge,
can lock the law

that roots them down:
stillness alone
to reinforce
and match their own.

The flame flares out,
the law holds good.
The old boar wheels
back into the wood.

Capitals

Moscow,
like a Christmas-tree,
glisters on the linen snow.
Fabergé red stars filigree
the mast-high spires, glitter and flow
over the square's starched sea
below.

Madrid,
a fortress on a height,
chessboard of stone, a granite grid
lifted and spread to the lancing light
staring down from the sun's arched lid:
of Europe's cities knight
and Cid.

Dublin,
in a Yeatsian haze,
Liffey waters strong as gin,
back-streets like a Chinese maze,
and Trinity, a palanquin –
the Book of Kells ablaze
within.

And Rome,
the white and marble rose
of Europe, rising from the foam
of all the fountains art unfroze
from conduits in time's catacomb:
which in their spray disclose
the dome.

RAYMOND GARLICK

Paris,
and the Seine's long psalm
holding in parenthesis
hundred-tapered Notre Dame –
pavilion of the genesis
of joy, and heaven's calm
chrysalis.

And Bonn,
empalaced on the Rhine,
where Beethoven looked out upon
symphonic counties-palatine.
Over river, bridge and swan
that fierce gaze, leonine,
once shone.

Cardiff
swirls about the numb
and calm cube of its castle cliff:
rune of departed power for some
to others towers a hieroglyph
of sovereign power to come
if if.

And last,
sun-ambered Amsterdam –
the churning hurdy-gurdy's blast
chiming with carillon and tram:
canal and concrete here contrast
their tenses, and enjamb
the past.

Europe:
young Ap Iwan's yard,
Gruffydd Robert's vision's scope,
Morgan Llwyd's hoist petard:
source to which our ballads grope –
context, compass-card
and hope.

RAYMOND GARLICK

Map reading

Look north if you like:
Eryri, water, Kirkcudbright,
the fingers of the Arctic sun
feeling out gold on the white
plains of the pole's Klondyke.

Look south even more:
Cardiff, the Bridge, and beyond
the Summer Country, Europe
shimmering up from the pond
of the Manche like a solar shore.

The west is all right:
the sea, the Republic, the crash
and spin of the ocean, furlongs
of light; only then bulks the brash
American shore, and the night.

Best avoid the east:
below the Dyke it's getting dark
in the tangled, litter-blown
Greater London park
of Britain, deceased.

Anthem for Doomed Youth

(Abertawe, 22 Tachwedd 1971)

My hope is on what is to come.
I turn in anguish from the servile, dumb

present – from an indifferent people, shut
to justice, crouching in the heart's dark hut.

I turn to the future, to a Wales hung
with the names, like garlands, of today's young.

Outside the court the three stood in the sun,
poised, at ease, in the soft chrysanthemum

light of Swansea, the bitter city. They
alone knew freedom on that icy day.

Policemen, advocates, recognised in those
the radiance of the uncorrupted rose

glowing above their court well's mantled scum.
Even the judge, that perched geranium,

saw it; and traded on it – to retail,
after the verdict, his unheard of bail,

honouring their integrity's claim
which he would deny when sentence came.

O unjust judge, mere expert in the sleight
of hand of law, do you sleep at night?

Be sure your victims sleep sounder than you
in the bitter place you condemned them to.

And you, Mr. Secretary of State,
setter up of committees, what fate

have the history books in store for you,
who can watch while the young are spitted through?

who can wait on a touring troupe's report
while conscience is crucified in court?

My rhyme tolls for you all, beats its slow drum.
My hope is on what is to come.

Ancestors

William Oliver maker
of winnowing machines, John Wood
labourer, in the fields of
the eighteenth century. You are good
forefathers for a man to have.
You might have understood

my making with words, my zest
for earth and spade. William Beere
tea merchant, savouring the joke.
And William Garlick, pioneer
of that name in Wales, who long
ago committed me here.

But of them all, the humble names
in the registers, I think of you
Nicholas Garlick, martyr,
and Derby Bridge your rendezvous,
in the armada year, with light.
You were an extremist too.

The Poetry of Motion

To see the Moscow-bound express withdraw
from Amsterdam; imperial, remote,
intent as a risen tsar returning
incognito. The destination boards,
in Latin and Cyrillic scripts, intone
a litany of cities: brown Berlin,
white Warsaw, and magnificent below
the dawns of three days' journeying, Moscow.

I once went to Italy
the whole way by wagon-lit,
Arnhem-Milan, on the Rome
express: its cabin a home
from home, inviolate cell
on that serpentine hotel
gliding through Europe. No one
but the steward and the sun
disturbed me for two whole days.
Washed by seas of light and haze
Germany and Switzerland
unfolded, flowered, to be scanned
by the wide picture-window –
whose flashing mirror, or glow
at sunset, signalled them peace,
wonder, and a heart at ease.

And then the Hoek, when the night-boat
slides in at dawn, and all those great
expresses stand – the *Lorelei*,
the *Scandinavie* and the rest,
like horizontal rockets poised
for count-down, lift-off, flawless launch;
waiting for some arch-guard to fire
the touchpaper and then retire
immediately as off we flare.

I think too of a tired express
that campaigned all day round Navarre
and Aragon and Old Castile
until, like an exhausted Cid,
at last it stumbled on Madrid.

But it's the old *Welshman* that I recall
from that steaming railway age best of all –
mid-morning train from antique Euston's drear
Abandon-hope-all-ye-who-enter-here
style of décor. Luncheon served about Crewe –
by the discobolus waiter who threw
in perfect parabola a full plate
of consommé when the train, a little late,
moved injudiciously. And after
these delights, Mr. Hughes Stationmaster
in rosebud, neatly furled, and yachting cap
waiting to welcome you (against the lap
of sea on the down platform) in the sails
of his regatta'd speech, home to Wales.

JOHN TRIPP
(*b.* 1927)

Diesel To Yesterday

There is downpour, always,
    as the carriages inch into Newport:
perhaps six times in ten years
    of a hundred visits to custom,
the entry to my country is uncurtained
    by rain or mist. I look
at the shambles of sidings and streets,
    the rust of progress and freight wagons,
the cracked façades of bingo cinemas.
    Sometimes I expect to see
the callous peaked caps and buttons
    of visa-checkers, cold sentries
on a foreign border, keeping out the bacillus
    in hammering rain and swirling fog.
Often I wish it were so, this frontier sealed
    at Chepstow, against frivolous incursion
from the tainting eastern zones.

Patience vanishes with frayed goodwill
   at the sight of the plump bundles
tumbling into Wales.
   They bring only their banknotes
and a petrol-stenched lust for scenery
   to shut in their kodaks,
packing out the albums of Jersey
   and the anthill beaches of the south.
They stand in line for pre-heated grease
   in the slums of crumbled resorts,
nose their long cars into pastureland
   and the hearts of ancient townships
that now are buried under chromium plate.

I catch myself out in error, feel
   ignoble in disdain.
The bad smell at my nostril
   is some odour from myself –
a modern who reeks of the museum,
   not wanting his own closed yesterday
but the day before that,
   the lost day before dignity went,
when all our borders were sealed.

Welcome To Wales

You drive in across this bridge they've built
or sleep through the railway tunnel
or step from a shaky plane on the coast.
The roads are quite modern, and the beer
is warm and generally flat.
The clocks keep the same time as Surbiton.

Our places of worship are more numerous
than the crumbling pubs, but their thin congregations
stay in bed. We have no
monopoly of compassion, but believe
no distance is too excessive
from a cold heart. Our schools
are full of children, and our seats of learning
turn out the usual quota of misfits.

Among the ancient customs, buttering-up tourists
is not one, so beware of the remnant of pride
hanging in corners. If you prick us,

we shall surely bleed. Here you can buy
what you purchase in Selfridges
and cut a small notch in your wallet for every snip.
There are plenty of bogus Tudor
expense-account restaurants; the hotels bulge
with rugby players, their supporters still happily dissecting
a try scored in 1912.
You will feel at home in the petrol fumes.

Our women are full and bloomy,
real women. Our girls
shuttle nicely in micro skirts.
(They are always a shock to the stranger.)

Our complaint is apathy, which would not
interest the visitor hungry for landscape.
We are not sure who we are, but the search
goes on. Experts fly in from abroad
to write big books about us,
to tell us who we are.
There's a splendid ritual in August
(swot up on the language first)
and singing high in the north
(book well in advance for your beds)
when the world comes rattling in motor cars
to our separate doorstep. You can eat
delicious flat cakes that are griddle-baked
and copy some recipes discovered in Caesar's time.
But our special flair is confusion: we have trouble
with our souls, and this could be tedious
if you bog yourself down in discourse
with local philosophers. On benches
in village squares, the very old
                              keep chiselling memories.

But make no mistake, and mark this well:
we do not sell ourselves cheap,
or short, despite what the experts say.

Eglwys Newydd

The village is straddled on both sides
of a main road. Sometimes it shakes
from heavy transport and rock blasting.
A shabby brook runs through it,

mossed blue slate and cheapjack granite
of functional dwellings, crumbling since Victoria.
The most terrible accent in Wales
ends here, and the authentic one begins a mile away
in Tongwynlais. The pubs are full of silence.
Oliver Cromwell spent a night in a house
that is now a greengrocer's.
                       It is one of those zones
for D.P.s between England and Wales,
a Gaza Strip where nobody belongs.
If you asked them how their search
for identity was getting on, they'd look blank
or say you needed certifying
in the asylum up the road.
                       It is one of the settlements
Rowland Lee would have praised,
being cleared of swarthy troublemakers
and neutered of Welshry. Dic Penderyn
would have yawned his head off.
                       Loyalty to the crown
hangs in pastry and sweet shops
when the ladies and gentlemen come
to open things. Controversy is swept with fag-ends
into the gutter.
                       I don't know why I live here.
I have been wating a long time
for my visa to Tongwynlais.

Capital

This will be the last ditch to fall
to the swing of its country.
Significance blowing down the hills
dies on the wind. Here the puffed
clink in their chains of office,
and the hagglers squat like a junta.

It is still as separate as an arm
lopped from its body: a strange sleeve
of territory spilled across the border.
What time has so carelessly mixed
clots here, where the ideals sag
and roots sprout only on the surface.

As long as I remember, the droll warmth
of its people has blurred
when our flag is lifted. Mouths are stitched.
Nothing is put to close scrutiny;
a knotted topic is flicked
into the bin, with a grin for Wales.

But now, in the distance, I think I hear
the young villagers build our future,
laying the first bricks of change.
This capital means less to them
than the land, where everything stems.
'Wait,' they are saying. 'Wait for us.'

On My Fortieth Birthday

When I was forty the stocktaker came
to take stock. He was dressed in black
like that old advertisement for Sandeman's port.
Let me see your books, he said.
I blew the dust off my ledgers
and showed him the blank pages.
These are nothing but blank pages, he said.
Are you trying to be whimsical?
He had the flat voice that BBC announcers use
when they describe calamity.
My plans are still maturing, I said,
I am on the point of doing something important.
An old lady in Port Talbot likes two of my poems
and she's ordered two copies for the library.
I am piling my rubbish against oblivion,
stacking it against the dark.
If you go up to Aberystwyth
you'll find my name misspelt in the dust.

He looked at me in contempt
right through to the lack of backbone.
Yes, he said, but what have you *done*?
What have you actually done with your lovely life?
Well, I said, it's like this...
I groped for the cudgelled album
where the corpses were kept.

Outside was the switchyard, with the expresses
coming at one another from all directions.
I hadn't heard a bird around here for years.
Loneliness came down like a lid.

I'll be back, old Sandeman said,
you'd better get those pages filled...

Headmaster

Now, thirty years on, I shift
nervously in respect, perhaps slur
my speech on the tavern court.
He is still formidable.

Under his arm is the fat
original Gibbon in faded red boards,
savoured with a wall-length stock
at his widower's villa.

He has a stick, and his limbs
are frailed and bent, but the awed clock
could stop in his Star Chamber
long back when he told me

I could amount to something, or
nothing. How many callow bluecoats
passed his window into the grey
mixer beyond? He saw them run

towards it, without literature
or history. Sometimes I think
his kind of iced wisdom is best –
the goodness of sad reason.

Fidgeting there, trying hard to account
for the locust, my chronicle bulges
to impress him. As I skulk off,
his example makes it seem nothing.

In Memory of Idris Davies
(for Glyn Jones)

He was short and sturdy, one of dim Picton's Silurians –
dark, tough, stocky, thick-necked and durable,
bantam of a race that went down before the blond Celts,
then packed the pits and Big Seats and choirs and scrums.
When you saw him in a drizzle on the Capitol steps

he wore a cloth cap, wool muffler, gloves and brown mac
with old wire specs askew, mended on wet-look solder,
one pebble-lens flattened tight to the eyeball.
He held his collier's Woodbine in the cup of his wounded hand,
easy and serene, without sulk or boiling mouth.

Rhymney and poverty made him. He was haunted to the very end
by the skull of want and the furious gospel
lashed from the radical pulpits. Green dawns of childhood
by the river and black alp, dust-hung summer afternoons
among nettles in the pityard with the lost ragged boys
led him and them to the customary crawl
under the earth, along the seams of Gwent,
thin layer of grime washed off into the evening tub.
Then the long lonely track to shape himself,
the bitter chronicle beginning to itch inside his mind.

Out of such parched soil, such pitiless rock
his harsh plant grew. No document was ever carved before
from this slab of ferocity and love –
a wept lament for all those diggers in the dark
and their broken kin, abandoned in the tunnels of the south,
a testament of disgust drilled at the core of wrong.
He never served an image of moonlit brooks
or salmon-running streams, or blue remembered hills.
His was a bedded landscape of human figures
bent but proud before a random wind.

Memory must have plagued him like a pox
as his exiled heart was shuttled about England,
as honesty tested his acceptance
through the soft quilted ease of Bohemia.
In the staff-rooms of mouldering schools,
what remark could have triggered a vision
that shot him straight back to his bleakest ridge?
In those gay nights of bellowing talk,
did the turnkey suddenly slide in his greasy coat
to show him the ramshackle beauty of Wales?

Stripped, bare, stark and pure the lyrics come,
hard and lovely as the place that formed him,
true as the tribute to his ravaged land.

DOUGLAS PHILLIPS

His goodness seeps down the years to remind us
of faith to be kept in the ruins. His last limp
over the mountain road, his suit hung loose on the frail bones,
will take him south again to the buttercup fields,
to the dream in the vale when he was young.
Your sad bells of Rhymney ring sweet and clear, Idris,
and the pigeons are homing. They are coming home.

JOSEPH P. CLANCY
(b. 1928)

Miscarriage

Friendship's folly, to utter
Strained words to your numbstruck face,
A worse thing, to be driven
To make verse by a friend's grief.

Let me not, if it must out,
Pretend to a true mourning,
Parade as if it mattered
A sorrow that's second hand.
What can I, this bleak springtime
That chilled buds, spilled more than blood
Know of this, not the simple
Anguish of an infant's death,
But hope's annihilation,
A loss without face or name,
A barren advent, a love
Still as a fallen nestling?

Not born of grief, this poem,
Not born of grief but of guilt
In my too great good fortune
And fear of tomorrow's cross.

DOUGLAS PHILLIPS
(b. 1929)

Maridunum

(The excavation of the Roman settlement in Carmarthen)

History hibernates here.
Beside this hedge, pregnant with hawthorn,
Earth's sleep is ending.
The grass of centuries is mown,
Soil pared more delicately than rosewood shavings,

- 269 -

Spades incised through clay and soft shale,
Seeking the faintly-perceptible outline of the past,
A fading copy, as elusive as inscriptions
On ancient parchments.

These are the cerements
Of a civilisation whose high tide flowed
From the world's middle sea
To this distant and outcast coast,
Leaving, when it ebbed, a few remains,
Sherds, tiles, coins,
Like shells and pebbles on receding shores.

Now the past reveals its fragrance
As herbs distil sweetness in a pomander,
Layer on layer of leaves and petals
Delicately aromatic,
Nestling in the enfolded strata of the earth.

Or like a paperweight
With roses inwrought
In its crystal calyx,
Preserving a perfection
Which time cannot shade.

Here we look through the glass of air
At the exposed soil,
And sense, beneath the roots of grass and flowers,
No musty fibres
Of withered relics,
But the warm arteries of a restored life.

BRIAN MORRIS
(b. 1930)

Dinas Emrys

They do not talk of Myrddin on the bridge at Beddgelert.
Words trickle over rocky lips – of fatstock, sheepdogs,
    the great fire
At Capel Curig. The bell-mouth of Llywelyn's faithful
    hound
Makes sweeter music in the tills.
                                            Leave it to educated men

ANTHONY CONRAN

Up the road, over the hill, in Caernarfon, another country,
To assign to shadowy Vortigern, Ambrosius (Emrys) and
The red and white dragons, by the pool, in the cave, under
    the hill,
Their *motifs* in the *Index of Folk-tales*. That old, stiffened
    legend
Is irrecoverably dead. No mileage in it. Not like Gelert.

The Swiss-clean cut rosebuds in every cottage kitchen
Flourished on a rich rotted compost of old Welsh lies.
As well one myth as another, tastes change, time and tide...
The Glaslyn chuckles by, nudging St. Celert's buried ribs,
Ambling through the pass to the capacious sea's lovely lap.
We are a gentle people, given to charity and abstinence.

ANTHONY CONRAN
(b. 1931)

Elegy for Sir Ifor Williams
(Englyn unodl union a englyn lleddfbroest)

Does a word as a widow in the brain
On the broad page of woe
Make outcry, sigh for him so
To sere an old heart's sorrow?

At a loss is Taliesin – the Black Book
Is bleak, and Aneirin;
On a bed where learning's been
The ravens take their ravin.

Sea-eagles feed at midday;
Too soon they peck at sinew;
Kite, crow and hawk make outcry;
Claws upon red flesh they cloy.

Where is Cynddylan's ransom – or Heledd's –
To make hale his wisdom?
As deep as the tongue is dumb
The drab dust keeps his custom.

At Catraeth troops took outrage – with the dawn
They died for the mead wage:
The quarrier of their courage
Lies raw to the Slayer's rage.

Three hundred, dead in a day, went warriors
Into war on foray:
We mind upon this Monday
What he was is locked away.

Death of a Species

Talk of old families – last remains
Of booted squires, generals, bishops.
A doddering aunt or two, a son
Not now distinguished from more common clay,
And here a daughter, though of a bastard line,
Shows in her tossing curls some hint
Of a too irksome nobility, long since
Defunct. A maiden aunt confesses
That in her youth her father (by all accounts
As fond a scholar as ever wrote bad verse)
Had tried to give her
Insight into wayward beauty, churches,
Manuscripts that garnered
Centuries for harvest – into rare
And lovely citadels he tried to bring her!
Boredom, dry dust, sad distraction then
From the gay world. She sighs, it is so late
Now, at this wilting time, to have to learn
These things...

       Talk of old families:
Among the teacups flowing into me
My ancestors! The tundra settles.
Huge snow against the wide plain blows.
Wool on my mammoth back stiffens with icicles
And wearily my awkward trunk gropes for mere moss
And my enormous knees kneel into sharp mud.

A million years from now, Siberian merchants
Collect at trading stations my dark white tusks.

Fledgling
(for Anna Daniel)

Dark speckle, half with down, half feathered,
A stump tail sprouted,
Wren fledgling sat in the road,
Its flying just started.

Shut resolute eyes had achieved
Two feet of flight;
It was too tired with that glory
To feel any fright.

Blind tyre of a car might roll
And rub out the fear
Of a world just glimpsed, just learnt,
If we left it here.

I like the clumsiness of honest mercy
With which you stoop
To free those incredibly long toes
From the road's grip.

How another girl would dance
In the picking it up –
Hold it to her like a babe,
Ladybird, buttercup!

But I'm relieved you do not make it yours
Like a casual thief:
Gravely you show it me, gravely lay it down
Into private green leaf.

GLORIA EVANS DAVIES
(b. 1932)

Holly Gone

Holly gone I discover
Commercially picked for wreaths;
Still searching
I turn this way and that in the deep snow
A puppet pulled by the breaking strings of the old year,
My eyes wet paint.

The freezing day
Cracks into mountain range after mountain range,
And the wind swears like a parrot on my shoulder.

HERBERT WILLIAMS
(*b.* 1932)

The Old Tongue

We have lost the old tongue, and with it
The old ways too. To my father's
Parents it was one
With the *gymanfa ganu,* the rough
Shouts of seafarers, and the slow
Dawn of the universal light.
It was one with the home-made bread, the smell
Of cakes at missionary teas,
And the shadows falling
Remotely on the unattempted hills.

It is all lost, the tongue and the trade
In optimism. We have seen
Gethsemane in Swansea, marked
The massacre of innocents. The dawn
Was false and we invoke
A brotherhood of universal fear.
And the harbour makes
A doldrum of the summer afternoon.

Even the hills are diminished.
They are a gallon of petrol,
There and back. The old salts
Rot. And the bread
Is tasteless as a balance sheet.

Oh yes, there have been gains.
I merely state
That the language, for us,
Is part of the old, abandoned ways.

And when I hear it, regret
Disturbs me like a requiem.

Like Father?

An urbane man, composed, aware.
Executive. Hair
Trimmed, like his opinions.
Smooth as paste.

A person to your taste?
You may prefer
Some others of his clan:
His father, Glyn,
A terror of a man,
Or Uncle Huw,
The Lenin of Fochriw.

They boozed and swore,
And played unholy war
With boss and scab.

So there he sits, the mob
Within his blood.

Pretending he's a lord.

BRYAN ASPDEN
(b. 1933)

News of the Changes

He wears Clarks Movers, his new shoes,
And carries papers to the typing pool,
The section's outmost chamber where
They press him for juice from the centre.
He tells them Colin's here and has made
A Maginot Line of cabinets and trays;
That Maureen's firm and will not move to Legal;
That John Morris the translator
Has changed rooms and taken his kettle.
Sweetened with news they loose him and he goes
Back to his office, where Llew's arrived to toy
With screens and arrows, bilingual signs—all the godwottery
Of order; until the morning's leaked away, and it's time
For sandwiches, and then his lunch hour walk.

He goes past the Pier Pavilion,
The Grand Hotel, The Pier, Happy Valley,
Alex Munro's open-air follies,
The Druids' Circle, the cable car station,
Queen Victoria in her stone pagoda,
Alice, and the White Rabbit, down the steps
To the beach. The tide's coming in. An oystercatcher

Scissors at its edge, and turnstones
Are dabbling their toes in its paper doilies.
As the rocks go under, barnacles
Unbuckle their shells and feed with their feet.
The waves revise their tenses, their soft mutations:
"Ll—", they say coming in; "L—", going out.

At two o'clock he returns to the Town Hall,
To his desk, and the silt of years clogging his in-tray;
Minutes of sub-committess; dictionaries, forms;
Sonnets; Catalan Grammar; *The Way to Write*.
He's done well from the changes. Is a senior fish
In the local government swim. Others
Are left dry and they complain—
Why should they work the word processor,
Learn floppy discs and software on MO1?
These bubbles of displacement stir
The shallows of the afternoon. He's had enough.
He clocks out early, escapes into the car park.
The Mini that he slipped a disc in's gone.
He drives home in the Mazda past Ffon Tom.

JON DRESSEL
(b. 1934)

You, Benjamin Jones

You, Benjamin Jones, dead seventeen
years of a weak chest and mill-dust
before I was born, known by me

through the passioned prisms of your
wife and daughter, my 'mamgu' and
mother; I could never pronounce the

Welsh, she became 'Mimi'...imagine, a
Puccini heroine from Llanelli, and her,
from middle years on, always close

to fifteen stone, though in the small gilt
wedding picture on my wall she is
lovely as Olwen resurrected

Victorian...and you, dashing as all
get-out in that wing-collar and brave
moustache; why in God's name did you

come to America, why did you come
to Pennsylvania to discover greed, get
mad, join the union, grub through strikes,

get scabbed, hymn your way west, losing
jobs, leading choirs, fathering eisteddfodau?
why? I found your trunk in Illinois, in a

cellar, the ivory baton, the warped books, the
Welsh words, strange beneath floodstains;
what drove you there, to the prairie, the

Mississippi, to die in 1918, forty-seven,
your cariad, your mortgage, five children at
your side? you sang The Star-Spangled Banner

as your eyes glazed, they said; God, no, Duw,
Arglwydd Dduw, I say, at dusk in this house
in Llansteffan's green October, what do I

know of you, of ash-blown grief, Benjamin Jones?

Dai, Live

Prytherch is dead. We have no right
to doubt it, let alone dispute. We must
contend with men we have in sight,

like Dai here, who is clean
as dirt. The rumor in the pub
is that he hasn't been seen

out of that ripening outfit
since the Investiture. It may
be a form of protest, though it

seems more likely, ten pints down,
he's just too whipped to shuck that
wind-grey coat, every button gone,

peel those frazzling sweaters, rife with him
and earth, lest those grime-stiff trousers
fall, or try to fall, before things dim.

Too whipped, perhaps, to kick those mud-
brindled boots to a corner, or toss
that crust of a cap to a bed-

post, if he has one. No farmer, Dai,
he digs around the village, roads,
sewers, God knows what, digs all day,

digs everywhere, turns up pints,
grubs of coins for the slot, studies men
who commute to Carmarthen, nods, squints,

grunts a little rugby, weathers at his end
of the bar like a cromlech, drones
like the surf when those with more voice bend

the last elbow in hymn, leaves alone
with a gutteral wave, boulders into night,
a man-shape hulking like an age of stone,

that knows no women, but lives with what it knows,
hard as breath, or a December rose.

The Drouth

A friend, a poet, wrote me near the end
of summer there had been a drouth
in Wales; hoarding for the roses,

water off between ten and six, things
like that; I hardly believed it,
it seemed like news of a blizzard

in Death Valley, but he spoke
dry truth; two weeks of sun in Sept-
ember, sails blazing on the Tywi,

reading in a garden warm with stone,
going barefoot like we'd never left
Missouri; Christ, I said, if this

holds we'll be breaking out the mandolins,
taking siestas on the dike, drinking ouzo,
pinching girls' behinds at the market;

of course it didn't; today the rain
drives in from sea as dense as Cal-
vin's breath, as a five-sharp hymn; only

the very close is green, slate
interposes, windows fog, the wind
tests every crevice and the land,

Welsh land, is wet, dissenting, glad.

Let's Hear It For Goliath

who never asked
to be born
either, let alone
grow nine feet

tall and wind
up a metaphor;
fat chance he
had of avoid-

ing the shove
from behind;
his old man
no doubt gave

him a sword
to teethe on,
and a scout
for the Philistine

host probably
had him under
contract by
the end of

junior high;
it was a fix;
and who wouldn't
have cursed

at the sight
of that arr-
ogant runt with
the sling, who,

for all his
psalms, would later
buy one wife
with a hundred

bloody pecker-
skins, and another
with a King's X
on Uriah; bah,

let's hear it
for Goliath, a big
boy who got
bad press but

who did his job,
absorbed a flukey
shot, and died
with a thud.

SAM ADAMS
(b. 1934)

Hill Fort, Caerleon

From this tree-finned hill
Breasting the breeze –
Leaf shadows like water shifting,
Sounds of water always moving
In the preening of so many leaves –
I can look down over old Caerllion.

In the aqueous rush of bracken fronds
Breaking round, and in a sound

Clearer now, once heard,
An unbroken hum
Like some instrument endlessly strummed
On one low note, or the tone

Of wires looped from pole
To pole vibrating through wood
Where we pressed our ears,
There is a sense of something living,
Breathing, watching here
As I push towards the rampart mound.

The path is blocked. A swarthy
Sentry bars my way, his spear-
Tip sparks with sunlight.
He challenges in accents I know well;
The words I recognise, but the sense eludes.
I am ashamed and silent. He runs me through.

Sliding

Do you remember the ritual of candle-wax,
The lanes of rubbed grass pale-gold like flax?
Do you remember how we used to slide,
Sharing the cardboard, down the mountainside,
You with your slim girl's thighs spread wide
Accommodating my narrow loins? Your hands
Held fast my summer shirt,
And when the ride began
You pressed your head against my back
And bit my shoulder till it hurt.

Do you recall the gasping flight
As the cardboard swished down the narrow track?
There were jarring bumps when your legs clung tight,
And I thrilled
At your light cries
Though I couldn't see for the dust in my eyes.
Too soon, too soon the final thump
Left us sprawled and stilled
At the foot of the tump.

Can you, in your mind's eye,
See us fly? –
Watch us, falling, die?

PETER GRUFFYDD

(*b.* 1935)

Digging Soil

I must feel this soil again
How it clutches with wet grasp
The arches of my boots
Sucks shine into the steel spade
Sinks brown pigment into my fingers

And is, in its volcanic universe
Of feeding life, mine, my blood
And sinew, giver and taker
Mother and whore to my flesh
Dark design of earth's skin
And a dry mystery in summer.

See it take rain until sogged
Grass can swig no more
And the apple tree glistens
With caves of light
Through flaking clouds:
Then soil resumes its drouth
An eternal itch in its myriad wombs.

Slate Quay: Felinheli

1

This will go too, this curve of shore
Which, bending the tangled Straits,
Looks over at fields that bulge smoothly
Under the folded church of Llanfairisgaer.

Today a brown clout of mist rushes
Over the grey, brawling waters.
The trees bow in anticipation
Curled by the wind's clinical hands
For the sudden drilling rape of rain
On their pale-bellied leaves.

Here, in this village which is asleep
And has not awoken for hundreds of years,
On its blue and grey quayside
Swept of slate piles and inhabited
Now by tatty dogs, lone walkers
The strident gulls and suave
Motor-cruisers, the lives of men
Sing in moist air and the spirit
Of human life wanders, inconsolable,
Pitting a faded emphasis against the end.

2

The small dog which ran, paused, poised
Pissed on a bollard then tracked on swiftly
Has it all his own way.
The bridge waits for the axe
The locks leak and spurt
The arrogant yachts bump the wall
And look as if it were not there.

An old woman calls the dog which, deaf,
Maps out again its world of odours.

Two times are here but one will conquer
As the sleepwalking people
Twitch obediently to their till's song.

SALLY ROBERTS JONES
(b. 1935)

Community

(Mr. Rogers, buried April 26, 1972)

There has been a death in the street.
Drawn curtains, collection for wreaths –
The historians call it Cymortha,
Assume that it vanished
In the steam of industrial birth.

We're the size of a village: forty houses,
A shop. Over fences the women gossip,

Watch weddings and growings – observe
The proper and ritual tact
Of those who must live with their kin.

No blood ties, it's true; our bonds
Are accent and place – and desire
For much the same ends. We are not
Political animals; held
An Investiture feast for the children,

And praised all that pomp. On Sundays
Expediency pegs out the washing:
If God is not mocked – well, He knows us ·
I suppose it was like this before
When Piety lay in the clouds, an oncoming thunder.

There has been a death in the street;
We are less by that much. Statistics
Cannot say what we lose, what we give:
Questionnaires for the Welfare Department
Tell industrious lies.

We adapt. To the chimneys, the concrete,
The furnace, the smoke, the dead trees.
Our fields are the names of roadways,
Our flocks and our language are gone:
But we hold our diminished city in face of the sun.

New World

In these neat boxes
The print of the Chinese woman
Is a world of culture.

Where is Aneirin now?
Or even that hippy, ap Gwilym?

Upstairs in their Swedish bunk beds
The statistical couple
Dream deeply of Yogi Bear and plastic ice-cream;

Below, in his hall, Cynddylan,
Roaring at 'Steptoe',
Waits for a double-bedtime;

Grandmother Heledd
Mourns, in a distant city,
Her long-dead kin.

The Gododdin are out on strike,
Rhiannon's at Bingo –
The *Sunday Times* reveals that Brân was a Jute.

In these cities of concrete egg-crates
There's no room for Pryderi:
The legends are all tucked up
In the old folks' Home.

Ann Griffiths

In little time I stake my claim
To all the panoply of fame.
My words are air, their manuscript
Forgetful flesh, a bony crypt
To lay these stillborn creatures in.

This foolishness of light intent
I turn to praise, my patterns meant,
Poor gift, for Him by whose free gift
My life is bought; the seasons sift
Away my youth, my fear, my sin.

The fire upon my hearth is tame,
God's gentle creature; now my name
Is signed in polished oak and brass,
My soul is singing, clear as glass,
Pure as this babe I bear within.

My songs as light as ash are spent;
My hope's elsewhere, a long descent
In flesh and land – and yet the air
Stirs with fresh music, calls me where
Intricate webs of words begin.

Lord, let me not be silent till
All earth is grinding in Your mill!

Illusions

We share this: that vanishing figure,
Morfudd or Dyddgu
(The name does not matter)
Who fades in the mist,
Dried spring of a flowing song.

These must be always beyond us:
Fulfilment would offer
Only a crust of dry bread.

Like Gwion's strange theft they enchant us:
We live in the wind, in the mist,
With the gull's eye see
Perfections minute as a sand grain –
What is Morfudd in this?
A lens or a burning mirror,
No more.
                    Till at length we may learn
To look past the image, accepting
The bread of our lives.
And then, that the rite in the woods
Is one with the words
That bind in the granite church:
That duty is freedom – that all
Abstractions are flesh at the last,
And 'Morfudd' as much
In the servant girl trysted and lost
As in Bwa Bach's wife.

The fountain is always beyond us. We need
The clear stream, not the muddy source,
The dream, not the dawn.

PETER PREECE
(b. 1936)

Cormorant

Later, a cormorant,
oil-black,
came up-wind
and stood on air;

he found and touched down
on a known rock,
settling through feather
spread and shake,
through folding wings,
posing in the manner
of a man at arms.

Black upon white,
cresting now that
guano-spattered rock,
master of ceremonial,
shifting feet on bits
of carapace and bone,
he scanned this corner
of his instinct feeding zone.

When hungry,
he was seen to dive,
dip down,
neck-twist, body-pull
splaying feet to thrust
him to his hunt;
then snap back
sharply into
surface air.

All this might well
continue
for a reasonable time,
if a death-black
man-made oil slick
doesn't coat his days
with slime.

GILLIAN CLARKE
(b. 1937)

Blaen Cwrt

You ask how it is. I will tell you.
There is no glass. The air spins in
The stone rectangle. We warm our hands

GILLIAN CLARKE

With apple wood. Some of the smoke
Rises against the ploughed, brown field
As a sign to our neighbours in the
Four folds of the valley that we are in.
Some of the smoke seeps through the stones
Into the barn where it curls like fern
On the walls. Holding a thick root
I press my bucket through the surface
Of the water, lift it brimming and skim
The leaves away. Our fingers curl on
Enamel mugs of tea, like ploughmen.
The stones clear in the rain
Giving their colours. It's not easy.
There are no brochure blues or boiled sweet
Reds. All is ochre and earth and cloud-green
Nettles tasting sour and the smells of moist
Earth and sheep's wool. The wattle and daub
Chimney hood has decayed away, slowly
Creeping to dust, chalking the slate
Floor with stories. It has all the first
Necessities for a high standard
Of civilised living: silence inside
A circle of sound, water and fire,
Light on uncountable miles of mountain
From a big, unpredictable sky,
Two rooms, waking and sleeping,
Two languages, two centuries of past
To ponder on, and the basic need
To work hard in order to survive.

Lunchtime Lecture

And this from the second or third millenium
B.C., a female, aged about twenty-two.
A white, fine skull, full up with darkness
As a shell with sea, drowned in the centuries.
Small, perfect. The cranium would fit the palm
Of a man's hand. Some plague or violence
Destroyed her, and her whiteness lay safe in a shroud
Of silence, undisturbed, unrained on, dark
For four thousand years. Till a tractor in summer
Biting its way through the long cairn for supplies
Of stone, broke open the grave and let a crowd of light
Stare in at her, and she stared quietly back.

As I look at her I feel none of the shock
The farmer felt as, unprepared, he found her.
Here in the Museum, like death in hospital,
Reasons are given, labels, causes, catalogues.
The smell of death is done. Left, only her bone
Purity, the light and shade beauty that her man
Was denied sight of, the perfect edge of the place
Where the pieces join, with no mistakes, like boundaries.

She's a tree in winter, stripped white on a black sky,
Leafless formality, brow, bough in fine relief.
I, at some other season, illustrate the tree
Fleshed, with woman's hair and colours and the rustling
Blood, the troubled mind that she has overthrown.
We stare at each other, dark into sightless
Dark, seeing only ourselves in the black pools,
Gulping the risen sea that booms in the shell.

Foghorns

When Catrin was a small child
She thought the foghorn moaning
Far out at sea was the sad
Solitary voice of the moon
Journeying to England.
She heard it warn 'Moon, Moon',
As it worked the Channel, trading
Weather like rags and bones.

Tonight, after the still sun
And the silent heat, as haze
Became rain and weighed glistening
In brimful leaves, and the last bus
Splashes and fades with a soft
Wave-sound, the foghorns moan, moon-
Lonely and the dry lawns drink.
This dimmed moon, calling still,
Hauls sea-rags through the streets.

GILLIAN CLARKE

Hay-Making

You know the hay's in
when gates hang slack
in the lanes. These hot nights
the fallen fields lie open
under the moon's clean sheets.

The homebound road is
sweet with the liquors
of the grasses, air
green with the pastels
of stirred hayfields.

Down at Fron Felen
in the loaded barn
new bales displace
stale darknesses. Breathe.
Remember finding
first kittens, first love
in the scratch of the hay,
our sandals filled with seeds.

Ram

He died privately.
His disintegration is quiet.
Grass grows among the stems of his ribs,
Ligaments unpicked by the slow rain.
The birds dismantled him for spring nests.
He has spilled himself on the marsh,
His evaporations and his seepings,
His fluids filled a reservoir.
Not long since he could have come
Over the Saddle like a young moon,
His cast shadow whitening Breconshire.

The blue of his eye is harebell.
Mortality gapes in the craters of his face.
Buzzards cry in the cave of his skull
And a cornucopia of lambs is bleating
Down the Fan of his horns.
In him more of October than rose hips

And bitter sloes. The wind cries drily
Down his nostril bones. The amber
Of his horizonal eye
Is light on reservoir, raven
In winter sky. The sun that creams
The buzzard's belly as she treads air
Whitens his forehead. Flesh
Blackens in the scrolls of his nostrils,
Something of him lingering in bone
Corridors catches my throat.

Seeking a vessel for blackberries and sloes
This helmet would do, were it not filled
Already with its own blacks,
Night in the socket of his eye.

Suicide on Pentwyn Bridge

I didn't know him,
the man who jumped from the bridge.
But I saw the parabola
of long-drawn-out falling in the brown

eyes of his wife week after week
at the supermarket cash-out.
We would quietly ask 'How is he?'
hear of the hospital's white

care, the corridors between her
and the broken man in the bed,
and the doctors who had no words,
no common supermarket women's talk.

Only after the funeral
I knew how he'd risen, wild
from his chair and told her
he was going out to die.

Very slowly from the first leap
he fell through winter, through the cold
of Christmas, wifely silences,
the blue scare of ambulance,

from his grave on the motorway
to the hospital, two bridges down.
A season later in a slow cortège
he has reached the ground.

ALUN REES
(b. 1937)

My Father's Father

(Er côf am Ezekiel Rees, Heolgerrig)

Don't say that he grew old. No, it was more
a growing into time before time grew
into his limbs like blight in an apple tree.

He was full-seasoned, for in his sapling days
he had bent with the wind. So, in his autumn wisdom,
his strong limbs held the postures of the wind.

The years on him were like moss, and in his head
two eyes like fledglings wise beyond their years
hopped, skipped and sang on the branches of his days.

Say that he made a bargain with the seasons
that he would honour them in return for honour,
that he would grow into them, as natural as a tree.

Say this, and remember the gentleness of his hands
tending his garden, and understand why now
all the leaves of his strong body green his grave.

Harry the Black

Overcoated throughout what we called summer,
he was one of the sights of our unsightly town,
an exotic break in the clouds of commonplace day,
squat and strange and burned an alien brown.

There were stories: he was a slave who ran away,
or a tribal chief in exile. He was half-blind,
and his faraway eyes told nothing, save he was lost,
wandering somewhere the trackless plains of his mind.

Taking, outside the church, what sun would shine,
sometimes, wearily, he would raise that clouded head
as though appealing to a half-remembered god
to pump the sun to splendour. But instead

of equatorial comfort came we boys
delighted by signs of awareness, however small,
in that dark totem around which we worshipped mischief.
His troubled peace was scattered in our squall.

Moved to stick-shaking rage, he'd hiss wordless curses,
helpless to avenge the thoughtless tricks we played.
Safe in our landscape, we escaped to leave him
more squat, more brown, more lost and more afraid.

J. P. WARD
(b. 1937)

Every Single Night

I get into bed.
A man climbs carefully in
Through a hole in my head.

He sweeps out a pile
Of straw, and lies down. The moon
Illumines his smile.

He's filthily dressed –
A squashed bowler and striped
Butcher's trousers. A clown's almost?

His manner appears
To ignore (though perceiving)
My presence. Why me? Christ knows.

He sleeps soundly. We share
All I own – he the boards, me the blankets.
By dawn he's not there.

Does he hear me here, cursing the poor?
But I don't. . . They never occur
To my mind at all.

Does he think of me, tossing, awake
On his account? I can't
Answer. He doesn't speak.

Will he ever have reason to go?
No less than for coming – I'd
Have thought, though by nature, can't know.

What nature have I,
When a tramp's got the grind
Of the world in his own

Rotting skull, and sets up like a lord in mine?

Unusual View Of The Town

No population, roofs that move
Under a slime of rain, and streets
To be assumed, ·not seen, in spates
Of chimney-pots. A mat of roof
I'd love to walk across and reach
That dismal sea. The ocean's bash
Of waves allures the patent tiles.

No one is ever seen, high up.
And yet I reassure myself
On that, for staring from this shelf
Unites the town and makes its map
Large and affectionate. Roofs lie
Like furrows. Nowhere near as high
As where I stand, gulls scream and dive.

A sense of rest. Banally, beds
Occur to me, under those eaves
And undulating stacks. Are lives
Of consequence in there? Tired heads
In daytime, sex and school of days
Take distant gun-grey waves to erase
Their questioning. Or heal with salt.

I try to hear the indifferent
Long chord of hidden cars. Smoke mists
And wipes and vanishes like ghosts

Of Father Christmas letters burnt
By children, surely dreaming in
Those attics. Daily in dry or rain
The long scene alters. When I climbed

The terraced row above to turn
And stare back down, the roofs appeared
A fraction smaller, like a herd
That moves off timidly or when
A townsman comes. Below, there'd been
Tall gabled windows in between
Sharp gutters. Two more points of view.

To Get Clear

I knew, all the rest of my life,
that I had seen it, cumulatively,
because of staying until rested in that
simple place of trees and water, and a house
with willow-pattern plates; and the
black cat came in as I put down this,
and growled, sliding the steel-blue
shine of his black body in and out
like a snake, against the table-leg, and
miaouing, telling me of his adventures
in the garden, and demanding food
peremptorily. So I got up, in my jeans
and with the sleeves pushed up to the
forearm, as the fashion is, and poured
a little milk, which it licked, as
though an ice-cream, as though the milk
had a hard edge of matter, which in
a sense milk does. Matter to us now
is mystery of course, that is where
those thinkers of our new past have
taken us. Matter is so nearly eternal
life, as MacDiarmid said; matter is
mysterious, it speaks to us and is
also what we are. How can that be? How
should we know? And yet we know.
    Walking along the lane, I met a
man, and it was Anselm, returning to
talk to me. He said he had thought,

and thought, as though along a renewed
lane, to thought's end, and that end
is Thou, O Lord Our God. I said it seemed
he had changed the gear of his language
deftly, with his left hand turned
upward; he said it was deliberate,
and that the nettles' points
at the roadside had brushed him as he
got out of that car, and goaded him
into that understanding.

EVAN GWYN WILLIAMS
(b. 1938)

Day trip

Between the ship's side and the quay, a gap
That reaches down. You can hardly discern
   The water except for intermittent
   Loops of light that curl and turn
Along her bulk, while overhead the seagulls snap
The crumbs thrown by children. Soon I hear frequent
    Throbbings move the stern.

Mufflered and squinting through the air I see
The whole grow smaller from where I stand, detail
   Merge until the light on that
   One windowpane becomes frail,
And baffled by approximations am only free
To gaze across the distance, the dull, grey mud-flat,
    And feel the deck's taut iron rail.

What is familiar must recede, the still moment
Smelling of rain, dust, or furniture in low
   Rooms, the knowledge we retain
Of silence after love. I see sharp light
In waves flicker, eyes in your head: as you invent
Again the stirrings of a 'child': distance as pain
    Only, this grow closer now.

And soon, like history, the essential facts
Shall emerge, become isolated and cold upon
   That other shore: absolving flesh,
   All things which, even now, belong
To evenings where desire lingered between the acts
Of love. What, I venture, remains always fresh,
    Alive, the singer or the song?

Yet this day trip is just rehearsal for the fact
Of leaving. You know this, walking to your lecture,
  Or sitting drinking tea with friends,
  Always alone, afraid and unsure –
What is love but the removing of the mask, an act
Of pain? Across the water's face vision ends,
    And so I turn toward the cure.

Grand entertainments on the pier, mild release
From an enduring grind of producing steel –
  Illusion, and the clown's key
  To happiness before you reveal
The self's truth: Odysseus in the violent sea. For ease,
You know, comes only in your being Penelope
    Awhile, obeying what you feel.

JOHN IDRIS JONES
(b. 1938)

Barry Island

Between the Haunted House,
The sea-blue wall of the Big Dipper,
The fruit machines, the trinket stall,
And the sea,

Going round and round,
Its horses on poles ascending and descending,
Words circulating round its roof
Reading: *Here are*
the ever popular
stud of galloping
horses and flying birds
patronised and enjoyed
by all classes.

Circulating, circulating,
Poised, clear—
All classes—
That's it, that's it,
That's how life should be.

MEIC STEPHENS
(b. 1938)

Ponies, Twynyrodyn

Winter, the old drover, has brought
these beasts from the high moor's hafod
to bide the bitter spell among us,
here, in the valley streets.
Observe them, this chill morning, as
they stand, backsides against the wind,
in Trevithick Row. Hoofs, shod with ice,
shift and clatter on the stone kerb.
Steam is slavering from red nostrils,
manes are stiff with frost and dung.

Quiet now, last night
they gallivanted through the village,
fear's bit in teeth. Hedges were broken,
there was havoc to parked cars. Yet,
despite the borough council's by-laws,
these refugees are welcome here.
Fed from kitchen and tommybox, they
are free to roam the grit backlanes,
only kids and mongrels pester them.

We greet them as old acquaintances
not because they bring us local colour,
as the tourist guides might say, but
for the brute glamour that is with them.
Long before fences and tarmac, they
were the first tenants of these valleys,
their right to be here is freehold.

Now, in this turncoat weather, as
they lord it through the long terraces,
toppling bins from wet steps, ribs
rubbing against the bent railings,
our smooth blood is disturbed
by hiraeth for the lost cantrefi,
the green parishes that lie beyond
the borders of our town and hearts,
fit for nothing now but sad songs.

These beasts are our companions,
dark presences from the peasant past,
these grim valleys our common hendre,
exiles all, until the coming thaw.

Hooters

Night after night from my small bed
I heard the hooters blowing up and down the cwm:
Lewis Merthyr, Albion, Nantgarw, Ty-draw –
these were the familiar banshees of my boyhood.

For each shift they hooted, not a night
without the high moan that kept me from sleep;
often, as my father beyond the thin wall
rumbled like the turbines he drove at work, I

stood for hours by the box-room window,
listening. The dogs of Annwn barked for me then,
Trystan called without hope to Esyllt
across the black waters. Ai, it was their wail

I heard that night a Heinkel flew up
the Taff and its last bomb fell on our village;
we huddled under the *cwtsh*, making
beasts against the candle's light until the sky

was clear once more, and the hooters
sounded. I remember too how their special din
brought ambulances to the pit yard,
the masked men coming up the shaft with corpses

gutted by fire; then, as the big cars
moved down the blinded row on the way to Glyntâf,
all the hooters for twenty miles about
began to swell, a great hymn grieving the heart.

Years ago that was. I had forgotten
the hooters: my disasters, these days, are less
spectacular. We live now in this city:
our house is large, detached and behind fences.

I sleep easily, but waking tonight
found the same desolate clangour in my ears
that from an old and sunken level
used to chill me as a boy – the inevitable hooter

that paralyses with its mute alarm.
How long I have been standing at this window,
a man in the grown dark, only my wife
knows as I make for her white side, shivering.

Elegy for Mr. Lewis (Welsh)

Sir, I was your pupil for five years
but you taught me nothing, except to recite
that verse about a little woman who sold black sweets,
and how to count up to ten. Without a doubt
you must have been the worst teacher in our school.

You won't remember me. I was the boy, no
duffer, who sat anonymous through your dreadful classes
and was never asked a question, but who still
recalls the famous sarcasm and the ferocious stick
by which a generation came to fear you.

I wonder what made you such a monster:
was it, perhaps, some private, ineffable grief
that you took out on us? No, I don't mean cancer
nor your flighty wife who ran away with an accountant,
but the more malignant knowledge that, for us,

Welsh seemed as obsolete as Etruscan
that only farmers and a few fanatics spoke.
After all, what did Glyndwr or Pantycelyn have
to say to us whose heroes were alive and relevant?
We cheered our own in cinema and stadium.

It's no secret that you failed at the job;
but why, so often from my desk in the back row, did
I catch you staring across the valley, tears
in your eyes, at the shining hill above Eglwys Ilan?
Old bully, ranting forever in my memory,

you've been dead these twenty years. Well,
I speak and love the language now, no thanks to you;
so please allow me, late as usual but not far wrong,
to raise my hand for once and make this reply:
Cymro, I know what drove you to despair.

MEIC STEPHENS

Elegy for Llywelyn Humphries

Liquor, wages, automobiles, women, dope –
your gang ran all the rackets in town.
Chicago your sweet moll, Al Capone your boss,
as in the old films with grin and gun
you swaggered through the glittering twenties.

This morning, picking up a magazine, I
happen to come across your obituary: death
at seventy-six in San Quentin hospital,
quietly, delivered by the cop cancer.
The photo shows you prosperous and gentle,

like a priest or grandfather, the scars
a boxer's perhaps but surely no killer's.
How strange then to discover that, in your day,
you swindled the state of a cool million,
sent your kid brother to the chair

and, these last years in the penitentiary,
read books on bees and economics; still more,
that your family was known to be Welsh –
farmers from some remote and derelict bro
sweating for a new deal in America.

Ah, Llywelyn, you were one of us, man!
I recognise you now and all your crooked kind:
small timers, fugitives from your people's past,
you got on in the big-shot world, but
had to face that most solitary music in the end.

So take it easy when I can't help wondering
who you might have been, with a name like that
and such remarkable enterprise, if only
you had crowed here in your own back yard.
Druan, I mourn a hoodlum, my compatriot.

GRAHAM ALLEN
(b. 1938)

Poem for my Father

Old fellow, old one,
    sing me a song out of the dark,
    a scullery one, and I'll beat time still
    on the tin-bath.
    How clear you looked free of the work's dirt
    and gay with evening, your time for taking the air
    – you'd think breathing it was a work of art,
    my mother said.

Sometimes before dressing, suds long at the elbow,
you had me punch away at your bicep:
always this strength; always the body,
you tested everything on it,
all life's fifty-year long shift:
suddenly, you must lie down with its strange stillness.

Older, I thought all you left of yourself
at home was a black ring round that bath,
water down the drain,
and me, cold leavings,
to remind my mother bitterly of you.

But do you remember sometimes on nights,
out of the street's noise never got used to,
you slept in my back-room, slipped carefully
into the rumpled shape of warmth I left you there,
each morning that ghostly crossing, you worn-out,
me head-full of Donne, Shakespeare and Keats?
– *Hyperion* to you was a beery windfall.

Now I get you into bed and out of it,
ashamed.
My body was never my meal-ticket
in the burrow of street and foundry under
the rattling viaduct, the canal's dark bridges.
Do you think if I could give you this strength

I wouldn't?
With finger-tip touch I steady your shoulders
pretending you sit alone on the brand-new commode.

Old fellow, old one,
sing me a song out of the dark,
twenty years later,
(must it be twenty years late?)
let the morning find
that shared shape in the bed,
 – no more cold crossings for us –
but the same flesh and warmth and need,
a father, a son.

PETER THOMAS
(*b.* 1939)

The Lascars

When I was a boy they came in blackness
from black ships together, gripping an unseen circle
protected from the pack of the crowd.
Lascars, my father would say,
they'll empty the pubs tonight,
 – and we'd see them in Wind Street by tailors' windows
huddled together, left alone.

One Monday, the *Evening Post* said blood had been found
on the pavement across the road from Sidney Heath's,
so *Lascars* my father said, and I stopped writing homework,
feeling the deft slit of the knife.

Then I was looking at coats in the window,
a man at the edge of means, indifferent to the town,
aching to be away. Quietly
they ringed me, staring into the same tailor's window,
dark in their quietness, unsure of the strange town,
nudging each other like schoolboys, they giggled
and fingered the frayed collars of loose shirts.

And *Lascars* I thought, as my dead father tugged,
but they smiled at me shyly, turning
to walk down Wind Street
to their ship.

BRAMWELL JONES
(*b.* 1939)

The Funeral

I

Death in the country is an event.
The old come out from behind their lives;
captains, farmers, ministers disturbed
into rain that covers women's tears.
The graveyard is an overgrown field.
Umbrellas flow through the silver gates,
spreading like a cautious delta stream
along faint green paths that circumscribe
watery marble kerbs and pass between
headstones ribbed with rain.
                                    The flow ceases,
arrested by mounds of dark brown earth
marking the verge of an open grave.

II

Rain adds to the rituals of death
glistening shoes, reprovingly set
against the field; an artist's contrast,
black against green as in a painting.

To the rituals of death rain adds
an unbroken counterpoint; sounds of
a persistent roll beating on tense
surfaces of stretched silk and nylon.

Through this come fragments. The unison
prayer of Welsh assembly: *Ein Tad yr
hwn wyt yn y nefoedd*. The blessing
Gras ein Harglwydd Iesu Grist. . . Amen.

Words half remembered, half understood;
words triumphantly free from meaning,
the poetry of a lost language.
They help me to concentrate on death.

CHRIS TORRANCE
(b. 1941)

Maen Madoc

the limestone pavement
partially submerged in grassy humps

a few red sandstone erratics
ponder the retreat of the ice

after climbing several
drystone walls &
"characteristic rubbly knolls"

there was the Stone
a sentinel on
the high & lonely moor
set into the matrix
of the Roman way, Sarn Helen

> The Court Jester
> By his artistry
> Influences affairs
> Of state in the
> Drenched lands
> Where an unbroken
> Dynasty of Kings
> Stretches back
> To a lone
> Standing
> Stone on
> A bald-
> Headed
> Conical
> Mountain
> primal inchoacy
> of pagan art

the yin & yang
firmly embossed
within the wheel
sections variant
fooling the eye
a vertiginous spiral

sheepshearing solstice
dry Westerly brings
summer heat
all growth
sunstretched

noisome flyswarms rocket
from dung soup
         ants eggs gathered
in galleries
         just under
the surface of
         the warm humus
circumnavigating
the mountain (Fan Llia)

the cycle
meanders
the perfect poem

fox's mask
expressionless
glares up at me
from the gutter
mangled remains
at Storey Arms

headwind baffling my strength
sit by Silurian erratic
crumbly conglomerate
menhir slab
laid
on the fair turf
of Mynydd Illtyd

megaphone echo
of a horseshow
in the mountains

silkiest maritime
summer high
swirling breezes the fields
the trees blurred washed out
cirrus tuffs moving up ahead in line

Boreas at my back
helps me up the cwm
at the head of Senni
to the Standing Stone, Maen Llia
rainspots dance in the
sunny cloudy wind.

JEREMY HOOKER
(b. 1941)

Gull On A Post

Gull on a post firm
In the tideway – how I desire
The gifts of both!

Desire against the diktat
Of intellect: be single,
You who are neither.

As the useful one
That marks a channel, marks
Degrees of neap and spring;
Apt to bear jetties
Or serve as a mooring;
Common, staked with its like.

Standing ever
Still in one place,
It has the look of permanence.

Riddled with shipworm,
Bored by the gribble,
In a few years it rots.

Desire which tears at the body
Would fly unconstrained
Inland or seaward; settle
At will – but voicing
Always in her cry
Essence of wind and wave,
Bringing to city, moorish
Pool and ploughland,
Reminders of storm and sea.

Those who likened the soul
To a bird, did they ever
Catch the eye of a gull?

Driven to snatch,
Fight for slops in our wake.
Or voice a desolation
Not meant for us,
Not even desolate,
But which we christen.

Folk accustomed to sin,
Violent, significant death,
Who saw even in harbour
Signs terrible and just,
Heard in their cries
Lost souls of the drowned.

Gull stands on a post
In the tideway; I see

No resolution; only
The necessity of flight
Beyond me, firm
Standing only then.

Brynbeidog

For ten years the sycamores
have turned about us, the Beidog
has run with leaves, and ice and sun.
I have turned the earth, thrown up
blue chip and horseshoe; from near fields
sheep and bullocks have looked in.

We have shared weathers
with the stone house; kept its silence;
listened under winds lifting slates
for a child's cry; all we have
the given space has shaped, pointing
our lights seen far off
as a spark among scattered sparks.
    The mountain above
has been rock to my drifting mind.

Where all is familiar, around us
the country with its language
gives all things other names;
    there is darkness on bright days
and on the stillest a wind
that will not let us settle,
but blows the dust from loved
things not possessed or known.

As A Thousand Years

Not a soul, only
a stubble field, bales
like megaliths; a flight
of trees over the Beidog,
and behind, darker green,
at the back of the sky,
the ridge damming
the sun; then,
    for a breath,
there was no sign of us.
Not a soul, only
light flooding this field,
bright as a marigold.

from *Englishman's Road*

Take a long view from Mynydd Bach: let your eye rise and fall
with ridges that stone walls or bent thorns follow – green dragon
backs, crested like petrified breakers; yet also the walls are always
climbing or in flight.

This is a country of vast spaces: it rolls with hidden hollows to the
mountains of the north, against the sweep of sea –

> preternatural grey,
> the mountains of Llŷn
> a chain of islands,
> or blue as spirit flame,
> or a lunula of beaten gold.

Here the buzzard with broad wings spread draws a widening
circle, ringing an intricate pattern of commons and enclosures,
whitewashed farms and red-roofed barns.

At night an irregular pattern of lights reflects the stars.

Here the western light is always changing, too quick for the eye
though it notes

> grey mystery
> of April, haunted
> by the curlew's salty cry,
> or August
> floating the hills,
> or Winter
> with a hard whiteness
> hammering the ground.

And what the light changes is only a face – face of a work vaster
and more laboured than the pyramids; but continuing. For this is
settled country, its pattern absorbent, deeply ingrained, but
unfinished; without the finality of a coiled fossil, though it too is a
life wrought in rock. And here these English words play on a
surface through which they cannot shine, to illumine its heart; they
can possess the essence of this place no more than the narrow road
under the Welsh mountain can translate its name.

> Lon Sais it is called,
> not Englishman's Road.

Two hundred years ago
> the first nightbuilders came

and on these commons they built,
        invoking an ancient but unwritten right.
Then it was said:

There shall not be any large farms or houses built on Mynydd
Bach but they shall be pulled down, but if any poor man shall
come, then we shall build a house and make a field and help him.

JOHN POOK
(b. 1942)

In Chapel

I follow my mother in from the car
Under the side-arch, up the steps
And into the vestry schoolroom where
On Sunday afternoons we kept

The faith and flirted with the girls.
Though everything has changed, it all stays
Here exactly as it was; the smells
Of flowers, polished wood, the mops

Behind the piano in the corner,
The heavy Bible resting on the lectern.
Now, on Saturday night, my mother
Comes with dahlias, daffodils, her turn

On 'Flower Rota', ready for the morning.
Two decades and its faces flip
My mind while she spends time arranging
Flowers, watering from the tap.

Predictably, like time, the jar fills up.
Tomorrow will see her worship here
As usual. Beer-dry, I think of the cup
She'll drink from. I shall be elsewhere.

Weekend At Home

Outside my window a lorry misses gear
Labouring towards Dyfnant Hill.
Potted plants rattle on the sill.
I have heard these sounds for twenty years

JOHN POOK

Cleave the air above this grey road.
The flower pot teeters on the ledge's
Lip, then settles back with age.
That lorry seems burdened with an old load.

Near the allotment children play,
Running into the patches we knew, their cries
Lilting away down the slope to the line.
Now their ghost train seems more real than I.

God, this is a calm place! The grass has been cut,
Even the wild dead sleep under tonsured green.
I sit at my typewriter looking serene,
Tapping like Catullus at my love and hate.

English Lesson

I read the class the old legend
of Brân, the son of Llyr,
and Branwen, Manawyddan,
Matholwch, king of Ireland
and the botched marriage with Wales.

Children believe in fables,
magic cauldrons, a giant
who wades across seas,
starlings with the power of speech.
But that Cornish facing door

on the island of Gwales
opening up an eighty years'
grief, what can I tell them of that
who are for ever slamming doors
joyously shut for the sheer hell of it?

CHRISTINE EVANS
(b. 1943)

Hâf Bach
(A 'little summer' in October)

The harvest was snatched weeks ago:
too late for anything

but pleasure now, lying all night
washed in wonder at the still-mildness
of the moonlit air.
We have thrown windows wide
to let it in.

The huge moon brims, begins to soften
round its edges.

It feels like sleeping on a vast resounding shore
within touch of the sea
though the air smells faintly of woodsmoke and apples
and it is quiet, except for young owls
learning to read
movement and shadow.
Question. And answer: warm flutter of breath.

This stormy summer threw down
and scattered grain, held berries back
from ripening. But, you tell me, everything does well
with so much spilling
and the known body of the fields we look out over
stroked smooth, lies tender and mysterious
with giving and more readiness to give.

In the morning, our windows
are momentary golden screens
steaming with moisture
that has gathered gentler than rain
like a slow-oozing, crystallising
joy. Next month, we know,
there'll be a hunter's moon.

CLIFF JAMES
(b. 1943)

Welsh Homer

To me there is more relevance in your single flight
than in a whole collection of Grecian tales, albeit in epic verse.

Your slight, curved breast prows through the winds' waves
each instinctive beat making your watch-tick heart race
as you thrust your grey, ocarina frame forward towards home.

For this you were hatched in a zinc-sheeted mountain loft.
Your bantam, white egg, khaki-blotched with droppings,
lay in a baking tin nailed to the wall.

You were as ugly as the others, large head and stretched-skin
    eyes,
tiny arteries, mapping penned veins and ridiculous
egg-toothed bill too heavy to raise.

When you were a squeaker you nervously pattered along
four-by-one, pinewood perches. Flapping desperately
cringing vainly to avoid the pesterings of the majoring cocks.

Your down, cartoon quiff, tea-cosy wattles and swollen black bill
made you a target for humans as well.
You, unlike most, achieved beauty with age.

And when you were ready the miner, your master,
threw you like a duster into the sky. You flapped
loosely at the air and your toes scraped the roof
like nails on a blackboard as you landed
and skidded on its striped corrugations.
You were afraid of the traps' double tappings
and had to be coaxed with dusty, orange Indian corn
to brave their metal contact and enter the cub.

And then the day when you flew with the flock.
The applause of taking-off and circling for height.
A squadron of grizzles, whites, blue-bars and blacks
who curved and banked and clipped, fluttered
like blown birch leaves as they reached each
determined limit in the meadow of their sky.

You were young and tumbled from their waving
feathered blanket, somersaulting, experimenting,
fast. While the man who helped you into the world,
gently scraping aside membrane and shell
with his thick, hard, black-nailed fingers,
watched you play and bit his cheek, hoping
you would avoid the wires that stretched
across the valley like a brace.

Today the man watches again as you, rubber ringed,
glide on landing-veed wings towards the white-
and black-striped strip. You have seen many places

and flown many miles. But this is your home
and this man is your God. The little man
from the tight, black places who sits and watches
his birds in the evenings as they dance in the sky
enjoying a freedom he can give but not have.
He sits now and watches you volplane,
then flap your wings wildly at the traps' jutting edge.
And as you hover the sound of your sweeping feathers
is the same as the sound of his clutching breath.

GRAHAM THOMAS
(b. 1944)

Lessons

All day he roams the garden
At the front of the house, choosing to walk
The grass before the path
Bare earth before the grass,
As though instinctively. This morning,
Walking together there, we hunted out
Fat bees and tiny spiders,
Ladybirds and worms – all
Those creatures they have taught him
To know as friends, as good
Tenants for the land to have. He takes it in
Without question now, each time he comes
Making a little ritual
Of stalking round the garden, saying
Hello to them again. But one day,
Without thinking, I killed some slugs
In front of him, turning the blade
Too deliberately home, remembering
Only after to explain
The trail of dying plants, the ugly
Residues of slime. He said
Nothing then, but today, as he held
His shining knife up tight above
His huge extended arm, I looked away.

At Ynysddu

There were two surprises for us
On the road that day. First

The mill, the one I should have known
Because of the name Cwmfelinfach;
And then, as the road arched upward
Over the mass of the hill, the bluebells
Studding the hedges all the way down
Past Islwyn's house. Unexpected,
Finding them there, and commoner too
Than willow herb on banks, in ditches
Beside the sudden stream, the school –
Heads of a vivid, spiky blue
That held us with their beauty, yet
Seemed alien for it somehow,
Out of place. I went expecting
The Big Tip and the shadowed streets,
The crumbling chapels with their high
Inscriptions hammered out in Welsh
All but forgotten. I saw them too.
But, driving to work each day, it was
The bluebells that I noticed, those
That come back every spring, the old
Promise to be true made good
Again and again. Turning my head,
I hoped to raise my eyes. Instead I saw
Only our own the alien now.

JOHN DAVIES
(b. 1944)

Mist

mist I have come to like
                    that lets things
    guess what they might be

    the shrubbery's tumbled cumulus
                    not the frozen lake
            a window
                            catching the sun

    outlines leave such space
    for what's not there
            to drift astonishingly in

that swing back there
becoming
a trapeze

the white odour of milk

through mist also
the gate's faint
harpsichord

How to Write Anglo-Welsh Poetry

It's not too late I suppose...
You could sound a Last Post or two,
and if you can get away with saying
what's been said, then do.

First, apologise for not being able
to speak Welsh. Go on: apologise.
Being Anglo-*any*thing is really tough;
any gaps you can fill with sighs.

And get some roots, juggle names like
Taliesin and ap Gwilym, weave
a Cymric web. It doesn't matter what
they wrote. Look, let's not be naive.

Now you can go on about the past
being more real than the present –
you've read your early R. S. Thomas,
you know where Welsh Wales went.

Spray place-names around. Caernarfon.
Cwmtwrch. Have, perhaps, a Swansea
sun marooned in Glamorgan's troubled
skies; even the weather's Welsh, see.

But a mining town is best, of course,
for impact, and you'll know what to say
about Valley Characters, the heart's dust
and the rest. Read it all up anyway.

A quick reference to cynghanedd
always goes down well; girls are cariad;
myth is in; exile, defeat, hills...
almost anything Welsh and sad.

Style now. Nothing fancy: write
all your messages as prose then chop
them up – it's how deeply red and green
they bleed that counts. Right, stop.

That's it, you've finished for now –
just brush your poems down: dead, fluffed
things but your own almost. Get
them mounted in magazines. Or stuffed.

Port Talbot

The breakers' jumbled yard: valley,
hills, strewn plain, reflect back
undulations of the sea.

Where steel and tidal water meet,
not turbulence and steam
but rust, what's left of heat,

is breaking down crisp ore
almost to the heart, the heart's
still beating core.

Mist's rolling-mills in sheets
send rain. There's sun. But night
alone here alters what it meets –

even when, silent, a furnace-flare
will flatter all the sleeping sky
like a dream of what was here,

three glimmering decades outstared
now by a ghost – and only
rust is eager and red-haired

in no-man's land, this town,
my town, whose thunder's the sound
of thunder running down.

At the Zoo

I've never been too keen on lions and
tigers, those decision-makers, frankly.
From my leafy covert here, all that
bunched exhibitionist-machismo just
to show off the quickest route from A to B
seems excessive. Why waste energy?

Elephants again: too many of them have
leant on me. Large-bottomed in middle age,
huge jowled but small of eye, they will
keep trumpeting as if I'm drunk or simple.
So I perch there, dull as an empty page,
eyes blank, too numb to be enraged.

I much prefer small things half-visible
and quiet (I don't know half their names)
that squirrel at the back of littered rooms,
doing interesting, shy things with straw.
Their lives seem to be an enigmatic game.
Trivial, I know. I like them just the same.

The boring task, that wastes our time, of
proving things to folk in next door's cage
doesn't seem to interest them at all –
they've opted out, signed off. So I watch
with quiet respect each quietly busy sage
twiddling, not tearing, towards old age.

Winter

all paths lead
here   curling leisurely
around the lake
or slicing trees
like a skater's traceries
dark on this sudden white
they come

– 319 –

                              to circle
                    the bandstand

       its worn loudspeakers
       are broadcasting snow   more snow
                                      notes falling
                  to faint applause of trees

                              the lawns listen
                                    muffled in white

        and footprints
                 fading
                             murmer
            no we have
                never
       been
                 here

NIGEL WELLS
(b. 1944)

Up

I approach gianthood warily
With great care, eyesight
Wedged unwinkingly wide
I'll not miss much

For the sudden rivering vein
And the slight but certain pressure
That tells the swelling bone
I wear my senses open now

Nails ripe with nerves
My neat white fingers
Drum-barrel on my lips

I run my seeing downwards
Trace my triggered self
No change. Yet

My gnat frame waits, grips its
Greeding size, aware of what it is
And what it may yet be

Oh I'll not be caught unawares
My flea-form's poised
My guard's up

Owl Wives

Owl wives

Come

Feathered ladies
Husbandless
And mean

When dog-breath
Stiffens
In bald yards

Come

From long perchings
On bad logs
Black reckonings
Under softened wood

Come

With mouse-bits
Clutched
In tidy claws

To line damp sills
And peer
Queer eyed
Through curtain chinks

Come

With clicking beaks
And woolly tongues

To sit the moon-hours
And the sleepers out

To knit
For sunken heads
Bad dreams

RICHARD POOLE
(b. 1945)

The Dark

And now, it seems, you are fearful
of the dark. You people black vacancies
with monsters of your own imagining.

I ridicule your child's fears.
'There's nothing to be frightened of,'
I hear myself saying, 'don't be absurd.'

But though I leave a light to burn
through darkness in your bedroom,
it cannot burn for ever against the night;

and with every good intention
I am simply a hypocrite –
for I too am frightened of the dark.

That once before I slept
in the perfection of absence
unknowingly, and undisturbed by dream,

is powerless to bring its consolation:
whose father lights a candle
in that infinite and that empty room?

TONY CURTIS
(b. 1946)

Neighbour's Pear Tree

Disturbed by the chatter
Of starlings gorging
From the rich, fat
Fruit, birds and pears both bursting

At the seams in a warm season,
We became aware of our neighbour's tree;
A nonentity since its springtime
Explosion of frail white.

Unpicked, these pears wasted
In our eyes. Despite noise
And clumsily-thrown sticks, pears, tasted
Vividly in the minds of the scrumping boys,

Maintained, obstinately, their hangings.
The bamboos and stones that bounced from boughs
To our garden are followed by clamberings
Wide-eyed over our wall now.

This sun-struck morning his tree is bare,
Fruit stolen or gathered,
Air doctored of sound.
We lie bathing and stare

Through the delivered branches lacing the sky.
Before the wall, bleeding gouts of flower up from the ground,
Our prim row of tended gladioli,
Climb strongly against the sticks I found.

Gambit

Sick of all his women
you tried to hit back with jealousy:
chose a name and a career,
researched your phantom lover

through encyclopaedias,
the business pages,
fleshed him with the jargon
of import/export.

Those absent afternoons,
did you walk the shops,
kick heels from a park bench?

Those obviously-stolen evenings –
was suspicion raised by your smudged face,
the cinema's smoke in your hair?

And when he confronted you,
believed your lies of an affair,
how smug he looked, so knowing and relieved
at what he took for your guilt.

Pouring a drink, he smiled through the back of his hand.
Giving his nose that characteristic rub,
"Join me," he said, "and
welcome to the club."

To My Father

Bellringing was another
of the things you didn't teach me.

How many crooked ladders did we climb?
How many belfries did we crouch in?
The musty smell of the years in the wood beams,
the giant domes balanced to move
against a man's pull.
Stories of jammed trapdoors and madness
in the deafening that draws blood.
Once you rang for the Queen
and I watched
all that pomp ooze into the cold stone of the cathedral.

I wanted to take the smooth grip of a rope
and lean my weight into it.
I wanted timing.
I wanted you to teach me
to teach my son's son.

Turning your back on that
brings our line down. What
have you left me? What sense
of the past? I could have lost myself in the mosaic
of Grandsires, Trebles and Bobs,
moved to that clipped calling of the changes.

I know now the churchbells' coming over the folded
town's Sunday sleep carries me close to tears,
the noise of worship and weddings and death
rolling out
filling the hollow of my throat.

The Spirit of the Place

Find me in the grass.

Find me in the West Wind.

I am between beats of the waves.
Winters I sleep in the seed potatoes
stocked in the dark.

Spring my sap works through tubers
stretching for light. Earth closes on me like a coat.

My engine coughs across the morning-grey farm.

I flower in the straight furrows of the angled steep fields.

I walk the coast path witnessing sun-rise
and fall of globes,

I am the flashing tinsel greed of sky mackerel.
The grey moving of tope deeply beyond Caldey.

I come blackly as cormorant.

With rain I will sweep the litter, rust the cans,
I will take buckets of brine and sluice the piss-smell
from the chapel of St. Govan.
I will erase the last scratch of writing,
save that in sand.

My weather eats the oiled guns of Castlemartin.

My surf rides in white, fucks fissures and cave.

I spread my legs in the cliff heather
move with waves.
My cries crack the headland's concrete bunkers,
spike the last war's ghost barrels.

Summers I twist lanes into blindnesses of faith.
I grit through carburettors till they phlegm to a stop;
my nails slough caravans into ditches.

I turn signs.

I rustle the paper bag dropped in the rabbit warren.

Autumn my dusk stirs mice through gaps;
they lodge in the galleries' ledgers,
shred and nest in the gift shop's trash.

I am the last revolution of the screws
of the last tanker nosing into the Haven;
I hang from the Cleddau Bridge,
stare out to the disappearing sea.
I scupper the moth-ball fleet.

My hands dip into rock-pools. Cool.
Anemones flower and close at my touch.

Nights I breathe Calor Gas.

Gulls are my envoys:
they glide and swoop above your heads,
they feed on your droppings.

There! See! And then!

What have you to say?

DUNCAN BUSH
(b. 1946)

Pneumoconiosis

This is The Dust,

black diamond dust.

I had thirty years in it, boy,
a laughing red mouth
coming up to spit
smuts black into a handkerchief.

But it's had forty years
in me now: so fine
you could inhale it through a gag.
I'll die with this now.
It's in me
like my blued scars.

But I try not to think about it.

I take things pretty easy
these days, one step at a time:

especially the stairs.
I try not to think about it.

I saw my own brother: rising, dying
in panic, gasping
worse than a hooked
carp drowning in air.
Every breath was his last
till the last.

I try not to think about it.

Know me by my slow step,
the occasional little cough, involuntary
and delicate as a consumptive's,

and my lung full of budgerigars.

Drainlayer

I made these mountains
I undig and heave and
bury; laid
these ducts dry to the mains

with the statutory fall.
Now earth to earth, where
must return,
sure as the apple, all

things earthly. The blade
cuts clean, and brightens;
glazes earth
the downthrust frees, the spade

flings. But I bury my own
work dark. Nothing stands
but me.
I lay veins, straight bone

in earth for earth my daughter.
My hollow son is
earth too,
exoskeleton of water.

Aquarium du Trocadéro

Here, in the terraced
gardens under the Musée de l'Homme
the stupefied,
reluctant fish stir behind glass.

The giant eel
swims 2 or 3 years
to reach the shallows
of its native river –

undulant, undinal
arrow of its unintelligible yearning,
it swallowed the Atlantic Ocean
through the slow
pulse at the gills.

Coiled like the Serpent
now in its illuminated, underwater tree
it is sleeping or dead.

The elvers
wave like weed. Born
in the tank, are they
incapable of memory or desire?

They mouth
the mollusc in the womb of rock,
like leeches.
The world blurs at the window.
They are at the source.

At other windows, tiny perch
hang
motionless,
like mobiles in the airless water,

and the sullen rainbow trout swerve
listless circuits
of their circulated tank.

The ferocious, brindled
pike cruise.

They have the neurasthenic, mad grin
and the water-cooled nervous system

of the Hollywood killer.
Here they dull like the fish in a case.

The fronts of the lighted tanks
are like Cinemascope screens in the dim light.

Lugubrious sunfish steer
towards the glass.

Found in the Garonne or the Pacific
currents, taken
from the cold Humboldt or the warm Gulf Stream,
the amnesic, doped fish wait.

Survivors of the Flood,
their boredom is cold-blooded
and absolute.
They are in their element.

PETER FINCH
(b. 1947)

A Welsh Wordscape

1

To live in Wales,

Is to be mumbled at
by re-incarnations of Dylan Thomas
in numerous diverse disguises.

Is to be mown down
by the same words
at least six times a week.

Is to be bored
by Welsh visionaries
with wild hair and grey suits.

Is to be told
of the incredible agony
of an exile
that can be at most
a day's travel away.

And the sheep, the sheep,
the bloody flea-bitten Welsh sheep,
chased over the same hills
by a thousand poetic phrases
all saying the same things.

To live in Wales
is to love sheep
and to be afraid
of dragons.

2

A history is being re-lived,
a lost heritage
is being wept after
with sad eyes and dry tears.

A heritage
that spoke beauty to the world
through dirty fingernails
and endless alcoholic mists.

A heritage
that screamed that once,
that exploded that one holy time
and connected Wales
with the whirlpool
of the universe.

A heritage
that ceased communication
upon a death, and nonetheless
tried to go on living.

A heritage
that is taking
a long time to learn
that yesterday cannot be today
and that the world
is fast becoming bored
with language forever
in the same tone of voice.

Look at the Welsh landscape,
look closely,
new voices must rise,
for Wales cannot endlessly remain
chasing sheep into the twilight.

We are in the Fields

we are in the fields

hidden by distance

the grass straining
under our feet

we talk, she and I,
the green intensity
of the landscape
filling our eyes

our words become birds
barely touching the air,
our faces smile,
our hands trace pictures
amongst the clouds,
our blood is love
and there is heat in our veins.

The sun turns to moon
and balanced in the sky
swollen stars
stream their gentle light
onto our bodies

time stops
and all
but the constellations
dancing on a distant horizon
returns to stillness

when dawn comes
it comes slowly
its light
half-afraid to move

my face is wet
her hands are muddy

and there are flowers
growing
in our clothes.

Acer

acum
    minature minat minet
    minum um
    atum
    atum atum
        away
i ffordd
i ffordd
i ffordd
     mapell
     schwern
     werini
       werin
     gwerin gwr
glab
    brumdoug
    doglab
    grand
    ent did
    arat ta ta te um
    ta ta t' um
    ta ta t' um
    ta ta t' um
mapbell bell
well na werin
erin schwe
wern wern
dogbell gwr
werin werin
brun well wern
werin werin
grand at chwer
werin werin
well na bell
werin werin
atum ffordd
werin ata
ffordd i schwern

ata werin
grand pell fern
werin werin
atum ata
felly
werin werin
werin werin
werin werin

PAUL GROVES
(b. 1947)

Heroine

She used to flash her fingers through the flame
Of her lighter. "Nothing to it."
She beckoned me to take part in her game.
I could not do it.
"Poltroonery!" (Where did she get that word?)
Beside her, my reserve was reprehensible.
She had a way of making the absurd

Appear supremely sensible.
Appearances were all. With sleight-of-hand
She waived responsibility, forsook
Caution, and inhabited a land
Within which my inhibited self shook
With genuine trepidation. She would sit,
Legs dangling, at a third-floor window, or

Balance on the handlebars with quite
Amazing calm while gathering speed, sure
That each calamity would pass her by.
We were college colleagues, yet I learned
Whereas she taught. The years mysteriously
Had gained her a maturity I yearned
To equal. Whence did she derive immunity?

How were so many safety measures spurned
With such alacrity, with such impunity?
She preached free love, and got her fingers burned
At last. The last I saw of her she had
Bowed like a branch beneath the weight of snow,
Mainlining, gaunt, pre-eminently sad.
I didn't know what to say, and still don't know.

PHILIP OWENS
(b. 1947)

Of One Dying

A portrait in the next room
tells me she was beautiful. Her mother's
eyes fill with memories.

The sclerosis has crippled her, and steroids
rendered her swollen, hairless. And now she gasps
with the spread pain of cancer.

Done with bravado and miracle
her ruthless refusal of the Sacrament
preserves a gentle candour

and we ask the questions, pointing
their tragedy. For strength alone
she accepts prayer, and together

flinching, we stare into the eye
of an unmoved ugliness which you cannot,
God, for all my helplessness and your
imposing grace, sanctify.

Croeso i Gymru

The coach waits, long, hot in the sun
stinking thickly of bananas and pop.
The trippers have gone from here, the

tight-packed coach park. On hazy beach
litter sand and sea with bared bodies;
stand sandalled, intent, in brazen bedlam

of amusement halls; bib beer
in brawling pubs. All this
is theirs and welcome. Not theirs

the basking country spread behind the
blaring town high in the sun's silence.

Soon they will have to drag back here
bedizened with baubles, sore with sand,
quit this blatant limbo littoral,

travel back wherever. Meanwhile
the driver sleeps in his glaring oven. Above,
seagulls tear screaming strips off a blazing sky.

STEVE GRIFFITHS
(*b.* 1949)

Just a Product of a Certain Situation

There was one I recognised in a train
I knew him immediately, once
he would have had a kid like me for dinner:
a bit of a devil at twenty-one, and a leader,
his hair black and combed thickly back like a star's.

Many were the stories of women he told
over a pint, his eyes laughing
through their bullets' confident trajectory
with the charm of olives, scattering the women
like chickens in a fictional yard.

I noticed the strong set of his shoulders
the chicken-fat with a furrow under his chin.
I thought he was studying me, too,
but he was casting the hard eye
on a round-faced girl beside me

who hid her burning face in a book of diagrams.
I moved, she looked up and smiled, he looked away
then took out a paper, removed the jobs column
with a studied tear, and folded the rest neatly
under his feet on the opposite place.

A nice unity of purpose, I thought.
But over his shoulder,
I saw the brutalities of disappointment hover
and the stories turn to betting,
the boasts settle like lees in his paunch.

Getting It Wrong, Again

Photographs, fading already, recall my discomfort.

Choristers were allowed to faint, and we did,
guards falling out honourably on parade

with a sense of our place in a world picture.

I did it too often, the honour was lost,
replaced with an inured suspicious sympathy;
the customers' eyebrows raised to heaven.

I played to the gallery with my voice,
I thought I had class. My solace
was the tender attention of illness.

Times change, and pretend positions
are recognised or lost; I am gummed in the present,
undefended from the past.

So many others are more resourceful,
they have invested in safe houses
and a repetitive future free from pain.

When the sun is shining,
they will not put their umbrellas away,
then they deny the existence of rain.

I might have followed, but again I got it wrong
and when out scavenging half-heartedly for bricks,
the heavy showers made my hair grow long.

There I am, leading the massed choirs into the wrong stall
at a celebratory service; at my back, the tall son
of the gardener, angrily poking me with his hymn-book;

in the scrubbed, anonymous line of distant faces
    where I belong.

NIGEL JENKINS
(b. 1949)

Yr Iaith

She who has forgotten
remembers as if yesterday
the scythe they left rusting
in the arms of an apple,
the final bang of the door
on those sheep-bitten hills.

In Abertawe, in Swansea
there were killings to be made,
and they politely made theirs.

She spent a lifetime loving
the taste of white bread, a lifetime
forgetting the loser's brown.
And on their middle floors
the brass gleamed, the crystal sang,
while away in the attic
dust fingered
the violins and the harp,
and far below stairs a discreet
and calloused tongue complained.

Years she remembers
of cuff-link and shoeshine,
but nothing, she says, nothing
of those dung-filled yards.

It's autumn now, an evening
that ends in colour t.v.
and the washing of dishes.
I ask her, as I dry,
Beth yw 'spoon' yng Nghymraeg?
Llwy, she says, *llwy, dw i'n credu,*
and she bites into an apple
that tastes like home.

Castration

Cutting, they called it –
but for all
his noise there was no
blood, no visible hurt:

just some thing in him
halted, to change
a bull-calf to a steer.

It didn't hurt, they said
as they caught and threw them,
locked each scrotum
for a second
in the cutter's iron gums.

The next one was mine:
round the yard we
chased him, brought him
down – hooves flying –
in a slither of dung.

They sat him upright,
like a man for barbering,
and I felt
in the warmth of his purse
for the tubes.
They gave me the tongs
and with all the steel
of my arms I
squeezed them home.

They fetched me another,
said he hadn't felt a thing.

But I wouldn't play.
With all that sky-wide bawling –
    sound his throat
    was never made for –
some nerve in me was severed.
There were words about
that weren't to be trusted.

Land of Song
(i.m. 1/3/79)

Oggy! Oggy! Oggy!
This is the music
of the Welsh machine
programmed – Oggy! – to sing
non-stop, and to think only
that it thinks it thinks
when it thinks in fact nothing.

Sing on, machine, sing
in your gents-only bar –
you need budge not an inch
to vanquish the foe,
to ravish again
the whore of your dreams,
to walk songful and proud

through the oggy oggy toyland
of Oggy Oggy Og.

Sing with the blinding hwyl
of it all: you are programmed
to sing: England expects –
my hen laid a haddock
and all that stuff.

Ar hyd y nos, ar hyd
y dydd – the songs, the song,
the hymns and bloody arias
that churn from its mouth
like puked-up S.A. –
and not a word meant
not a word understood
by the Welsh machine.

Oggy! Oggy! Oggy!
shame dressed as pride.
The thing's all mouth,
needs a generous boot
up its oggy oggy arse
before we're all of us sung
into oggy oggy silence.

SHEENAGH PUGH
(*b.* 1950)

Shoni Onions

He comes with autumn, when the leaves flake
from the rusty branches. His old bicycle
itself's a twisted tree, its creaking black
hung heavy with the long strings ripened full.
He is at the end of things; a sure sign,
the sad smile wrinkled in his golden skin.

There used once to be more of him, they spoke
a tongue that was the one half of a code
between old neighbours, a key to fit the lock
of cousins' speech, distanced but understood.
He sells in English now; his customer
or he mislaid the other words somewhere.

The boats that took our coal to Brittany
once brought him back; surely they don't still run?
Only old custom's sake now brings him by,
each year the same, a little older grown,
a taste sharp as nostalgia on his wares
startling the tongue; stinging the eyes to tears.

Coming Into Their Own

I like to think of a day for all those
who have been unloved in legend; the crooked man
who married Morfudd, the mocked Menelaus,
Conchubhar, Mark of Cornwall, all whose pain

has been a good joke since the troubadours.
Always in the way, the comic hindrance
to the real hero; butts of tolerance.
Tristan had his day; it will come yours.

Stand up, sad, jealous, commonplace,
and make a flag out of the loneliness
you were supposed to suffer out of sight.
Embarrass us; make us admit to it.

King Sigurd and King Eystein

(From an incident in *Heimskringla Saga: Snorri Sturlusson*)

'When I went to fight in Saracen country,
seven times I had the victory,
and where were you, kinsman Eystein, then?'

Northwards in Vaage, building the fishermen
smoke-houses; they have work all seasons now.

'In Apulia I did not see you
on my crusade; where were you at that time?'

Setting up inns on the road out of Trondheim
where night frosts used to freeze the traveller.

'I saw Christ's tomb; I did not see you there.'

At Agdaness the ship-grave, I had made
a harbour, to save men's lives when I am dead,
and but for my life, it would be worse for them.

'What were you doing, brother, when I swam
the Jordan river, or when I tied a knot
by the bank, and promised my kinsman should come out
on that holy journey and untie it again?'

I was bringing under our rule the Jemte men,
not with war, but with good words. And a man unties
the knot he finds, kinsman, where he is.

King Billy on the Walls

I can remember looking up at him
on many a Belfast wall; King Billy, bright
in his chalk colours, riding a white horse,
larger than life, twice as victorious.

If I saw him again, perhaps I'd see
the sick, frail Dutchman with the tired eyes
who looked down on the drums, the exuberance,
the orange sashes, with an embarrassed air,

wondering when he became so popular.
And now he looks on fear and scattered flesh
and brutal faces, thinking of the years he lost
fighting the French, the Irish, his wife's father...

He was a gentle man, and all his life
a soldier, and now, trapped in the crude chalk
both friends and enemies use to picture him,
his eyes can still rest nowhere but on pain.

HILARY LLEWELLYN-WILLIAMS
(b. 1951)

Two Rivers

It was here, in the long red meadow
two princes fought a battle
in old times, in the shadow
beneath this hill
in this dark sorrel
where children roll and squeal
flattening pathways in the brushed grass.
This ridge, the high seat
its flank woods heavy with summer—
was this where he raised his spear,
stood lightly rehearsing the blow

while the villagers swarmed below
with pop and crisps and bright-striped folding
chairs, men in tweed caps, women
in pale blue nylon housecoats
faces pink in an unaccustomed sun?

And the one they fought for—was she
there in the crowd with her schoolfriends
pressed round her, craning for a sight
of blood? Or sitting high
as a bird, like a Carnival Queen?
Or did she stand alone with her hair down,
her fingers twisting together, down by the river
to her knees in plumes of meadowsweet?

I think she turned her face when the blow fell
and the crowd yelled and horns blared
towards the place where the two rivers meet.

Two rivers, brown and muscled, struggle
endlessly in a pool. Warm afternoons
in our own short summer, I've gone there
to skinny-dip, the shock
of water raising up gooseflesh.
Feeling the two floods not quite equally cold:
    one with a little sun in it
    one with the mountain in it
and my body between the two
touching them both, as she once used to do.

Was it here, to this shadowed pool
when the show was over
she fled with her nine maidens
pursued by redfaced men, her triumphant lover?
Along the footpath from the post office
they ran to fetch her; but she'd flown
with her white turned face into the alder scrub
in a flurry of wings and claws.

Now they have lost her in the long
meadow; and their darkness is complete.

She flies high
here, in the woods, at night—
I've heard her thin cry, where the rivers meet.

PETER THABIT JONES
(b. 1951)

Modris

Modris sits on the warm doorstep,
Wearing a pullover knitted
By his blind sister.
He grins at fresh girls clip-clopping
In high, platform shoes
Down the sun-blurred street;
Tut-tuts at the old Indian
Doctor's sons playing
Football against a garage door;
Accepts homemade cake
From the young wife across the road;
Gives children hot mints;
Asks me about Keats.
Goes in about ten in the night.

I live three houses away.
Midnight, I can hear him coughing.

ROBERT MINHINNICK

(b. 1952)

Sap

Where the stream ox-bowed
And we stood on a bulwark
Of planks and turf, the current
Made its darkest passage,
A black stillwater, treacherous
Beneath a sheen of scum.

Once, and only once, a trout rose,
Its lean sides gleaming like
A knife between the stones,
Crimson shadow at its belly.
Yet how often was the only sound
Not the Ffornwg or our
White thrash after fish,
But the thinnest flute of the sap
Maintaining its single note
A long minute in my head
As I imagined that pressure
Of water rising through the trees,
Streams moving vertically
And spilling in a silent turbulence
Along the boughs, a river

Flowing there beneath the bark,
The sap, singing, even as flesh
Leaned white and stunned
Against the visible current,
And the *gwrachen* like a small
Green stick swam past the hand.

The Boathouse

The sawyers lie outside the shed,
Their blades motionless for the first
Time today, the men silent, sprawled
On a floor of white dust, their
Haversacks before them and behind
The heaps of sawn wood, the logs stacked
Like new loaves, the smell as sweet.

In my mind they will sit there forever,
The village men in feudal grouping,
Craftsmen of the estate,and my mother
Saying 'good morning sir' to the gentleman
As he passes, to the brassy heads
Of cartridges in his twill. A smile
For the girl remembered always.

It's finished now. The whole place
Closed down. Employment's found outside
The creamery, the vinery and grange
Farm that fed inherited wealth,
That tiny, epic world once sufficient
To itself, working perfectly and
Observed from the boathouse by this

Trespasser hidden amongst anglers'
Tackle, the moss-covered lake sliding
Under the boards. Suddenly everyone
Had fallen asleep—nurserymen,
Chauffeurs, kitchenmaids—the hour
Went unstruck. There was nothing
But silence and the soft putrescence

Of the boathouse, the shoals of ochre
Mud where water stood. Through a rotten
Lath the lake slipped in; vans arrived,
I heard the barking of the country
Auctioneers, 'good morning sir
Sir sir' of my mother talking to the dead,
A population slamming doors on a way of life.

After a Friendship

Still clear, that morning his family moved,
The lorry carrying furniture and people
Towards Swansea. I never waved
But breathed at the window the sweet-stale

Air of the empty house. And walked home.
If there was grief I have forgotten it,
But from then on things were not the same.
Grammar-school, homework, rugby-kit

Filled my time. I learned to become
Invisible and wrote the days' timetable
In an exercise book. My uniform
Had a heart-shaped badge and its black wool

Steamed in the rain. We were all proud.
And seven years passed like the days'
Seven lessons and he slowly dwindled
From my mind, a small ghost who preys

Now suddenly but for good reason
On imagination and memory.
It was never repeated, that season
Of friendship: a ten-year-old boy

With mad eyes, a truant, a sleeper-out
In haystacks brought down his fist
With a cobble in it and a gout
Of blood fell like a grape into the dust.

Fear and learning; deliberate
Childish violence. Like steel and flint
We sparked each other to the great
Discovery of ourselves. And went

Our ways. Children with their tough minds
Would understand. Seeing my blood
Did not scare us. It ran for the parting of friends.
We both knew we were going away for good.

The House

I lie across the rafters of the loft
Holding the torch. From the junction box
Wires twist into darkness, a crumbling
Skein of red and black under sackcloth
Of webs. For three stifling hours

In the attic's heat I have cursed
This challenge, frustrated by
Electricity – the merciless current
That will not come. And the silence
Of the house offers no clue. Matching

Myself against its fifty years,
The solid rooms and gables of this redbrick
Terrace, I must establish my own
Permanence. For territory is not
Bought or sold but fought over: it is

The first instinct, the small, unremarkable
Warfare of our lives. Yet crouched in this
Hot attic room my sweat has turned to ice.
The torchbeam's yellow cylinder
Identifies the dust, shapes from life

That have served their time and been abandoned
By the house. And I stare, fascinated,
At the dead. The faces of those who once called
This house home. Like them, like this frail
Blade of light, the house has swallowed me.

The Children

Their squints and stammers disappeared,
The crooked teeth straightened somehow.
Difficult to tell if they need you now,
These fastidious young, your children,
Sipping glittering gin through their own ice.

Talk of experience, you're still the novice:
Already they have covered the world,
England, France, it's a motorway ride
In a friend's car, the music blasting
As they overtake your careful saloon.

Yet you still pretend to know these strangers,
Passing round photographs of children
They used to be, the horses ridden,
The mountains climbed. Look closer, you think,
And you will see yourself, a figure

In the background smiling at something
Out of the picture. Yet you will wonder
At your own permanence. Make supper then,
You're good at that, but already
They are waving goodbye through the frozen

Brilliance of windscreens, driving
To a life where their backs form a tight
Circle. Are you ever discussed?
There's never a silence in their intricate conversations;
And they forgot to mention when they are coming again.

The Drinking Art

The altar of glasses behind the bar
Diminishes our talk. As if in church
The solitary men who come here
Slide to the edges of each black
Polished bench and stare at their hands.
    The landlord keeps his own counsel.

This window shows a rose and anchor
Like a sailor's tattoo embellished
In stained glass, allows only the vaguest
Illumination of floor and ceiling,
The tawny froth the pumps sometimes spew.
    And the silence settles. The silence settles

Like the yellow pinpoints of yeast
Falling through my beer, the bitter
That has built the redbrick
Into the faces of these few customers,
Lonely practitioners of the drinking art.
    Ashtrays, a slop-bucket, the fetid

Shed-urinal, all this I wondered at,
Running errands to the back-doors of pubs,
Woodbines and empty bottles in my hands.
Never become a drinking-man, my
Grandmother warned, remembering Merthyr
    And the Spanish foundrymen

Puking their guts up in the dirt streets,
The Irish running from the furnaces
To crowd their paymaster into a tavern,
Leather bags of sovereigns bouncing on his thigh.
But it is calmer here, more subtly dangerous.
    This afternoon is a suspension of life

I learn to enjoy. But now
The towel goes over the taps and I feel
The dregs in my throat. A truce has ended
And the clocks start again. Sunlight
Leaps out of the street. In his shrine of glass
  The landlord is wringing our lives dry.

MIKE JENKINS
(b. 1953)

Chartist Meeting
(Heolgerrig, 1842)

The people came to listen
looking down valley as they tramped;
the iron track was a ladder
from a loft to the open sea –
salt filling the air like pollen.

Each wheel was held fast
as you would grip a coin;
yet everything went away from them.
The black kernel of the mountains
seemed endless, but still in their stomachs
a furnace-fire roared,
and their children's eyes hammered
and turned and hollowed out a cannon.

Steam was like a spiral of wool
threaded straight down the valley,
lost past a colliery.
The tramways held the slope
as though they were wood of a pen.
Wives and children were miniatures
of the hill, the coal engrained
in enclosures on their skin.

They shook hands with the sky,
an old friend; there, at the field,
oak trees turned to crosses
their trunks bent with the weight
of cloud and wind, and harsh grass
from marshes that Morgan Williams,
the weaver, could raise into a pulpit.

A thousand listened, as way below them
Cyfarthfa Castle was set like a diamond
in a ring of green,
and the stalks of chimneys
bloomed continuous smoke and flame.

The Welsh that was spoken
chuckled with streams, plucked bare rock,
and men like Morgan Williams
saw in the burnt hands a harvest of votes.

Martins

A line of martins
bring to the wire
their abrupt, reed-splitting
calls. Each tick
they weed from their feathers
is a phrase to repeat.

They look so balanced there,
the sun giving a tulip's shine.
Their wings spread suddenly
as if you could see petals emerging
in a second. They stretch
the bounds of your sight
as they dart down a chasm
of flies above the stream.

Returning to the wire
they cut contours in the air
with scythe-shaped wings.
Mid-air contact, when flies caught
are planted from beak to beak,
sends two songs together,
their seedbursts shaking open wings.

Look closer: the martin's thumb of a head
is animated by signals, as if vibrations
from the wire had become the steady drone
of insects, a burr catching its eyes.
It is hard to think of this bird
cupped in a close cave of a nest,
when you have seen it garden
the air with its feeding flight.

CHRISTOPHER MEREDITH

(b. 1954)

Jets

All day the jets have rifled through the air,
Drilled through the lessons that I've tried to give,
Scabbing the blue with vapour for a scar,
Passing the dummy-bombed hamlets with a wave.

I've comforted myself. I'm not sot bad,
I've thought, in spite of the raised voice, the sudden squall—
If discipline and strictness knocks them dead
At least I'm not out there learning to kill.

And each frail cliché rears to the surface,
Writhes in the strong light, dies, and having sunk
Leaves me to know I work for who in office
Shuts books to put more octane in the tank.

What *I* would does not possess our minds.
This boy, the fat one, has been rifled too,
Belongs to the plane and every bomb it sends,
Absorption melted from his ragged row

Of words. Just now, he, my bluntest blade
Inevitably felled first in any game,
Looked from the tortured page, the word-wrought board,
To a sky where steel hammered its own scream—
And smiled.

CATHERINE FISHER
(b. 1957)

Severn Bore

Somewhere out there the sea has shrugged its shoulders.
Grey-green masses slip, rise, gather
to a ripple and a wave, purposeful, arrowing up
arteries of the land. Brown and sinuous, supple
as an otter, nosing upstream under the arching
bridge, past Chepstow, Lydney, Berkeley where a king
screamed; Westbury, where old men
click stopwatches with grins of satisfaction;

slopping into the wellingtons of watchers,
swamping the nests of coots, splashing binoculars.
And so to Minsterworth meadows where Ivor Gurney's ghost
walks in sunlight, unforgotten; past lost
lanes, cow-trodden banks, nudging the reeds,
lifting the lank waterweed,
flooding pills, backwaters, bobbing the floats
of fishermen, the undersides of leaves and boats,
and gliding, gliding over Cotswold's flawed
reflection, the sun swelling, the blue sky scored
with ripples, fish and dragonfly, stirred
by the drip and cloop of oars; and finally, unheard,
washing into the backstreets of the town to lie
at the foot of the high
cathedral, prostrate, breathless,
pilgrim from a far place;
refugee
from the ominous petulance of the sea.

Acknowledgements

The editors wish to thank the following: Meic Stephens, Literature Director of the Welsh Arts Council, for proposing this book and helping to make it possible; the Librarian of Trinity College, Carmarthen, and his staff; Kathleen H. Jordan Power and *The Anglo-Welsh Review* No. 56 for 'The Epitaph of Sir Griffith ap Rhys'; Gerald Morgan and *The Anglo-Welsh Review* No. 35 for 'On the Welch'; Ivor Waters for 'Chepstow: a Poem'; Revd Hugh Thomas of Ruthin for information on Thomas Hughes; Sam Adams and *The Anglo-Welsh Review* No. 52 for information on T. J. Ll. Prichard.

For Ernest Rhys: 'Wales England Wed' from *Wales England Wed*, 'The Ballad of the Homing Man' from *Welsh Ballads*, to J.M.Dent Ltd. and to the Estate of Miss A.S.Rhys.

For W.H.Davies: all poems from *Collected Poems*, to Jonathan Cape Ltd. and the W.H.Davies Estate.

For A.G.Prys-Jones: 'The Ploughman' from *Poems of Wales*, to Basil Blackwell Ltd. and to the author; 'Henry Morgan's March on Panama' from *Green Places*, to Gwasg Aberystwyth and to the author; 'Cors-y-Gwaed' from *High Heritage*, to Christopher Davies Ltd. and to the author; 'Unfortunate Occurrence at Cwm-Cadno' from *A Little Nonsense*, to D.Brown & Sons Ltd. and to the author.

For Dudley G. Davies: both poems from *The Boat-Race and other poems*, to The Alden Press and Mr. A.R.Davies.

For David Jones: extracts from *In Parenthesis*, *The Anathemata* and *The Sleeping Lord*, to Faber & Faber and to the Estate of David Jones.

For Gwyn Williams: 'City Under Snow' and 'St. Ursula of Llangwyryfon' from *Inns of Love*, to Christopher Davies Ltd. and to the author; 'Wild Night at Treweithan' and 'Pelagius' from *Foundation Stock*, to Gwasg Gomer and to the author.

ACKNOWLEDGEMENTS

For Idris Davies: all poems from *The Collected Poems of Idris Davies*, to Gwasg Gomer and to Mr. E.Morris and the Estate of Idris Davies.

For Glyn Jones: all poems from *Selected Poems*, to Gwasg Gomer and to the author.

For Vernon Watkins: 'Foal', 'Returning to Goleufryn', 'Crowds' and 'Music of Colours: The White Blossom' from *The Lady with the Unicorn*, 'Music of Colours: The Blossom Scattered', and 'The Heron' from *The Death Bell*, 'The Replica' from *Cypress and Acacia*, 'Taliesin and the Mockers' from *Affinities*, to Faber & Faber and to Mrs G.Watkins.

For Lynette Roberts: 'Poem from Llanybri' from *Poems*, to Faber & Faber and to the author.

For Jean Earle: both poems from *Trial of Strength*, to Carcanet Press and to the author.

For Tom Earley: 'Lark' from *The Sad Mountain*, to Chatto & Windus and to the author.

For Elwyn Davies: 'Portrait of Auntie Blodwen' from *Words Across the Water*, to Christopher Davies Ltd. and to the author.

For R.S.Thomas: 'A Peasant' and 'Reservoirs' from *Selected Poems 1946-1968*, to Granada Publishing and to the author; 'The Welsh Hill Country' and 'Cynddylan on a Tractor' from *An Acre of Land*, to The Montgomeryshire Printing Co. and to the author; 'Welsh History' from *Song at the Year's Turning*, 'Expatriates' from *Poetry for Supper*, 'A Line from St. David's' from *The Bread of Truth*, 'A Welshman in St. James's Park' from *Pieta*, 'Sir Gelli Meurig' and 'Llanrhaeadr Ym Mochnant' from *Not That He Brought Flowers*, to Rupert Hart-Davis Ltd. and to the author; 'Other', 'The Bright Field', 'The Empty Church' and 'The White Tiger' from *Later Poems*, to Macmillan Ltd. and to the author.

For Dylan Thomas: all poems from *Collected Poems*, to J.M.Dent Ltd. and to the Estate of Dylan Thomas.

For Clifford Dyment: 'Derbyshire Born, Monmouth is My Home' from *Collected Poems*, to J.M.Dent Ltd. and to the Estate of Clifford Dyment.

ACKNOWLEDGEMENTS

For Alun Lewis: 'Raiders' Dawn', 'All Day it Has Rained',
    'Post-script: for Gweno', 'The Sentry', 'The Mountain
    Over Aberdare', 'The Mahratta Ghats', 'In Hospital,
    Poona (1)' and 'The Jungle' from *Selected Poems*, to Allen &
    Unwin and to Mrs G.Lewis; 'Goodbye', to Mrs G.Lewis.

For Keidrych Rhys: 'Interlude' from *The Van Pool and other
    poems*, to George Routledge Ltd. and to the author.

For Roland Mathias: all poems from *Burning Brambles: Selected
    Poems 1944-1979*, to Gwasg Gomer and to the author.

For Emyr Humphreys: both poems from *Ancestor Worship*, to
    Gwasg Gee and to the author.

For John Stuart Willliams: both poems from *Banna Strand*, to
    Gwasg Gomer and to the author.

For Harri Webb: 'The Nightingales', 'Epil y Filiast', 'Synopsis
    of the Great Welsh Novel', 'Cywydd o Fawl', 'Thanks in
    Winter' and 'The Stone Face' from *The Green Desert*, 'Abbey
    Cwmhir' from *A Crown for Branwen*, to Gwasg Gomer and to
    the author.

For Robert Morgan: both poems from *The Night's Prison*, to
    Rupert Hart-Davis Ltd. and to the author.

For Leslie Norris: 'The Ballad of Billy Rose' from *Finding Gold*,
    'Water' and 'Early Frost' from *Ransoms*, 'Stone and Fern',
    'Barn Owl' and 'Elegy for David Beynon' from *Mountains,
    Polecats and Pheasants*, 'Ravenna Bridge' from *Water Voices*, to
    Chatto & Windus and to the author.

For T. Harri Jones: all poems from *Collected Poems*, to Gwasg
    Gomer and to the Estate of T.H.Jones.

For Ruth Bidgood: 'Chimneys', 'Burial Path', 'All Souls'' and
    'Standing Stone' from *Lighting Candles* (published by Poetry
    Wales Press); 'Dragon', to the author.

For Dannie Abse: 'Socialist Revolution in England', 'Return to
    Cardiff', 'Not Adlestrop', 'Peachstone', 'New Diary' and
    'Cousin Sidney' from *Collected Poems 1948-1976*, 'X-Ray'
    from *Way Out in the Centre*, to Hutchinson and to the author.

For John Ormond: 'My Grandfather and his Apple-Tree', 'The
    Key', 'Certain Questions for Monsieur Renoir', 'Ancient
    Monuments', 'Definition of a Waterfall' and 'Lament for a

ACKNOWLEDGEMENTS

Leg' from *Definition of a Waterfall*, to O.U.P. and to the author; 'Design for a Quilt', to the author.

For Alison Bielski: both poems from *Across the Burning Sand*, to Gwasg Gomer and to the author.

For Raymond Garlick: 'Note on the Iliad', 'Still Life' and 'Capitals' from *A Sense of Europe*, 'Ancestors', 'Map Reading' and 'Anthem for Doomed Youth' from *A Sense of Time*, 'The Poetry of Motion' from *Incense*, to Gwasg Gomer and to the author.

For John Tripp: 'Diesel to Yesterday', 'Welcome to Wales' and 'On My Fortieth Birthday' from *The Province of Belief*, 'Eglwys Newydd', 'Capital', 'Headmaster' and 'In Memory of Idris Davies' from *Collected Poems 1958-1978*, to Christopher Davies Ltd. and to the author.

For Joseph P.Clancy: 'Miscarriage' from *The Significance of Flesh*, to Wiegand and Kennedy and to the author.

For Douglas Phillips: 'Maridunum' from *Poems 74*, to Gwasg Gomer and to the author.

For Brian Morris: 'Dinas Emrys' from *Stones in the Brook*, to Gwasg Gomer and to the author.

For Anthony Conran: All poems from *Poems 1951-1967*, to Christopher Davies Ltd. and to the author.

For Gloria Evans Davies: 'Holly Gone' from *Her Name Like the Hours*, to Chatto & Windus and to the author.

For Herbert Williams: 'The Old Tongue' from *Dinosaurs*, to The Triskele Press and to the author; 'Like Father' from *Poems 69*, to Gwasg Gomer and to the author.

For Bryan Aspden: 'News of the Changes' from *News of the Changes*, Poetry Wales Press.

For Jon Dressel: 'You, Benjamin Jones', 'Dai, Live' and 'The Drouth' from *Hard Love and a Country*, to Christopher Davies Ltd. and to the author; 'Let's Hear it for Goliath', to the author.

For Sam Adams: both poems from *The Boy Inside*, to The Triskele Press and to the author.

ACKNOWLEDGEMENTS

For Peter Gruffydd: both poems from *The Shivering Seed*, to Chatto & Windus and to the author.

For Sally Roberts Jones: all poems from *The Forgotten Country*, to Gwasg Gomer and to the author.

For Gillian Clarke: 'Blaencwrt', 'Lunchtime Lecture' and 'Foghorns' from *The Sundial*, to Gwasg Gomer and to the author; 'Hay-Making', 'Ram' and 'Suicide on Pentwyn Bridge' from *Letter from a Far Country*, to Carcanet Press and to the author.

For Alun Rees: both poems, to the author.

For J.P.Ward: 'Every Single Night' from *The Other Man*, to Christopher Davies Ltd. and to the author; 'Unusual View of Town' and 'To Get Clear' from *To Get Clear*, to the author (published by Poetry Wales Press).

For Evan Gwyn Williams: 'Day Trip' from *The Clown and other poems*, to The Triskele Press and to the author.

For John Idris Jones: 'Barry Island' from *Barry Island and other poems*, to John Jones (Cardiff) Ltd. and to the author.

For Meic Stephens: 'Ponies, Tynyrodyn', 'Hooters' and 'Elegy for Llywelyn Humphries' from *Exiles All*, to The Triskele Press and to the author; 'Elegy for Mr Lewis (Welsh)' from *Green Horse*, to Christopher Davies Ltd. and to the author.

For Graham Allen: 'Poem to my Father' from *Out of the Dark*, to The Triskele Press and to the author.

For Peter Thomas: 'The Lascars' from *The Trailing Cord*, to Christopher Davies Ltd. and to the author.

For Bramwell Jones: 'The Funeral' from *Cadence Notes*, to The Triskele Press and to the author.

For Chris Torrance: 'Maen Madoc' from *Citrinas: The Magic Door Book 2*, to The Albion Village Press and to the author.

For Jeremy Hooker: 'Gull on a Post', 'As A Thousand Years' and 'Brynbeidog' from *A View from the Source*, 'Englishman's Road' from *Englishman's Road*, to Carcanet Press and to the author.

For John Pook: all poems from *That Cornish Facing Door*, to

ACKNOWLEDGEMENTS

Gwasg Gomer and to the author.

For Christine Evans: 'Hâf Bach' from *Cometary Phases*, Seren Books.

For Cliff James: 'Welsh Homer' from *Poems 72*, to Gwasg Gomer and to the author.

For Graham Thomas: both poems from *The One Place*, to the author (published by Poetry Wales Press).

For John Davies: 'At the Zoo', 'How to Write Anglo-Welsh Poetry' and 'Port Talbot' from *At the Edge of Town*, to Gwasg Gomer and to the author; 'Mist' and 'Winter' from *The Silence in the Park*, to the author (published by Poetry Wales Press).

For Nigel Wells: both poems from *The Winter Festivals*, to Bloodaxe Books and to the author.

For Richard Poole: 'The Dark' from *Words Before Midnight*, to the author (published by Poetry Wales Press).

For Tony Curtis: 'Neighbours' Pear Tree' from *Album*, to Christopher Davies Ltd. and to the author; 'Gambit', 'To My Father' and 'The Spirit of the Place' from *Preparations*, to Gwasg Gomer and to the author.

For Duncan Bush: 'Pneumoconiosis' and 'Drainlayer' from *Three Young Anglo-Welsh Poets*, to the Welsh Arts Council and to the author; 'Aquarium du Trocadéro' from *Aquarium*, to the author (published by Poetry Wales Press).

For Peter Finch: 'A Welsh Wordscape' and 'We Are in the Fields' from *End of the Vision*, to John Jones (Cardiff) Ltd. and to the author; 'Acer' from *Connecting Tubes*, to Writers' Forum and to the author.

For Paul Groves: 'Heroine' from *Academe*, Seren Books.

For Philip Owens: both poems from *Look, Christ*, to Gwasg Gomer and to the author.

For Nigel Jenkins: all poems from *Song and Dance*, to the author (published by Poetry Wales Press).

For Sheenagh Pugh: 'Shoni Onions' from *Crowded by Shadows*, to

ACKNOWLEDGEMENTS

Christopher Davies Ltd. and to the author; 'King Sigurd and King Eystein', 'King Billy on the Walls' and 'Coming Into Their Own' from *What a Place to Grow Flowers*, to The Triskele Press and to the author.

For Hilary Llewellyn-Williams:'Two Rivers' from *Book of Shadows*, Seren Books.

For Peter Thabit Jones: 'Modris' from *Clocks Tick Differently*, to The Celtion Publishing Co. and to the author.

For Robert Minhinnick: 'Sap' from *A Thread in the Maze*, 'After a Friendship', 'The House', 'The Children' and 'The Drinking Art' from *Native Ground*, to The Triskele Press and to the author; 'The Boathouse' from *Life Sentences*, to the author (published by Poetry Wales Press).

For Mike Jenkins: both poems from *The Common Land*, the author (published by Poetry Wales Press).

For Christopher Meredith: 'Jets' from *Snaring Heaven*, Seren Books.

For Catherine Fisher: 'Severn Bore' from *Immrama*, Seren Books.

Index of Titles

INDEX OF TITLES

Index of First Lines